The Nature of the New Firm

The Nature of the New Firm

Beyond the Boundaries of Organizations and Institutions

Edited by

Killian J. McCarthy

Research Associate, University of Groningen, The Netherlands

Maya Fiolet

Research Associate, VU University Amsterdam, The Netherlands

Wilfred Dolfsma

Professor, University of Groningen, The Netherlands, and corresponding editor of the Review of Social Economy

Edward Elgar

Cheltenham, UK • Northampton, MA, USA

Published by
Edward Elgar Publishing Limited
The Lypiatts
15 Lansdown Road
Cheltenham
Glos GL50 2JA
UK

Edward Elgar Publishing, Inc.
William Pratt House
9 Dewey Court
Northampton
Massachusetts 01060
USA

A catalogue record for this book
is available from the British Library

Library of Congress Control Number: 2011925753

ISBN 978 1 84980 393 9

Typeset by Servis Filmsetting Ltd, Stockport, Cheshire
Printed and bound by MPG Books Group, UK

Contents

Contributors

Alexander S. Alexiev is Assistant Professor in Strategy and Innovation at the Department of Management and Organisation of VU University Amsterdam, The Netherlands. He is a graduate from the PhD and research master programs of the Erasmus Research Institute of Management (ERIM). His dissertation research includes a publication in the *Journal of Management Studies* and he has made presentations at numerous international conferences in the field. The focus of his research is on management behaviors and organizational features that can support organizational learning, innovation and effective strategic decision making.

Nima Amiryany is conducting PhD research on organizational learning through technology acquisitions. He is especially interested in how knowledge sharing (on an employee level) takes place within acquisitions of high-tech firms and how firms can learn from their acquisitions in order to enhance innovation. With his research, he aims to contribute to the strategic management literature, and more specifically to the literature of the knowledge-based and dynamic capabilities views of the firm. He has a background in business administration with a specialization in knowledge management.

Claire E. Ashton-James is Assistant Professor in Psychology at the Rijksuniversiteit Groningen, The Netherlands. She holds a PhD in social psychology from the University of New South Wales, Australia. Before moving to the Netherlands, she taught markets and management studies at Duke University, USA, and completed a post-doctoral fellowship at the University of British Columbia, Canada. Her research interests include nonconscious social influences on thought, emotion, and behavior, power, and emotions.

Sjoerd Beugelsdijk is full Professor of International Business and Management at the University of Groningen, The Netherlands. His research interests are in the fields of international business, institutional economics and comparative economic organization theory. He received his PhD from Tilburg University (The Netherlands) in 2003, for his thesis on the relationship between culture and economic behavior. In 2004, he visited Copenhagen Business School, the European University Institute in Florence, and Case Western Reserve University in Cleveland, Ohio. In 2006, he received a three-year research grant from the Netherlands Organization for Scientific Research, which allowed him to spend some time at the Center for Strategic Management and Globalisation in Copenhagen in 2007, and the IGIER research institute of Bocconi University (Milan) in 2008. His current research concentrates on three main areas: institutions and the geography of the multinational firm; culture, institutions and economic performance; and innovation, social capital and institutions.

Myriam Cloodt is Assistant Professor in Entrepreneurship and Innovation at Eindhoven University of Technology, The Netherlands. Her research interests mainly include open innovation, strategic technology alliances, mergers and acquisitions, and corporate entrepreneurship. Her work has been published in *Research Policy*, *Business History*, *Business History Review*, and *International Studies of Management and Organization*. She co-authored (with Wim Vanhaverbeke) the chapter 'Open innovation in value networks', in H. Chesbrough, W. Vanhaverbeke and J. West (eds), *Open Innovation: Researching a New Paradigm* (Oxford University Press, 2006).

Ard-Pieter de Man is Professor of Management Studies at VU University Amsterdam and principal consultant at Atos Consulting, The Netherlands. His research concerns alliances, networks and innovation. He is the (co-) author of about thirty articles and nine books, mainly on alliances. His interest in alliances and networks is not only academic, as he has worked as a consultant for a variety of companies and governmental institutions in Europe and the USA.

Wilfred Dolfsma is an economist and philosopher, and holds a PhD in economics from Erasmus University, Rotterdam, The Netherlands. He is Professor of Innovation at the University of Groningen, The Netherlands, and is corresponding editor for the *Review of Social Economy*. His research interests are innovation and technological development, media industries, consumption, and the developments in and effects of intellectual property rights (IPR). His *Institutional Economics and the Formation of Preferences* (Edward Elgar, 2004) won him the Gunnar Myrdal Prize. His most recent books include *Media & Economics* (ed. with Richard Nahuis, 2005), *Knowledge Economies* (Routledge, 2008) and the *Companion to Social Economics* (ed. with John Davis, Edward Elgar, 2008).

Anca Dranca-Iacoban studies human resource management and organizational behavior in the Faculty of Economy and Business, Groningen University, The Netherlands. She focuses, in particular, on organizational behavior. She has a bachelor's degree in organizational psychology from the University of Bucharest, Romania. With a background in a student NGO, where she focused on human resources, her research interests include leadership and the influence of power on behavior, cognition and affect.

Geert Duysters is Professor of Entrepreneurship and Innovation at Eindhoven University of Technology and Tilburg University, The Netherlands. He currently acts as the scientific director of the Brabant Center of Entrepreneurship. He also holds a professorial fellow affiliation with UNU-MERIT. He holds a PhD in economics and has worked at the University of Maastricht and the TU Eindhoven as researcher, assistant professor, associate professor and full professor. He was an alliance expert for the European Commission and the OECD. From 2000 to 2003 he was Director of the Eindhoven Centre for Innovation Studies (ECIS). He also acted as Associate Dean of the Faculty of Technology Management from 2004 to 2006. His academic research mainly concerns international business strategies, innovation strategies, corporate entrepreneurship, mergers and acquisitions, network analytical methods and strategic alliances.

Maya Fiolet has a background in economics with a specialization in management. She graduated from the VU University Amsterdam, The Netherlands, where she is currently a PhD candidate in the Department of Organization Science, in the Faculty of Social Science. Her PhD research focuses on entrepreneurship in the care for the elderly.

Yolanda Grift is Assistant Professor in Econometrics at the Utrecht University School of Economics (USE), The Netherlands. She studied econometrics at the University of Amsterdam and received her PhD in 1998 with her thesis 'Female Labour supply: the influence of taxes and social premiums'. The analysis of the time allocation between spouses in the household is still one of her research fields. Recently, she has done some research into the transition of secondary school to the university with respect to the mathematical knowledge and skills of first-year students. Since 2005 she has been involved in research on the influence of works councils on firm performance in collaboration with the members of the chair of institutional economics at USE.

Peter Groenewegen is Professor of Organization Science at the Faculty of Social Sciences and member of the Network Institute at the VU University Amsterdam, The Netherlands. His research is directed at the internal and external role of networks in modern organizations. He has published on the development and cooperation of science and technology organizations as well as on environmental policy issues. Currently he is involved in projects on the dynamics of networks in organizations, communities and crisis management. Externally his current research concerns field-level changes as a consequence of the actions of new entrants and social movements on incumbent networks.

Michael A. Hitt is Distinguished Professor of Management at Texas A&M University, USA and holds the Joe B. Foster Chair in Business Leadership. He received his PhD from the University of Colorado. He has co-authored or co-edited 26 books and authored or co-authored many journal articles. A recent article listed him as one of the ten most cited authors in management over a 25-year period. In 2010 The Times Higher Education listed him among the top scholars in economics, finance and management and first among management scholars (tied) with the highest number of highly cited articles. He has served on the editorial review boards of multiple journals and is a former editor of the *Academy of Management Journal*. He is the current co-editor of the *Strategic Entrepreneurship Journal*. He received the 1996 Award for Outstanding Academic Contributions to Competitiveness and the 1999 Award for Outstanding Intellectual Contributions to Competitiveness Research from the American Society for Competitiveness. He is a Fellow of the Academy of Management and the Strategic Management Society, a Research Fellow of the National Entrepreneurship Consortium, and he received an honorary doctorate from the Universidad Carlos III de Madrid. He is a former President of the Academy of Management, a Past President of the Strategic Management Society and a member of the *Academy of Management Journal's* Hall of Fame. He received awards for the best article published in the *Academy of Management Executive* (1999), the *Academy of Management Journal* (2000), and the *Journal of Management* (2006). In 2001, he received the Irwin Outstanding Educator Award and the Distinguished Service Award from the Academy of Management. In 2004, he was awarded the Best Paper Prize by the Strategic Management Society, and in 2006, he received the Falcone Distinguished Entrepreneurship Scholar Award from Syracuse University.

Marleen Huysman is Professor of Knowledge and Organization in the Faculty of Business Administration, VU University Amsterdam. Her research interests are related to knowledge networks, a practice-based approach to organizations, organizational learning, distributed knowledge sharing and integration, and new forms of organizing. Her research has appeared in various international articles, books and edited volumes. She currently heads the research group Knowledge, Information and Networks at the VU University Amsterdam.

Justin J.P. Jansen is Professor of Corporate Entrepreneurship at the Rotterdam School of Management, Erasmus University, The Netherlands. He received his PhD Cum Laude from Erasmus University in 2005. His research addresses leadership, organizational learning, ambidexterity, and corporate entrepreneurship and has appeared in the *Academy of Management Journal*, the *Journal of Business Venturing*, the *Journal of Management Studies*, *Leadership Quarterly*, *Management Science* and *Organization Science*.

Hsin-Hsuan Meg Lee is a PhD candidate at Amsterdam Business School, The Netherlands, and a lecturer in marketing. Her research focuses on corporate social responsibility, particularly in the field of corporate communication and consumer behaviors on social media. She holds an MSc in marketing from the University of Strathclyde, and an MSc in applied animal behaviours and animal welfare from the University of Edinburgh.

Killian J. McCarthy is an economist and strategist. He read for a PhD in the economics of corporate strategy at the University of Groningen, the Netherlands, and wrote on the topic of mergers and acquisitions. His research interests include business and industrial organization, and strategy, but he has also published on the topics of corporate tax competition, money laundering and criminal finance, as well as the influence of media power on both consumer and business sentiment. He holds a first-class Bachelor's degree in business from University College Cork, Ireland, which he earned with a double-major in economics and law, and two 'cum laude' Master's degrees in economics, from the Utrecht University School of Economics, the Netherlands, and the University of Vienna, Austria. In addition, he is currently reading a bachelor of laws at the University of London, UK.

Tiago Ratinho is currently working on his PhD thesis at Nikos, the Dutch Institute for Knowledge-Intensive Entrepreneurship. He research analyses the impact of business incubation, showing how incubation processes work, unravelling complex relationships between business support and firm performance. His research interests are in the fields of entrepreneurship, small business management, technology transfer and organizational change. He graduated in industrial engineering (Évora) and holds an MSc in engineering policy and management of technology (Lisbon). His work is published in international journals (*Techovation*) and international conferences (Academy of Management meetings, Babson College Research Conference on Entrepreneurship).

G.J. (Joost) Rietveld is pursuing a PhD at the London-based Cass Business School, City University, in the field of strategic management in the digital games industry. He has particular interest in the strategic implications of the advent of digital distribution channels, and the post-acquisition integration process of high rise acquisition targets. In his research, he is supervised by Professor Joseph Lampel, known for his contributions in the fields of strategic management and cultural industries. Joost holds a BSc in business with a specialization in small business and entrepreneurship and strategic management of innovations, and an MSc in strategic management of innovations, both from the University of Groningen, the Netherlands.

Saraï Sapulete is an economic PhD candidate with a sociological background. She is interested in organizational processes and studies the effects of works councils in organizations at the Utrecht University School of Economics, The Netherlands. In her past education and research at the University of Groningen (BSc in sociology, MSc in human behavior in social contexts) she has focused on social capital and social networks in organizations. She is currently studying the effect of works councils by means of different methods, including experimental economics and social network analysis.

Astrid A. ter Wiel is a PhD candidate at the Faculty of Economics and Business Administration at the VU University, Amsterdam, The Netherlands. After obtaining her MSc in industrial engineering and management at the University of Twente, she worked as a consultant – with PwC Consulting and Significant B.V. – in the Netherlands and as a manager of a developing aid project at two local universities in Kampala, Uganda. In 2008, she started her research at the VU in which she focuses on interorganizational collaboration and relationship management. She teaches in the areas of strategy, organizational behavior and procurement.

Annette van den Berg is Assistant Professor in Institutional Economics at the Utrecht University School of Economics (USE), The Netherlands. She studied economic history at Leiden University and graduated from the Economics Faculty of the University of Amsterdam with her thesis: 'Trade union growth and decline in the Netherlands'. Her research still focuses on labor relations, with special attention to the role of workers in the corporate governance debate and the influence of works councils on firm performance.

Frans A.J. Van den Bosch is Professor of Management of Interfaces between Firms and their Environments at the Department of Strategic Management and Business Environment, RSM Erasmus University, Rotterdam, The Netherlands. His current research interests include managerial and knowledge-based theories of the firm; strategic renewal

and corporate entrepreneurship; intra- and interorganizational governance structures; corporate governance and corporate responsiveness;
and integrative strategy frameworks. He has published several books
and papers in journals such as the *Academy of Management Journal*, the
Journal of Business Venturing, the *Journal of Management Studies*, *Long
Range Planning*, *Management Science*, *Organization Science*, *Organization
Studies* and *Business and Society*. He is an editorial board member of,
among others, the *Journal of Management Studies*, *Long Range Planning*
and *Organization Studies*. He is co-director of the Erasmus Strategic
Renewal Center (ESRC) and chairman of the Advisory Board of Erasmus
Research Institute of Management (ERIM).

Arjen van Witteloostuijn is Research Professor of Economics and
Management at the University of Antwerp in Belgium, and Professor of
Institutional Economics at Tilburg University and Utrecht University,
both in the Netherlands. In the 1980s, 1990s and 2000s, he was affili-
ated with the University of Groningen, University Maastricht (both the
Netherlands) and Durham University (United Kingdom), and he visited
New York University (the USA) and Warwick Business School (the UK).
He holds degrees in economics, management and psychology. In 1996–98,
he was Dean of the Maastricht Faculty of Economics and Business
Administration. He is a (former) member of the editorial board of, for
example, the *Academy of Management Journal*, the *British Journal of
Management*, *Industrial and Corporate Change*, the *Journal of International
Business Studies*, *Organization Studies* and *Strategic Organization*. Apart
from many (chapters in) books, and articles in Dutch dailies and journals,
he has published widely in a variety of disciplines, such as accounting
(for example, *Accounting, Organizations and Society*), economics (for
example, the *International Journal of Industrial Organization*), management (for example, the *Academy of Management Journal*), public administration (for example, the *Journal of Public Administration Research
and Theory*), political science (for example, the *American Journal of
Political Science*), psychology (for example, *Personality and Individual
Differences*) and sociology (for example, the *American Sociological
Review*).

Paul W.L. Vlaar obtained his MSc in economics from Wageningen
University, The Netherlands, and his PhD from RSM Erasmus
University (both cum laude). He is currently the Commercial Director of
Aannemingsbedrijf Ooijevaar, a Dutch construction firm, and Associate
Professor at the VU University, Amsterdam, The Netherlands. His
research concerns interorganizational cooperation, new business devel-
opment and strategic change, and has been published in *MIS Quarterly*,

Organization Studies, Group & Organization Management, and several edited books. His first book was *Contracts and Trust in Alliances: Creating, Appropriating and Discovering Value* (Edward Elgar, 2008) followed by *Strategy at Every Corner! Inspiration for a New Breed of Strategists* (Synspire Publishing, 2010).

Henk W. Volberda is Professor of Strategic Management and Business Policy and Director Knowledge Transfer at the Rotterdam School of Management, Erasmus University, The Netherlands. He is director of the Erasmus Strategic Renewal Centre (ESR) and Fellow and Director of the Strategy Research Program of the Erasmus Research Institute of Management (ERIM). He is also Chairman of the top institute INSCOPE: Research for Innovation, board member of the Netherlands Institute for Social Innovation (NCSI), and Vice-President of the European Academy of Management (EURAM). His research on strategic flexibility and organizational renewal received many awards, including the Erasmus University Research Award 1997, the Igor Ansoff Strategic Management Award 1993, the ERIM Impact Award 2003, 2005 and 2007, the ERIM Top Article Award 2007 and the SAP Strategy Award 2005. His work on strategic renewal, coevolution of firms and industries, knowledge flows, new organizational forms and innovation has been published in journals such as the *Academy of Management Journal*, the *Journal of Business Venturing*, the *Journal of Management Studies*, the *Journal of International Business Studies*, *Long Range Planning*, *Management Science*, *Organization Studies*, and *Organization Science*.

Charles B. Weinberg is SMEV Presidents Professor and Chair of Marketing at the Sauder School of Business, University of British Columbia, Vancouver, Canada. His research interests include marketing management in public and nonprofit organizations, services management and marketing, and the development and application of marketing models and analytical techniques to a broad range of business and non-business settings. Recent published work has focused on competitive dynamics and timing strategies (with particular application to the arts and entertainment industries), the marketing of safer sex, and competition among nonprofit organizations. He is a former editor of *Marketing Letter* and former area editor of *Marketing Science*.

Raymond O.S. Zaal has been a PhD researcher at Nyenrode University, The Netherlands since 2009. He holds a Bachelor's degree in engineering and two Master's degrees in business administration, from Erasmus University, Rotterdam and the University of Rochester (USA). He is a senior lecturer and developer in several educational programs at Inholland

University for Applied Sciences and works as a management consultant. He is currently working on a PhD thesis on integrity management. His research is on the banking and real estate sectors in The Netherlands, focusing on the relationship between organizational aspects and ethical behavior, specifically the effectiveness of performance measurement and reward systems and ethical cultural practices as organizational instruments to reinforce ethical behavior.

Introduction

Killian J. McCarthy, Maya Fiolet and Wilfred Dolfsma

1 THE THEORY OF THE FIRM

In his seminal paper, 'The nature of the firm', Nobel Prize winning economist Ronald Coase (1937) introduces transaction cost theory, and defines the firm in relation to the market. Coase suggests that, given the presence of imperfect information, production will be centralized in the firm when the costs of doing so are cheaper than the costs of coordinating production through the market price exchange mechanism. The firm therefore is defined as a 'system of relationships' (ibid.), or as a 'nexus for a set of contracting relationships among individuals' (Jensen and Meckling, 1976, p. 8), which only 'comes into existence at the direction of the entrepreneur' (Coase, 1937, p. 393).

Figure 0.1 summarizes the Coasian argument. Here the vertical axis measures cost differences between internal organization and market transactions, and the horizontal axis measures asset specificity, denoted by k. The ΔY curve measures the differences in production costs when an item is produced in a vertically integrated firm, and when it is exchanged through a market transaction. It is positive at every level because outside suppliers can always aggregate buyer demands, and take advantage of economies of scale and scope to lower production costs below the production costs of the firm. The ΔY cost difference curve is downward sloping because higher levels of asset specificity (k) implies more specialized uses for the input, and fewer outlets for the outside supplier, and so increased asset specificity reduces the possibility of scale- and scope-based advantages.

Next, the ΔX curve measures differences in exchange costs when an item is produced internally, and when it is purchased from an outside supplier. It is positive for low levels of asset specificity, because then transaction costs are low, but quickly becomes negative as the levels of asset specificity increase. Higher levels of asset specificity suggest higher levels of transaction costs, and beyond point k^* these costs are so large that vertical integration is more efficient than market exchange. Finally, the ΔZ curve is the

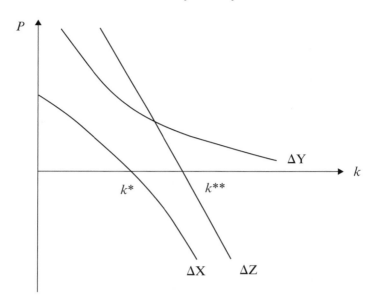

Figure 0.1   The boundaries of the firm

vertical summation of the ΔX and ΔY curves; it represents production and exchange costs under vertical integration, minus production and exchange costs under market transactions. When positive, the market exchange is preferred, and when negative the exchange costs of using the market more than offset the production cost savings, and vertical integration is preferred. Point kk^* then becomes the black and white Coasian boundary.

2   THE BLURRING OF BOUNDARIES

According to Klein (1983, p. 373), however, in reality 'such a sharp distinction does not exist'. In its simplest form, Coase's model offers clear and distinct boundaries between firms and markets – and hence between firms themselves which, it is suggested, are connected through markets – but does not allow for boundaries or subdivisions within firms. It is well known, however, that multiple markets exist within the firm, and that boundaries are blurring not only between firms, but even between the firm and the state.

In the aftermath of the financial crisis, for example, the boundaries between public and private have become increasingly unclear. As state actors in the US and Europe have slowly acquired ever more significant shares of private firms, while public and non-profit organizations adopt business practices, the question of where exactly the state stops and private industry begins is becoming an increasingly difficult question to answer.

Between organizations too, boundaries are becoming increasingly blurred. The rising popularity with which 'joint service centres' are being created, for example, raises some interesting questions. From a policy perspective, for instance, is it optimal to allow competitors to enjoy scale economies in the provision of 'non-core' products and services? And, from the firm's perspective, is it really beneficial to create joint ventures in, for example, research and development (R&D), when the resultant subsidiaries do not demonstrate strong ties to their parents? The existence of such 'intermediate forms' of activity, operating between firms and markets, however, draws into question the applicability of Coase's theory (Richardson, 1972).

Klein (1983, p. 373) suggests that Coase must also be updated to consider 'transactions occurring within the firm as representing market relationships', because as the state plays more of a role in internal governance, the functional areas of the firm have to adapt. Different product lines and/ or projects, for example, are increasingly encouraged to adopt a market mechanism, and to compete for resource allocations. Between firms, competitors can be welcomed into the fold (creating a patent pool) as alliance partners competing with another set of firms cooperating as an alliance to create a dominant design (standard). Traditional boundaries between 'them' and 'us' are continuously challenged on multiple levels relevant from an economic or business perspective.

3   CHANGES IN THE THEORY OF THE FIRM

A number of theories have been put forward to explain the blurring of Coasian boundaries: the managerial, the behavioural, and the Schumpeterian approaches.

Of these, the managerial theories – as developed by Baumol (1959 and 1962), Marris (1964) and Williamson (1996) – probably takes the dimmest view of the blurring boundaries. Managerial scholars suggest that managers seek to maximize their own utility, and that it is an asymmetry in the interests of the manager and the owner that explains the deviation from the behaviour suggested by transaction cost theory. More recently this has developed into 'principal–agent' analysis (Spence and Zeckhauser, 1971), which suggests that managerial behaviour arises either because the agent has greater expertise or knowledge than the principal – that is, the owner or shareholder – or because the principal cannot directly observe the agent's actions. The principal–agent problem is a leading explanation for the observed destruction of value, for example, in the case of mergers and acquisitions (Martynova and Renneboog, 2008).

The behavioural approach – as developed in particular by Cyert and March (1963), and which builds on Herbert Simon's work in the 1950s – is somewhat more forgiving, and suggests that 'limited cognitive ability' causes 'bounded rationality' but also 'framing', and that it is this which results in non-Coasian outcomes. Behavioural scholars suggest therefore that the blurring of boundaries is not evidence of self-interested managerial behaviour, but of the fact that a human manager cannot possibly weigh up all the costs and benefits of an action, and cannot therefore always adhere to the one best solution suggested by Coasian theory. Rather, managers tend to 'do the best they can', and it is this that sometimes leads to the selection of a suboptimal alternative. Furthermore, Cyert and March argued that the firm cannot be regarded as a monolith, which scrutinizes every decision against a single utility-maximizing condition. Firms and organizations, they suggest, are composed of different individuals and groups, each of which has its own aspirations, and often conflicting interests, and therefore organizational behaviour is the weighted outcome of these conflicts, rather than the actions of a single individual.

4   THE RISE OF THE KNOWLEDGE ECONOMY

In the Schumpeterian literature, and in a knowledge economy, the firm is seen in a different light. Rather than a simple 'nexus of contracts', the firm is seen to be a creator of knowledge through localized search efforts in and around production (Nelson and Winter, 1982; Rosenberg, 1982; Nelson, 1991). Such efforts, however, often require knowledge exchanges between individuals, between firms, and between firm and non-firm actors. And if the flows of knowledge, and the extent to which firms draw upon external capabilities rise sufficiently, then the boundaries of the firm blur.

Developments in information and communication technologies, and a more liberal anti-trust environment for interfirm cooperative arrangements, have facilitated this expansionary process, and encouraged the proliferation of cooperative ventures, by removing some of the constraints which had the capabilities for industrial growth centralized within large firms (Langlois, 2002). The result is a shift towards a more open structure of interfirm network relationships, and a decline in the relative significance of the traditional pyramid-like structure of organizational hierarchy. The result is that firms became specialist 'integrators' of different systems of knowledge, each of which was derived from internal and external sources

(Ernst and Kim, 2002), and embedded in a series of internal and external business networks (Forsgren et al., 2005).

This process of business network formation simultaneously, however, not only blurs the boundaries between firms, but also erects new boundaries within the firm. In an environment of open structures, subsidiaries, for example, or other subunits, may independently choose to initiate and/ or participate in different networks, and do so at such a frequency that the company's headquarters is unable to fully understand the diversity of its networks, as they develop. In addition, a given business network may connect a selection of internal and external actors, so that parts of the network belong to some common corporate group, but there are other subunits of the same group that may have no association with this network. So, if an entrepreneurial initiative begins in conjunction with network partners, the relevant focus of analysis may become the localized network, rather than the firm as such. As a result, the barriers to knowledge exchange between different units of the business in large firms can, it is suggested, become as much of an issue as the boundaries between firms, with the result that tension may develop between the local interorganizational networking relationships of an intrafirm unit and its wider international networking relationships with other parts of its corporate group.

5   ON THE NATURE OF BOUNDARIES

The boundaries of the firm are therefore active and dynamic places. Boundaries are typically contested, and have been compared to rivers, which 'tend to stick in their places, doing damage when they wander'.[1] Borders should not, however, be treated as a negative of behaviours elsewhere. In some academic domains, this is well understood.

Law, for instance, draws boundaries between what is allowed and what is not allowed.[2] At the same time, however, the law relies on boundaries for it to be effective. Without impregnable geographical boundaries, at least to some extent, the law is toothless. And enforcement of the law boils down to keeping the boundaries in place.

In sociology and anthropology, inclusion and exclusion, and the active contestation of their implied boundaries, is a long-standing research theme. What is included and what is excluded defines communities as well as organizations and firms: 'They' do not belong to 'us' (Elias and Scotson, 1965; Barth, 1970; Dolfsma et al., 2009). By establishing a border, a relatively stable sphere is created, which is safe and predictable in relation to an outside that is not. The inside/outside distinction that boundaries create 'lies at the collective' (Falk, 1994, p. 121). Boundaries will thus function not only as thresholds, controlling inflow and outflow, but also as binding structures, producing and reproducing internal unity (Llewellyn, 1994, p. 14). The boundaries created to impose homogeneity and certainty create a common institutional 'furniture' that allows for interpretation and coordination without direct involvement of a specific individual in a specific role.

Boundaries can be persistent, but also remarkably fluid under pressure. Boundaries are not simply residuals, to be changed at will. Transaction cost economics, as we have seen, takes the romantic view that boundaries are perfectly flexible, to the point where they are inconsequential. Much has been written about where the boundaries of the firm for instance are, but little about what actually occurs at the boundaries (Casson and Wadeson, 1998). The economy, for example, is an open system (Grunberg, 1978), which makes interactions with an environment inevitable. Hence, there is a need for active boundary maintenance, controlling which information is exchanged with the environment (Weber, 1968; DiMaggio and Powell, 1983; Llewellyn, 1994). Some measure of inertia is implied, and this explains, for example, why the supposed globalization of management practices does not materialize (Pot, 2000). But a change in the permeability of a boundary, may mean that (communication) costs increase, or decrease (Casson and Wadeson, 1998).

6   THE NATURE OF THE NEW FIRM

In this volume, we enquire into the 'nature of the new firm'; that is, the firm that has emerged from the blurring of traditional Coasian transaction cost boundaries.

In Part 1 we look at the blurring of boundaries within firms, and begin with an overview by Beuglesdijk which unites the three chapters, and marks their contributions. In Chapter 1, Ashton-James et al. study the nature of managerial power within the firm, and show, with reference to the merger process, how the manager's 'experience' of power can destroy value within the firm. In Chapter 2, Zaal studies unethical behaviour, and discusses how the organizational architecture of the firm can be used to reinforce ethical behaviour. Building on the findings of Ashton-James et al., particular attention is paid here to the assignment of decision rights, the structure of performance evaluation and the reward systems. And finally, in Chapter 3, Alexiev et al. look at the role of 'advice seeking' on the whole process. The authors consider how top management teams connect to their internal and external environments and, using data from a cross-industry study of Dutch firms, investigate the relationship between 'advice seeking', and the degree of comprehensiveness, or level of rationality, in the strategic decision-making process. In line with the story of Part 1, they find that external advice seeking is an important factor in the decision-making process.

In Part II we move to look at the blurring of boundaries between firms, and again begin with an overview, by Dolfsma and Duysters, which first introduces, and then unites the four chapters in Part II. In Chapter 4, Hitt and Ratinho begin with a discussion of institutions. They suggest that specific regulatory, political and economic institutions, as well as the emergence of a global economy, has affected the strategic behaviour of firms, both domestic and foreign. The strategic challenge that this poses to firms is lucidly illustrated in their contribution, and the authors make clear that firms need to develop strategic positions in their value chain if they hope to maintain a competitive advantage, and appropriate rents from their investments and innovative activities. In Chapter 5, Rietveld shows how choosing a position in a chain is not self-evident, even for established players. Rather than developing these key capabilities oneself, Rietveld shows that a firm may be forced to seek cooperation with another firm, thereby relinquishing a large part of the proceeds to this other firm.

In Chapter 6, Amiryany et al. suggest that serial acquirers can build the capabilities to share knowledge across boundaries, and investigate the micro-foundations of the so-called 'knowledge-sharing capability'. They suggest that knowledge transfer between cooperative units, and across the boundaries of the firm, is dependent upon the levels of integration. In Chapter 7, ter Wiel and Vlaar point out that the accumulation of experience in collaborating with other firms does not always contribute to a firm's competitive position. The authors argue that experience with one type of collaborative relationships is different from experience with another, and thus that lessons learned from repeated interactions with one party might not be transferable to another. Worse, they suggest that experience with certain types of collaborative relationships may even be detrimental to the performance of other types of relationships.

Finally Part III concludes with a discussion of the blurring of boundaries between public and private, profit and non-profit sectors, and deals with the issues of trust, and of boundaries between workers and management, between the clients of the organization, and the building of relations in the market. Groenewegen introduces this discussion, with an overview that unites the last three chapters. In Chapter 8, Sapulete et al. begin with a discussion on the connections between workers and management function, and argue that trust in the relationship between the two is crucial to understanding the effect of works councils on productivity during reorganizations. When trust is present, they suggest, works councils and management can be considered as part of a closely-knit network, which enhances the functioning of organizations, while a disjointed network leads to conflict, distrust and lower productivity. Organizations struggle, however, with the control issues related to networked organizing when hierarchical lines are blurred. This has frequently been shown to be the case when a network-like perspective is applied to the core of organizing, and is the subject of Chapter 9. Here, Fiolet discusses the changing patterns of activity in organizations, and suggests that this reflects this need for exploration into new forms of organizing. Fiolet suggests that due to external changes in mission, there is an increased need to change from internal logics to demand-driven care. This new logic crosses the boundary between two forms of control, one derived from care demands, the other from cost control. The process requires the development of trust relations, it is suggested, between different departments and disciplines in health-care organizations. Fiolet's research indicates that new organizational forms increasingly emerge as a consequence of a patchwork of solutions to the problems of organizations. And, echoing prior contributions to this volume, she suggests that managerial responsibility requires some degree of control, but that the new services also require management control. Finally, in Chapter 10, Weinberg and Lee explore the blurring of boundaries between the internal and the external, public and private. In both the research and management domains, networks are a key concept, enabling proper external positioning of the organization. Therefore external relations and positioning also become increasingly important to all organizations, and marketing tools are of increasing importance in finding audiences for both social and non-profit organizations, as argued by Weinberg and Lee. Marketing, they suggest, can be described as establishing relations with new publics, and in order to succeed in marketing, trust is subsequently seen to be an essential ingredient. Thus for marketing to work effectively, the authors suggest that the organization needs to pay attention to building relationships with the public, and make clear that networks are of broader importance. The growth in the number of non-profit providers catering for the same social needs, they suggest, shows that networking with 'competitors' is essential for success.

NOTES

1. *The Economist*, December 19, 1998 'Good Fences', pp. 19–22.
2. We would loosely define a boundary as an institution or set of institutions that separates two or more relatively homogeneous entities.

REFERENCES

Barth, F. (ed.) (1970), *Ethnic Groups and Boundaries*, London: Allen & Unwin.

Baumol, W.J. (1959), *Business Behaviour, Value and Growth*, New York: Macmillan.

Baumol, William J. (1962), 'On the theory of expansion of the firm', *American Economic Review*, **52** (5), December, 1078–87.

Casson, M. and N. Wadeson (1998), 'Communication costs and the boundaries of the firm', *International Journal of the Economics of Business*, **5** (1), 5–27.

Coase, R.H. (1937), 'The nature of the firm', *Economica*, N.S., **4** (16), 386–405.

Cyert, Richard and James March (1963), *Behavioral Theory of the Firm*, Oxford: Blackwell.

DiMaggio, P.J. and W.W. Powell (1983), 'The iron cage revisited: institutional isomorphism and collective rationality in organizational fields', *American Sociological Review*, **48** (2), 147–60.

Dolfsma, W., R. van der Eijk and A. Jolink (2009), 'On a source of social capital: gift exchange', *Journal of Business Ethics*, **89** (3), 315–29.

Elias, N. and J.L. Scotson (1965), *The Established and the Outsiders: A Sociological Inquiry into Community Problems*, London: Cass.

Ernst, D. and L. Kim (2002), 'Global production networks, knowledge diffusion and local capability formation', *Research Policy*, **31** (8–9), 1417–29.

Falk, R. (1994), 'The making of global citizenship', in B. van Steenbergen (ed.), *The Conditions of Citizenship*, London: Sage, pp. 127–40.

Forsgren, M., U. Holm and J. Johanson (2005), *Managing the Embedded Multinational: A Business Network View*, Cheltenham, UK and Northampton, MA, USA: Edward Elgar.

Grunberg, E. (1978), '"Complexity" and "open systems" in economic discourse', *Journal of Economic Issues*, **12**, 541–60.

Jensen, M.C. and W.H. Meckling (1976), 'Theory of the firm: managerial behavior, agency costs and ownership structure', *Journal of Financial Economics*, **3** (4), October, 305–60.

Klein, B. (1983), 'Contracting costs and residual claims: the separation of ownership and control', *Journal of Law and Economics*, **26** (2), 367–74.

Langlois, R.N. (2002), 'Modularity in technology and organization', *Journal of Economic Behavior and Organization*, **49** (1), 19–37.

Llewellyn, S. (1994), 'Managing the boundary – how accounting is implicated in maintaining the organization', *Accounting, Auditing & Accountability Journal*, **7** (4), 4–23.

Marris, R. (1964), *The Economic Theory of Managerial Capitalism*, London: Macmillan.

Martynova, M. and L.D.R. Renneboog (2008), 'A century of corporate takeovers: what have we learned and where do we stand?', *Journal of Banking and Finance*, **32** (10), 2148–77.

Nelson, R.R. (1991), 'Why do firms differ, and how does it matter?', *Strategic Management Journal*, **12** (1), 61–74.

Nelson, R.R. and S.G. Winter (1982), *An Evolutionary Theory of Economic Change*, Cambridge, MA: Harvard University Press.

Pot, F. (2000), *Employment Relations and National Culture: Continuity and Change in the Age of Globalization*, Cheltenham, UK and Northampton, MA, USA: Edward Elgar.

Richardson, G.B. (1972), 'The organisation of industry', *Economic Journal*, **82** (327): 883. doi:10.2307/2230256.

Rosenberg, N. (1982), *Inside the Black Box: Technology and Economics*, Cambridge and New York: Cambridge University Press.

Spence, Michael A. and Richard Zeckhauser (1971), 'Insurance, information, and individual action', *American Economic Review*, **61** (2), 380–87.

Weber, Max (1968), *Economy and Society*, New York: Bedminster.

Williamson, O.E. (1996), *The Mechanisms of Governance*, Oxford and New York: Oxford University Press.

PART I

Within the firm

Introduction to Part I: Organization theorists struggling with a view of humankind – power, ethics and top management teams

Sjoerd Beugelsdijk

All three chapters in Part I are rich and the information density is high. They are all well embedded in the relevant literature and provide a number of useful additions to this literature.

Chapter 1, by Ashton-James et al., provides a social view on mergers and the destruction of value in mergers. Given the dominance of the finance-based view on mergers, their approach is a welcome addition to the debate on this topic and the question whether and how they destroy value. Their core argument is that managers have unique opportunities to create or destroy value in the conclusion of a merger, owing to their position of power. Ashton-James et al. carefully describe the merger process in different steps. For each step they analyze the role of the manager. Embedded in an otherwise standard theory of power, they distinguish between a pre-merger stage, a post-merger stage, and the underlying motivation of the merger. In the pre-merger stage, managerial hubris (overconfidence) may lead the firm to pay a premium in the merger process. The post-merger stage leaves most room for value destruction according to the authors, and they point at a lack of the proper skills (communication and emotional intelligence). Finally, the motivation of the decision to merge may be blurred as well, because it may be driven by self-enhancement and/ or self-protection. These stages are then analyzed in more detail, based on a set of behavioral assumptions derived from 'power theory': powerful managers are 'optimistic, action-oriented individuals, prone to overconfidence, risk taking, and illusions of control' (p. 24). They conclude their chapter with a carefully crafted 'laundry list' of practical implications.

Although Ashton-James et al. start their chapter by arguing that managers can also add value, the authors are concentrating on reasons why and how managers destroy value. Except for a limited number of more positive remarks, the authors have a rather pessimistic view on the role of managers in the merger process. The reality is that for mergers to occur, key decision makers also need to have a powerful position. It is not that successful mergers are associated with managers that are *not* powerful. Power is not necessarily a bad thing. This raises the question *under what conditions* do powerful managers create or destroy value? A contingency approach to the role of managerial power in mergers is a next step and provides an interesting avenue for further research (Chapter 2 by Zaal illustrates this, see my discussion below).

Moreover, Ashton-James et al. are right that managers may destroy value, but how many opportunities for value creation by merging are missed, precisely because of managerial power, and the entrenched positions that key decision makers take? The point is that while we can observe mergers and whether they fail or not, we cannot observe 'failed attempts to merge'. The population of actual observations does not include this category, and no one knows how large this group actually is. Hence, the argument that powerful managers destroy value can actually be extended to the sample of 'failed attempts to merge'. The sample studied by the authors is relevant because it is the subsample we can actually observe, but the flipside of the merger medal also includes firms that would benefit from merging, but actually fail to do so. In other words, the theory developed by the authors applies not just to failed mergers, but also to failed attempts to merge.

Chapter 2 by Zaal is directly related to the previous one by Ashton-James et al. Instead of a focus on powerful managers, he concentrates on employees and argues that ethical behavior of employees is embedded in the overall organizational architecture. Managers do play a crucial role, though, because they are key decision makers guiding the development of a certain organizational architecture. Zaal starts from the observation that (un)ethical behavior is a function of both individual and organizational characteristics, but that research has shown that strategies focusing on the former have been ineffective. This is why he turns to the role of organizational architecture. In a way he complements Ashton-James et al. by providing a contingency approach of (un)ethical behavior. Although Zaal does not refer to this theory, it strongly resembles the theory on organizational citizenship behavior (OCB). Under what conditions do employees behave as good 'citizens'?

After establishing that organizational culture plays a role as well, Zaal concentrates on 'hard' organizational structure, more specifically to the assignment of decision rights, the structure of performance evaluation, and the role of reward systems. For each of these, he carefully describes how they promote (un)ethical behavior. A key underlying assumption in his arguments is that ethical behavior is 'defined as employee behavior that is consistent with the norms and values, rules and obligations *of the stake-holders of the organization*' (p. 45; emphasis added). By doing so, Zaal has a view of ethical behavior that is driven by purely external factors. This is a risky statement, because what if the stakeholders define an unethical aggregate goal? The case of Enron comes to mind, in which a top-down defined, collectively shared unethical approach was the norm, supported by a specific internal reward system and performance evaluation.

In this view, employees are implicitly assumed to be ethically naive and can only be guided by proper incentives and external pressure. In doing so, Zaal sees a role for key decision makers. This is an interesting position given the negative role ascribed to such powerful managers in the first chapter by Ashton-James et al. Both Zaal and Ashton-James et al. have a negative view of humankind, the former of employees, and the latter of managers. However, Zaal is clearly struggling with this view of employees and managers. He implicitly ascribes a certain moral superiority to top managers when curbing the potentially unethical behavior of employees. Key decision makers are seen as angels in such an approach. However, he also writes that a participatory management style is associated with ethical superiority, linking hierarchy and power with negative effects. All this is related to an age-old question: are people intrinsically ethical or intrinsically unethical? And more broadly, who guards the guardian? Is that institutionalized by means of an internal bottom-up process or 'imposed' by external stakeholders?

The relative importance of internal or external influences on key decision makers is the focus of Chapter 3. Alexiev et al. aim to understand the decision-making process among top managers by focusing on the behaviors that link managers with their external and internal environments, and understand the forces that influence this behavior. In doing so, they study the strategy process as a whole, and concentrate on decision comprehensiveness. This is defined as 'the extent to which an organization attempts to be exhaustive or inclusive in making and integrating strategic decisions' (quoted from Fredrickson and Mitchell). Alexiev et al. distinguish between top managers that are externally oriented and those that are internally oriented (seeking advice from external or internal sources). Although they propose that both are linked positively to decision comprehensiveness, firms differ in their preference for internal or external advice seeking depending on what is common in their external environment. Industries differ, and the need to adapt to the external environment (isomorphism) is argued to determine the preference for either internal or external advice seeking.

The authors test their argument by an empirical analysis of five industries with a total sample of 659 respondents. They indeed find that both internal and external advice seeking has positive effects on decision comprehensiveness, but also that it varies across industries. In other words, top decision makers use a variety of sources of information, and in some industries this is more internally oriented, whereas in others it is more externally oriented. By emphasizing the role of a firm's institutional environment, Alexiev et al. clearly show the importance of applying a contingency approach in understanding the foundations of decision making among top managers. Hence, whereas Ashton-James et al. propose that powerful managers may destroy value in mergers, Alexiev et al. show that this may not be a generic phenomenon because the overall decision-making process is not uniform across industries. The contribution by Alexiev et al. is also important in the context of Zaal's discussion of the organizational architecture and the impact on promoting (un)ethical behavior. Whereas Zaal struggles with the question whether people are naturally inclined to behave ethically or need to be curbed by top management, Alexiev et al.'s analysis suggests this is also affected by the firm's need to adapt to the local environment, and is externally determined.

In sum, all three chapters try to increase our understanding of the decision-making process and the role of managers in this process. All three make a contribution to the literature and in that respect they are self-standing. They are linked, as described above, but they also reflect a broader struggle of organization theorists that is related to the view of humankind. Do people in a position of power by definition frustrate merger processes? Do people behave intrinsically ethically or not? Is the need to search for external or internal advice imposed by the external environmental pressures or a decision independently made by (top) managers? Such questions touch upon core methodological and philosophical predispositions. Hence, these chapters are not just self-standing contributions to ongoing debates, but reflect a fundamental struggle of organization theorists to understand the role of individuals (agency) in organizations (structure), and how organizations shape individuals.

1. Power, and the destruction of value in mergers and acquisitions

Claire E. Ashton-James, Killian J. McCarthy and Anca Dranca-Iacoban

1 INTRODUCTION

Between 1995 and 1999, US$9,000 billion was spent by North American and Western European firms on mergers and acquisitions (M&As);[1] – a near incomprehensible figure which, by way of comparison, was about seven times the UK's GDP, and more then twenty times that of the Netherlands (Schenk, 2003) in the same period. So large was the expenditure that, as a percentage of US GDP, M&As soared from 1.6 percent in the 1960s, to 3.4 percent in the 1980s, to a staggering 15.4 percent at the height of the 'fifth merger wave' in 1999 (Mergerstat, 2006). And as the 'sixth merger wave' unfolded (2003–08), records were again broken, when 'the value of M&A averaged $10 billion a day' (*The Economist*, April 8, 2006).

Positive as this may at first appear, the fact that the impact of M&A activity on the performance of the firm is, at best, 'inconclusive' (Roll, 1988; Haspeslagh and Jemison, 1991; Sirower, 1997), and at worst 'systematic[ally] detrimental' (Dickerson et al., 1997), is nothing short of troubling. Some studies have reported that the combined average returns (CAR) – that is, the average net change in value, accrued to the shareholders of both the acquiring and the target company and caused by a merger – are positive but small (Campa and Hernando, 2004). Others still occasionally find no significant effects on performance (Stulz et al., 1990). The 'overwhelming majority', however, find that 'M&A activity does not positively contribute to the acquiring firm's performance' (King et al., 2004, p. 196), or its profitability, as variously measured (Ravenscraft and Scherer, 1987, 1989; Bühner, 1991; Berger and Humphrey, 1992; Simon et al., 1996; Rhoades, 1998). A consensus of estimates places the M&A failure rate somewhere in the range of 65–85 percent (Puranam and Singh, 1999), a figure which Moeller et al. (2005) translate into annual losses of $60 billion.

The paradox is that mergers should, however, create value. Because – according to efficiency theory – mergers are an alteration to the boundaries of the firm, which occur either because the manager attempts to cut costs – by internalizing those transactions that had previously been negotiated on the market – or to expand revenues – by seeking out scale economies in new products and markets (Besanko et al., 2006). And they will only be concluded when the shareholders of both the target and the acquirer possess a symmetric expectation of a realizable gain (Weston et al., 2004). The scale of the destruction thus creates important questions about the effectiveness with which the firm's boundaries can be altered by the manager.

A number of firm- and deal-specific explanations have been put forward to explain why mergers fail. Chatterjee (1986) and Gugler et al. (2003), for example, show that the 'degree of relatedness' between the target and the acquirer is a significant explanatory variable in predicting post-merger performance. Moeller et al. (2004) and, more recently, Weitzel and McCarthy (forthcoming), show that size matters, and find that larger acquirers underperform their smaller rivals, while Chang (1998) and Officer (2007) provide evidence that acquirer returns in publicly listed targets differ significantly from private targets. Jensen (1986, 1988, 2003) shows that the presence of 'free cash' (or excess liquidity) affects performance, because it liberates the firm from the so-called 'discipline of debt'; a conclusion confirmed by Hitt et al. (1998) from the perspective of leverage. Carline et al. (2002) find significance in deal values, suggesting that the bigger the deal the poorer the performance, and Moeller et al. (2005) find that merger waves significantly impact average deal value. Haunschild (1994), Hayward and Hambrick (1997) and Hitt and Pisano (2003) all find evidence that the payment of 'premiums' – that is, the payment of a sum on top of the firm's market value – predicts poor performance, while Jensen and Ruback (1983) and Betton and Eckbo (2000) find that hostility also plays an important role in merger success.

In this chapter we introduce managers' 'experience of power' as an explanation for the observed destruction of merger value. We argue that the extant literature adopts a predominantly finance-oriented perspective in attempting to understand success and failure – within which it is assumed that M&As are a 'closed system' – with little room for human influence or interference. We suggest, however, that managers have unique opportunities to create or destroy value in the conclusion of a merger, owing to their position of power, and we adopt a multidisciplinary approach to understanding and predicting success and failure, by synthesizing new research on the impact of power on judgment and decision making with existing research on mergers and the merger process.

We begin, in Section 2, with a review of the merger process, within which we consider the explanations – both financial and psychological – for why mergers destroy value. In Section 3, we examine 'managerial power' – a psychological factor known to affect key aspects of judgment and decision making – as an important and yet unexplored element of value creation (and destruction), and we then build a conceptual model, which systematically describes how power affects value. In Section 4 we identify the limitations of our analysis, and suggest some practical implications of our theoretical model in the light of these limitations, and in Section 5, we conclude with a discussion of our future research directions.

2 UNDERSTANDING MERGERS AND ACQUISITIONS

The Merger Process

The various stages of the merger process can be describes as the: 'pre-merger' (planning), 'during-the-merger' (realization), or 'post-merger' (integration) stages (Appelbaum et al., 2000a,b; Cartwright and Cooper, 2000; Jansen and Pohlmann, 2000). To understand the scope of managerial power, it is necessary to understand each stage.

The pre-merger stage consists of a number of 'planning' and 'positioning' decisions (see Figure 1.1). The decision to merge is made by a few top executives – if not a single CEO or chairperson – who makes a decision either to cut costs, by internalizing operations that had previously been negotiated on the market, or to expand revenues, through the attainment of scale economies. 'Searching' and 'screening' (that is, the 'due-diligence process') come next, as target companies are considered on the basis of their projected earning potential and strategic fit (be it in products, markets, location, or resources). Based on the (legal and financial) health of these companies, top-level negotiations can then begin.

The contract is signed in the during-the-merger phase. During this phase 'integration planning' also occurs (Burgelman and Grove, 2007), redundancies are defined, and the merger announcement is planned and then executed.

In the post-merger phase, strategic capabilities are integrated in an effort to realize synergies, and thereby create value. This stage involves strategic interactions between the managers of different hierarchical levels, and between colleagues of partner organizations. Effective communication, an understanding of and respect for each other's organizational structure and

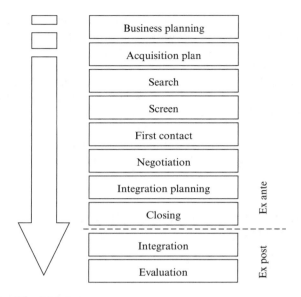

Figure 1.1   The M&A process

culture are essential for the transfer and integration of capabilities, and the creation of value (Haspeslagh and Jemison, 1991).

Merger Motives and the Destruction of Value

Synergistic savings and economies in scale and scope – and thus the creation of value – are among the most commonly cited merger motives (Gaughan, 2007).

A merger of two firms is thought to result in: (a) cost synergies, as labor forces are reduced, and administration and production costs are stream-lined (Carey, 2000); (b) market power gains, as a reduction in the level of competition allows for wealth to be transferred from the firm's customers and suppliers to its shareholders (Chatterjee, 1986); (c) financial gains, as a merger produces a company with a reduced tax profile (Devos et al., 2008); and (d) scale and scope economies, as a firm exploits the opportunity to expand and diversify into new products and regions (Besanko et al., 2006).

However, there are also subtle psychological reasons for mergers that are widely unacknowledged but implicitly understood (Cartwright and Cooper, 1990). Fear of obsolescence, personal interest, and the desire for power, prestige and empire are examples of such psychological motives (Shleifer and Vishny, 1989). Each is connected to the managers' egocentric needs to increase or maintain personal power; indeed several scholars and independent consulting firms have recognized that M&As are often born out of the 'personal whims' of egotistical CEOs, looking for excitement, a feeling of control or influence over the direction of the company, the need to gain collective influence, to entrench themselves in an irreplaceable position within the firm, or simply following an urge for empire building (McKinsey & Associates, 1988; Halpern, 1983; Cartwright and Cooper, 1990).

It is perhaps not surprising that mergers motivated by economic considerations – that is, by the attainment of 'synergies' – are generally more successful than those motivated by ego protection or agency (Weitzel and McCarthy, forthcoming). But studies suggest that even these often fail to produce non-negative returns (Cartwright and Cooper, 1993; Appelbaum et al., 2000a,b; Martynova and Renneboog, 2008).

There are several reasons why mergers might fail (Trautwein, 1990). Understandably, many of these have to do with failures in the strategic, financial and economic decision-making processes. For example, underprivileged due-diligence analyses, poor selection decisions, a lack of pre-planning, a strategic and financial mismatch, a failure to correctly estimate the value of the target, and unpredicted changes in market conditions can all contribute to poor performance (Fairburn and Geroski, 1989; Cartwright and Cooper, 1990; Rockness et al., 2001). Furthermore, a number of firm- and deal-specific characteristics – such as size, relatedness, and ownership structure, the levels of hostility, liquidity and methods of payment – have been found to play an important role in moderating the probability of success and failure.

Human factors, however, and the psychology of the manager, are a much-neglected explanation for the destruction of value, because it is assumed that mergers are a 'closed system', with little room for human influence or interference. Estimates suggest, however, that managers may be responsible for between one-third to one-half of all merger failures (Cartwright and Cooper, 1990; Dannemiller Tyson, 2000).

The Psychology of the Manager

The manager can influence and undermine the M&A process at both the pre- and post-merger stages (see Weitzel and McCarthy, forthcoming for an overview).

Managerial influence on pre-merger processes
A number of theories explain value destruction at the pre-merger stage. The theory of managerial hubris (Roll, 1986, 1988) for example, suggests

that managers may have good intentions in initiating mergers, and that they may aim to increase the value of the firm. The theory suggests, however, that being overconfident, managers typically overestimate their ability to create synergies. Overconfidence leads to overpaying (Hayward and Hambrick, 1997; Güner et al., 2008), which in turn dramatically increases the probability of failure (Dong et al., 2006). By contrast, Jensen's (1986) theory of managerial discretion claims that it is not managerial overconfidence that drives unproductive acquisitions, but rather the overconfidence of shareholders in managers. Jensen suggests that this allows them to make quick strategic decisions, and to engage in large-scale strategic actions with little analysis or accountability (Martynova and Renneboog, 2008). The managerial theories of the firm (Marris, 1964) are, however, less kind. They suggest that managers may intentionally act as value destroyers, because they pursue self-serving acquisitions. The theory of managerial entrenchment (Shleifer and Vishny, 1989), for example, claims that unsuccessful mergers occur because managers make investments that minimize the risk of replacement, or allow for increases in wealth, power, reputation and fame.

Managerial influence on post-merger processes

Irrespective of their initial motivation, the goal of the post-merger processes is to integrate the two organizational structures and cultures. And here the potential for value destruction is immense (Burgelman and Grove, 2007). Critical to the success of this stage is the managers' capacity to effectively communicate organizational goals across hierarchical levels, and between organizations. Furthermore, an understanding and respect for the organizational structure and culture of both the target and the acquirer are essential for an effective transfer and integration of capabilities (Haspeslagh and Jemison, 1991). It is perhaps not surprising, therefore, that failures at this stage have been attributed to the absence of emotionally intelligent leadership (Cartwright and Cooper, 2000).

A Gap in the Literature

Clearly, the manager occupies a position of power, and can influence both the organizational strategy of the firm, and group decision processes, to destroy value. Yet little is known about the manner in which the manager affects value in M&As, beyond the fact that hubris, or motives for self-protection (entrenchment) or self-enhancement (empire building) destroy value. There is therefore an important gap in our understanding of the psychology of the manager. The goal of the present research is to correct this, and to investigate 'power' – a psychological factor known to affect key aspects of judgment and decision making – as an important and yet unexplored element in the creation and destruction of value.

3   THE IMPACT OF MANAGERIAL POWER ON THE M&A PROCESS

It has been empirically demonstrated that individuals in a position of power have a unique capacity to affect the thoughts, feelings, and even behaviors of others.[2] More recent research reveals that the 'experience of power' itself has the capacity to influence the thoughts, feelings, and behaviors of powerful individuals themselves, often to destructive ends. In other words, individuals in a position of power are influenced by it to think and act in ways that they would not otherwise. In this section, we consider the nature of managerial power, and explore how this can affect judgment and decision-making processes that are critical to M&A processes.

Power Affects Thought and Behavior

Power is 'experienced' when individuals have asymmetric responsibility for and control over valued resources in social relations (Fiske, 1993). Managers, responsible for the division of a firm's resources to a greater extent than other organizational members, are thus in a position associated with the experience of power.

The potential for power to influence managerial judgment and decision-making processes stems from the fact that power fundamentally alters individuals' psychological states. The most influential and empirically supported theoretical framework for understanding the psychological effects of power is known as the 'power approach theory' (Keltner et al., 2003). This theory posits that elevated power activates what social psychologists refer to as the 'behavioral approach system' – which increases one's sensitivity to rewards – while powerlessness activates the so-called 'behavioral inhibition system' – which triggers a sensitivity to threats. Although at first both are probably unfamiliar, we suggest that both will have been experienced by the reader: in response to positive environmental feedback (receiving praise, for example), one feels motivated to approach, or to take action towards the achievement of our goals; in response to negative environmental feedback (receiving criticism, for example), one becomes more inhibited, and proceeds with caution and consideration. Thus the activation of behavioral systems will vary from situation to situation. However, people in a position of power, it is suggested, will more often than not find themselves in an approach state rather than in an inhibition state.

The power-induced activation of the behavioral approach system has important cognitive and behavioral consequences. In the following, we shall discuss how the experience of power: (i) focuses the individual's attention on rewards and opportunities, rather than on threats; and (ii) reduces social attentiveness. These effects are particularly important in the context of M&As, where vigilant decision making, and behavioral caution, reduce the potential for errors in the pre-merger planning and post-merger integration stages.

Attention to opportunities and rewards

Much research – directly flowing from this power-approach theory (Keltner et al., 2003) – has shown that the powerful appear to be optimistic, action-oriented individuals, prone to overconfidence, risk taking, and illusions of control.

Power increases optimism and risk taking   Research has shown that power induces a general sense of optimism. Powerful individuals, it has been shown, tend to believe that their future holds in store both more positive and fewer negative events (Anderson and Galinsky, 2006). These optimistic views of the world increase the attraction of the powerful to risk, in terms of both exhibiting greater risk preferences as well as making riskier choices (Anderson and Galinsky, 2006; Maner et al., 2007). The risky decision making and behavior of the powerful is also facilitated by their tendency to focus their attention on the potential rewards, rather than on the potential threats in their environment. When presented with a selection of alternatives, therefore, they are more likely to see the potential gains associated with each option, and to become blind to the potential losses.

Power increases illusions of control   Power not only transforms individuals into optimists and risk takers, but it also increases their general sense of control, even in situations where this control is illusory. In other words, powerful people are more optimistic, and take more assertive action, because they experience a heightened sense of control. This sense of control can, however, result in both positive and negative downstream consequences. For instance, an illusion of control allows the powerful to achieve seemingly unreachable goals by pursuing low probability alternatives (Taylor and Brown, 1988). But as pointed out by Galinsky et al. (2010), the relationship between power and illusory control might also contribute to an escalation of commitment, leading them and others down disastrous paths of entrapment.

Social attentiveness
Perhaps because they are less reliant on others for access to valued resources, people in a position of power are less attentive to the thoughts and feelings of others (for example, Galinsky et al., 2006), and are less concerned with social norms – unless, of course, these others are seen by the powerful to be instrumental in achieving self-interested goals, in which case they show increased attentiveness to the thoughts and feelings of others (Overbeck and Park, 2006).

Power reduces perspective taking and compassion   The powerful are notoriously poor perspective takers. Galinsky et al. (2006), for example, found that the powerful are less able to take the visual perspective of others, to take others' background knowledge into account, and to correctly identify others' emotional expressions. This lack of understanding of others' point of view and feelings impairs communication.[3] Research has shown that power also impairs compassion, however, and blinds people to the feelings of others. The powerful are less accurate, it has been shown, in comprehending others' emotional states (ibid.), and show diminished reciprocal emotional responses to another person's suffering (feeling distress, for example, at another person's distress). Van Kleef et al. (2008) found that emotional disengagement of the powerful from others was driven by power-related differences in the motivation to affiliate and connect with others.

There is, however, one caveat to this: power makes people more inclined to view others in an instrumental manner, as a tool toward the achievement of their own goals. For example, a series of studies by Overbeck and Park (2006) showed that when the powerful are pursuing 'people-centered' goals they individuate their targets by paying increased attention to and remembering more unique information about them. Similarly, Gruenfeld et al. (2008) found that power increases objectification, which they define as relating to social targets, based on their utility for achieving self-relevant goals. As we discuss below, this tendency for powerful individuals to view others in an instrumental manner can have both positive and negative consequences for the realization of value in the M&A process.

The powerful think abstractly   Finally, Smith and Trope (2006) found that the powerful engaged in more abstract thinking than the powerless, who demonstrate more concrete thinking. Abstract thinking is used to identify the relationship between the individual parts and the whole – it is the ability to see the big picture. Concrete thinking, on the other hand, is detail oriented. Thus, Smith and Trope found that the powerful are better able to recognize patterns in the environment and capture the gist of large amounts of information efficiently and effectively, but are often less capable of effectively operationalizing their plans.

On the effects of power on thought and behavior

In sum, we suggest that the manager's 'experience of power' activates the behavioral approach system, which: (i) focuses his/her attention on rewards and opportunities, promoting overconfidence, risk taking, and an illusion of control; and (2) reduces his/her social attentiveness, which impairs perspective taking and compassion, but increases divergent and abstract thinking. We now turn to the implications of these cognitive and behavioral consequences of power for the management of the M&A process, in an effort to better understand the creation and destruction of value.

Managerial Power in the Merger Process

Power in the pre-merger stage

As outlined in Figure 1.1, the pre-merger stage involves planning an acquisition, searching, and screening, and results in the selection of a firm with which to merge. Contact is then made, and negotiations are held between top managers on the terms of the merger or acquisition, followed by integration planning, and closing.

Several of these steps may be critically affected by the psychology of the manager, who is in a position of power and therefore may be prone to power-related biases (opportunity seeking and social inattentiveness). We have also established that the manager's psychological state is largely affected by his or her experience of power, which focuses attention on opportunities and rewards. This attentional bias towards rewards rather than threats may lead to overconfidence (hubris), which motivates managers to enter into mergers and make acquisitions that are high risk. Indeed, power is also associated with optimism and high-risk decision making, as managers in a position of power experience an illusion of control over the outcomes of their decisions. Berkovitch and Narayanan (1993) find strong evidence of hubris in US takeovers, and Goergen and Renneboog (2004) find the same in a European context. The latter estimate that about one-third of the large takeovers in the 1990s suffered from some form of hubris. Malmendier and Tate (2005) show that overly optimistic managers, who voluntarily retain in-the-money stock options in their own firms, more frequently engage in less profitable diversifying mergers. Rau and Vermaelen (1998) find that hubris is more likely to be seen among low book-to-market ratio firms – that is, among the so-called 'glamor firms' where managerial discretion is greater – than among high book-to-market ratio 'value firms'. Thus, we suggest that power may motivate managers to enter into mergers that have a high risk of failure, thereby increasing the potential for value destruction from the outset.

Whatever the motive, once a merger or acquisition has been planned, managers *search and screen* potential candidates for the merger. Optimally, this process is systematic and detail oriented. Power interferes with concrete thinking, however, and detail-oriented processing, and hence may impair the managers' attention to detail in the search and screening process. The rise of management theory, and the idea that 'good managers can manage anything' (Weston and Mansinghka, 1971; Gaughan, 2007), it is generally agreed, further diminished the managers' attention to detail in the 1960s, and inspired the third merger way (ca. 1960 to 1969) to diversify. In this case, and in any subsequent case where the manager does not pay adequate attention, the suggestion is that power increases the potential for value destruction, by undermining the process by which the manager chooses a firm with whom to merge, or to acquire.

After the target has been selected, and – typically informal[4] – first contact with the chosen firm has been made, the *negotiation process* – in which a buying price is settled – begins. Research by Van Kleef et al. (2006) demonstrates that in the realm of negotiation, power has the potential to facilitate the creation of value. As mentioned above, power reduces social attentiveness; the powerful are better able to turn a blind eye to the suffering of others. Consequently, power protects negotiators from being swayed by the strategic displays of emotions that are designed to induce concessions. Thus, high-power negotiators are less likely to concede to an angry opponent compared to low-power negotiators (ibid.). Similarly, in a bargaining context, high-power negotiators are more likely to make a first offer compared to their less powerful partners (Magee et al., 2007). These studies showed that by making the first offer, the powerful garnered a distinct financial advantage. Thus, in the negotiation phase of the M&A process, the power bestowed upon the manager may, we suggest, impart a distinct organizational advantage.

Finally, and as argued by Cartwright and Cooper (2000), many M&As fail due to poor *integration planning*. Organizational and cultural clashes, duplication, and a failure to streamline the operation of the firm can all result in the destruction of significant value (Weston et al., 2004). Given that power reduces social attentiveness, and in particular leads to poor perspective taking and a tendency to view others in an instrumental manner, it is likely that managers experiencing power may pay less attention to this aspect of the M&A process than necessary for a smooth post-merger integration. Thus, value can again be destroyed in this stage, too.

Power in the post-merger stage

In the post-merger stage, the manager oversees the *integration* of skills and resources necessary for the achievement of synergies, and the creation of value.

The integration stage involves retrenchment and reallocation of employees, as well as hiring of new middle managers. As discussed earlier, the success of this stage depends on the effective communication of organizational goals within and across organizations. Managerial communication is potentially impaired, however, by the experience of power, which leads individuals to focus on 'the gist', and to address problems at a higher level of abstraction, which can lead to communication distortions between high- and low-power individuals, who tend to think more concretely.

We have seen, however, that managers with enhanced abstract thinking capacity have the ability to see the big picture. Coupled with optimism, this can be used to generate and successfully communicate 'grand visions for the future', and thereby motivate subordinates to pursue a common goal. Hence, while power is, in general, an obstacle to communication, it may also facilitate motivational leadership.

As demonstrated by Galinsky et al. (2008), however, we have suggested that the powerful have a reduced capacity for perspective taking which results in a tendency to assume that others have access to private knowledge. In a merger process, this would inevitably impair the communication of details that are essential to employees' understanding of the situations and problems that arise amidst organizational change.

Destructive as it may be in terms of communication, it is possible that the experience of power can have positive consequences for the merger, in terms of *hiring* decisions. Gruenfeld et al. (2008) create a hiring situation, in which some job candidates were better fits for specific positions (for example, a salesperson needed to be extroverted). In this situation high-power individuals were better able to select the candidate whose attributes best matched the hiring criterion. In addition, managers may be better able to make difficult *restructuring* decisions (that is, laying off employees), because of their instrumental view of organizational members. In support of this, Lammers and Stapel (2009) found that in a medical simulation, high-power senior surgeons' more objective view of patients helped them to administer a painful but effective medical treatment. Low-power nurses and junior surgeons were hindered from doing so, because they focused too much on the pain and suffering caused by it. Thus, while the relationship between power and objectification might be dysfunctional for social relationships and communication with lower-level managers and employees, it may be functional for the attainment of organizational goals.

Finally, we suggest that managerial power is most likely to affect the *evaluation* of merger success, and re-evaluation of integration plans, by biasing managers towards the perception of opportunities and rewards and hindering attention to threats and obstacles. Paired with an illusion of control, the powerful may see real threats as mere 'setbacks', influencing their willingness to re-evaluate pre-merger integration plans. This promotion- rather than prevention-focused interpretational bias maximizes, rather than minimizes, we suggest, the potential for value destruction.

The effects of power on the merger process
In summary, we suggest that managerial power may influence the M&A process by: introducing overconfidence to the merger motives (value destruction); reducing the rigor of the search and screening process (value destruction); facilitating negotiations and bargaining (value creation); reducing motivation to invest in integration planning (value destruction); impairing the communication of organizational strategies (value destruction); enhancing the communication of organizational goals (value creation); aiding the objectivity with which restructuring (hiring and firing) decisions are made (value creation); and placing a positive bias on the evaluation of post-merger processes (value destruction). These, and the potential, practical, consequences of them on the merger, are documented in Table 1.1.

Thus, while power clearly provides managers with key competencies in the negotiation of the merger, the communication of organizational goals, and strategic restructuring, there are several phases of the M&A process that may be undermined by managerial power, if that power is allowed to lead organizational policy unchecked. In the next section, we discuss strategies for utilizing managerial power in mergers, and strategies for managing the influence of the powerful in the M&A process. First, however, it is important to address the limitations of our analysis for understanding the impact of managerial power on M&As.

4   DISCUSSION

Theoretical Limitations

Our preceding discussion of the effects of manager power on M&A success suggests that it can increase the probability of value destruction in many ways due to the fact that power increases attention to rewards or opportunities and decreases social attentiveness. An important caveat to

Table 1.1   The effects of power on the merger process

Psychological construct	Effect on the merger process	Effect on shareholder value	Merger stage
	Overconfidence in the initiation of an (ill-advised/unnecessary) merger	−	2
Abstract thinking	Reduced search and screen	−	3
Reduced social attentiveness	Facilitated negotiation and bargaining	+	5 & 6
Poor perspective taking	Failure to plan for integration	−	7
Abstract thinking	Impaired ability to communicate strategic strategies	−	7
Abstract thinking	Enhanced ability to communicate organizational goals	+	7
Reduced social attentiveness	Increased objectivity in restructuring (hiring and firing decisions)	+	9
Optimism	Positive bias in the evaluation of the merger	−	10

this perspective, however, is that while power has these effects, in general, there are certain individuals that will be immune to these effects of power. Indeed, there are certain groups of individuals for whom power only serves to increase attention to threats and attention to social relationships.

Individual differences in manager psychology
Recent research lends credence to Abraham Lincoln's intuition that 'nearly all men can stand adversity, but if you want to test a man's character, give him power'.

Research indicates that power increases the correspondence between individual traits and behavior (Galinsky et al., 2008), with their personalities being better predictors of their thoughts and behaviors than are the personalities of the powerless. The implication of this is twofold: (a) the effects of power should be attenuated by the possession of personality traits that are inconsistent with the general effects of power on people; and (b) the effects of power should differ across cultures that vary in their conceptualizations of the self in relation to others (Zhong et al., 2008).

A number of recent studies have provided support for the idea that power reveals the person's true *personality*. Chen et al. (2001) found that so-called 'communally-oriented people' act more selflessly, and 'exchange-oriented people' act more selfishly, when allowed to experience power. The authors argued that power activated social responsibility goals in 'communals', and self-interest goals in 'exchangers', thus leading to different behavioral outcomes. Similarly, Galinsky et al. (2008) found that in a negotiation task, high-power participants' social value orientations were better predictors of their interest in trusting and building a relationship with their negotiation partner than their partners' reputations. In contrast, baseline participants' interest in relationship building was more a function of their partner's reputation than of their social value orientations. In sum, the behaviors of the powerful will be in line with their personality when these personality traits conflict with the expressions of power exhibited by the general population.

Individuals' differences that are rooted in *culture* have also been shown to moderate the effects of power on cognition and behavior. Zhong et al (2008) show that the effects of power on attention to rewards are culturally bound: whereas Western cultures automatically associate power with freedom and reward, Eastern cultures automatically associate power with restraint and responsibility. The implication of this is that Western managers in a position of power show an attentional bias towards rewards, while Eastern managers may focus attention on responsibilities and potential threats to organizational performance. Furthermore, members of Western and Eastern cultures differ in their construal of the 'self'; Western cultures stress the autonomy and separateness of the self, whereas East Asian cultures tend to have interdependent self-construals that emphasize the importance of social connectedness and of being embedded in larger groups. Thus, Galinsky et al. (2003) finds that among Westerners, power increases self-interested claiming in a commons dilemma. In contrast, Zhong et al. (2008) showed that among East Asians, power led to reduced claiming from a commonly shared resource pool.

In sum, while there are consistent and predictable effects of power on cognition and behavior observable among the general population, certain individuals and groups will tend to reveal power differently. As discussed below, the moderating role of personality and culture on the effects of power are important to keep in mind when considering the management of power in the M&A process.

Practical Implications

With a new-found understanding of the potential for power to influence managers' thoughts and behaviors in destructive ways at specific stages of the M&A process, it is clear that management needs to be managed during the M&A process. In particular, based on our foregoing review and synthesis of research on power and merger processes, we can identify four key phases of the M&A process in which the negative effects of power on managerial decision making can be curbed:

1. *The acquisition plan should be checked for signs of overconfidence or hubris* Our results show that powerful managers are likely to be overly optimistic in their decision to merge, taking on 'hopeless cases', or paying 'premiums',[5] even when paying such premiums drastically increases the pressure on the acquiring firm to create returns (Haunschild, 1994; Hayward and Hambrick, 1997), and are thought to be *per se* excessive (Hitt and Pisano, 2003; Krishnan et al., 2007),

2. *The search and screening process should be carried out by less-powerful organizational members* Our results show that powerful individuals rely more on abstract thinking, and are less detail oriented, both of which undermine the process by which a manager chooses a firm with which to merge, or to acquire. Coupled with the outdated idea that a 'good manager can manage anything' (Weston and Mansinghka, 1971), this can lead to a merger of poor strategic fit, and may be used as an explanation for why mergers by 'glamor acquirers' – planned by liberated, independent and empowered managers – typically perform less well than 'value firms' – concluded by managers clearly supervised by the firms' other stakeholders (Rau and Vermaelen, 1998).

3. *Integration planning and post-merger integration management should be drafted by a human resources (HR) manager or an external organizational consultant who understands the importance of cultural integration and communication of organizational goals, and is at the same time sufficiently independent from the employees to guard against sympathetic rather than efficient restructuring* Our results show that powerful managers are good at communicating the 'bigger picture', but not the methods by which this might be attained. Powerful managers are good at cutting costs – possibly explaining why workforces are often so ruthlessly cut in mergers (for example, Krishnan et al., 2007) – but poor at perspective taking, paying little attention to the 'human side' of integration planning. An HR manager, we suggest, would bridge the gap between the 'big picture' of the manager and the concrete perspective of the employees, taking into account both the culture of the acquirer and the target, as the failure to do so is a chief reason for the merger to go sour.

4. *The post-merger evaluation process should be undertaken by the manager, in cooperation with lower-level managers, and a third-party*

*consultant, in order to objectively check the reliability of the evalua-
tions* Our results show that egotism and optimism are likely to lead
the manager to judge his/her failures with bias, and to consider real
threats to the long-run sustainability of the firm as little more than
short-term setbacks. This is an obvious threat to the firm, as 'those
who do not learn from their mistakes are destined to repeat them'.

The ideal approach to the management of power in the M&A process
would be to recruit a manager with a personality profile that would
capture the value of power at the negotiation and integration (restructuring) phases, without compromising value at the planning, searching and screening, integrating (communication), and evaluation stages.
Identifying the selfish, the harassing, and the volatile is critical for creating
value efficiently and effectively in M&As. Managers of the M&A process
cannot, we suggest, simply be technical experts or analytically skilled, but
must also be individuals who take their group members' perspectives, who
value their relationship with their peers and subordinates, and who derive
self-esteem by enhancing the well-being of others, rather than relying on
self-enhancing strategies such as empire building for self-esteem and a
sense of personal security.

Another possibility, however, would be to heighten the risk perception
and social attentiveness of the powerful. One possible way to increase
perspective taking would be to hold the powerful accountable (Tetlock
et al., 1989). Powerful individuals who know that they will have to justify
their actions are more likely to consider the social consequences of their
decisions and to take others' interests into account (Tetlock, 1992; Lerner
and Tetlock, 1999). For example, US presidents exhibit greater cognitive
complexity after having been elected, when they become accountable to a
variety of constituents, than before election (Tetlock, 1981).

5   CONCLUSIONS

Mergers and acquisitions are big business: 29,312 firms were merged or
acquired in 2008, at a cost of $2.56 trillion to the shareholder (WilmerHale,
2009).

Mergers should allow the firm to cut costs, and/or expand revenues
(Besanko et al., 2006), and as such are critical for the firm seeking to increase
its global reach and competitiveness (Lasserre, 2007). The 'overwhelming
majority' of studies, however, find that they 'do not positively contribute to
... performance' (King et al., 2004, p. 196). Furthermore, estimates suggest
that as many as 65–85 percent fail (Puranam and Singh, 1999).

The extant literature adopts a predominantly finance-oriented perspective in attempting to understand success and failure, and assumes that M&As are a 'closed system', with little room for human interference, in spite of the fact that estimates suggest that managers may be responsible for between one-third to one-half of all merger failures (Cartwright and Cooper, 1990; Dannemiller Tyson, 2000). In this research we suggest that managerial power is thus a long-neglected moderator of merger performance, because managers have a unique opportunity to create or destroy value in the merger process. Consequently, we adopt a multidisciplinary perspective, which puts the manager under the microscope.

In the process, we show that the manager's 'experience of power' leads to overconfidence, results in risk taking behavior, and may lead the manager to believe the old – and defunct – adage that a 'good manager can manage anything'. At the pre-merger stage, this results in value destruction, because mergers may be unnecessarily pursued, and targets sought out and approved, on the basis of fuzzy and subjective concepts, such as 'instinct' and 'gut feeling', rather than rigorous economic analysis.

Right or wrong, our findings suggest that the manager's experience of power may facilitate the negotiation and bargaining processes during which the merger is agreed, and may increase the probability that value will be created. Powerful managers, we suggest, are also better able to communicate the grander goals of the merger, and their lack of emotional empathy will aid in the objectivity with which they restructure the organization, and 'cut the dead wood' to realize synergies.

We suggest, however, that a general disinterest in the detail, and an inability to communicate the day-to-day details of the integration plan, will typically result in value destruction. Powerful managers, we suggest, will simply not invest in the 'nitty-gritty' of integration planning, and will prefer instead to take a 'hands-on approach'. Furthermore, and in the evaluation stage, we suggest that powerful managers are less likely to be harsh on themselves, and will consider 'failures' as mere 'setbacks'.

To ensure that value is created, we thus argue that an awareness of the role of managerial power is necessary, and claim that to manage the M&A process, the manager – that is, the person in a position of power – needs to be managed. We suggest that by understanding the systematic effects of power on the thought processes and behaviors of managers, the constructive forces bestowed upon the manager by power – in negotiations and restructuring, for example – can be harnessed, while its more dysfunctional effects on performance can be mitigated. In doing so, we hope to contribute to the understanding of both scholars and practitioners in the field, and demonstrate that the boundaries of the firm can be altered, but only with due care.

NOTES

1. Although technically inaccurate, we use the terms 'merger' and 'acquisition' synonymously in this study.
2. Take for instance, Milgram's classic study (1963) in which participants obediently delivered what they thought were 440-volt shocks to anonymous strangers at the insistence of an experimenter – a person in a position of relative power. People in a position of power, it was shown, are capable of influencing the decisions and behaviors of others, to destructive ends.
3. Galinsky et al. (2006) presented participants with a scenario in which an individual responded to a very bad restaurant experience by (sarcastically) remarking that it was a 'marvellous experience. Just marvellous'. The powerful inaccurately predicted that others would see the world as they saw it (that is, that the message was sarcastic) even though these others lacked access to the private knowledge of the experience.
4. Burgelman et al. (2004), in describing the merger between Compaq and HP, report (p. 5): 'Compaq's CEO, Michael Capellas, called HP's CEO, Carly Fiorina, to discuss a joint research and development (R&D) deal, but the conversation turned to acquisition'.
5. A 'premium' is a proportion of the expected synergy gain from the combined firm, which is paid to the target and offered in excess of the firm's stand-alone valuation (Weston et al., 2004; DePamphilis, 2008).

REFERENCES

Anderson, C. and A.D. Galinsky (2006), 'Power, optimism, and risk taking', *European Journal of Social Psychology*, **36**, 511–36.

Appelbaum, S.H., J. Gandell, B. Shapiro, P. Belisle and E. Hoeven (2000a), 'Anatomy of a merger: behavior of organizational factors and processes throughout the pre- during- post-stages (part 2)', *Management Decision*, **38** (10), 674–84.

Appelbaum, S.H., J. Gandell, H. Yortis, S. Proper and F. Jobin (2000b), 'Anatomy of a merger: behavior of organizational factors and processes throughout the pre- during- post-stages (part 1)', *Management Decision*, **38** (9), 649–62.

Berger, A.N. and D.B. Humphrey (1992), 'Megamergers in banking and the use of cost efficiency as an antitrust defense', Finance and Economics Discussion Series 203, Board of Governors of the Federal Reserve System, Washington, DC.

Berkovitch, E. and M.P. Narayanan (1993), 'Motives for takeovers: an empirical investigation', *Journal of Financial and Quantitative Analysis*, **28** (3), 347–62.

Besanko, D., D. Dranove, M. Shanley and S. Schaefer (2006), *Economics of Strategy*, 4th edn, New York: Wiley.

Betton, S. and B.E. Eckbo (2000), 'Toeholds, bid jumps, and expected payoffs in takeovers', *Review of Financial Studies*, **13** (4), 841–82.

Bühner, R. (1991), 'The success of mergers in Germany', *International Journal of Industrial Organisation*, **9** (4), 413–53.

Burgelman, R.A. and H.S. Grove (2007), 'Let chaos reign, then rein in chaos – repeatedly: managing strategic dynamics for corporate longevity', *Strategic Management Journal*, **28**, 965–79.

Burgelman, R.A., R. Pearl and P.E. Meza (2004), 'Better medicine through information technology', Stanford Business School Case SM-136, Stanford, CA.

Campa, J.M. and J. Hernando (2004), 'Shareholder value creation in European M&As', *European Financial Management*, **10** (1), 47–81.

Carey, D. (2000), 'A CEO roundtable on making mergers succeed', *Harvard Business Review*, **78** (3), 145–54.

Carline, N., S. Linn and P. Yadav (2002), 'The impact of firm-specific and deal-specific factors on the real gains in corporate mergers and acquisitions: an empirical analysis', University of Oklahoma Working Paper, Oklahoma City, OK.

Cartwright, S. and C.L. Cooper (1990), 'The impact of mergers and acquisitions on people at work: existing research and issues', *British Journal of Management*, **1**, 65–76.

Cartwright, S. and C.L. Cooper (1993), 'The role of culture compatibility in successful organizational marriages', *Academy of Management Executive*, **7** (2), 57–69.

Cartwright, S. and C.L. Cooper (2000), *HR Know-How in Mergers and Acquisitions*, London: Institute of Personnel Development.

Chang, S. (1998), 'Takeovers of privately held targets, methods of payment, and bidder returns', *Journal of Finance*, **53**, 773–84.

Chatterjee, S. (1986), 'Types of synergy and economic value: the impact of acquisitions on merging and rival firms', *Strategic Management Journal*, **7**, March/April, 119–39.

Chen, S., A.Y. Lee-Chai and J.A. Bargh (2001), 'Relationship orientation as moderator of the effects of social power', *Journal of Personality and Social Psychology*, **80**, 183–7.

Dannemiller Tyson Associates (2000), *Whole-Scale Change: Unleashing the Magic in Organizations*, San Francisco, CA: Berrett-Koehler.

DePamphilis, D.M. (2008), *Mergers Acquisitions and Other Restructuring Activities*, Burlington, MA: Elsevier.

Devos, E., P.R. Kadapakkam and S. Krishnamurthy (2008), 'How do mergers create value? A comparison of taxes, market power, and efficiency improvements as explanations for synergies', *Review of Financial Studies*, **22**, 1179–211.

Dickerson, A., A.H. Gibson and E. Tsakalotos (1997), 'The impact of acquisitions on company performance: evidence from a large panel of UK firms', *Oxford Economic Papers*, **49** (3), 344–61.

Dong, M., D. Hirschleifer, S. Richardson and S.H. Teoh (2006), 'Does investor misevaluation drive the takeover market?', *Journal of Finance*, **61** (2), 725–62.

Fairburn, J. and P. Geroski (1989), 'The empirical analysis of market structure performance', in J.A. Fairburn and J.A. Kay (eds), *Mergers and Merger Policy*, Oxford: Oxford University Press.

Fiske, S.T. (1993), 'Controlling other people: the impact of power on stereotyping', *American Psychologist*, **48**, 621–8.

Galinsky, A.D., D.H. Greenfeld and J.C. Magee (2003), 'From power to action', *Journal of Personality and Social Psychology*, **85**, 453–66.

Galinsky, A.D., J.C. Magee, D.H. Gruenfeld, J. Whitson and K. Liljenquist (2008), 'Power reduces the press of the situation: implications for creativity, conformity, and dissonance', *Journal of Personality and Social Psychology*, **95**, 1450–66.

Galinsky, A.D., J.C. Magee, M.E. Inesi and D.H. Gruenfeld (2006), 'Power and perspective not taken', *Psychological Science*, **17**, 1068–74.

Galinsky, A.D., D. Rus and J. Lammers (2010), 'Power: a central force governing psychological, social and organizational life', in D. De Cramer, R. Van Dick and J.K. Murninghan (eds), *Social Psychology and Organizations*, New York: Psychology Press.

Gaughan, P.A. (2007), *Mergers, Acquisitions and Corporate Restructurings*, London: John Wiley.

Georgen, M. and L. Renneboog (2004), 'Shareholder wealth effects of European domestic and cross-border takeover bids', *European Financial Management*, **10** (1), 9–45.

Gruenfeld, D.H. M.E. Inesi, J.C. Magee and A.D. Galinsky (2008), 'Power and the objectification of social targets', *Journal of Personality and Social Psychology*, **95**, 111–27.

Gugler, K., D.C. Mueller, B.B. Yurtoglu and C. Zulehner (2003), 'The effects of mergers: an international comparison', *International Journal of Industrial Organization*, **21**, 625–53.

Güner, A.B., U. Malmendrer and G. Tate (2008), 'Financial expertise of directors', *Journal of Financial Economics*, **88** (2), 323–54.

Halpern, P. (1983), 'Corporate acquisitions: a theory of special cases? A review of event studies applied to acquisitions', *Journal of Finance*, **38**, 297–317.

Haspeslagh, P.C. and D.B. Jemison (1991), *Managing Acquisitions: Creating Value Through Corporate Renewal*, New York: Free Press.

Haunschild, P.R. (1994), 'How much is that company worth? Interorganisational relationships, uncertainty and acquisition premiums', *Administrative Science Quarterly*, **39**, 391–411.

Hayward, M.L.A. and D.C. Hambrick (1997), 'Explaining the premiums paid for large acquisitions: evidence of CEO hubris', *Administrative Science Quarterly*, **42**, 103–27.

Hitt, M., J. Harrison, R.D. Ireland and A. Best (1998), 'Attributes of successful and unsuccessful acquisitions of US firms', *British Journal of Management*, **9**, 91–114.

Hitt, M.A. and V. Pisano (2003), 'The cross-border merger and acquisition strategy: a research perspective', *Management Review*, **1**, 133–44.

Jansen, S.A. and N. Pohlmann (2000), 'Anforderungen und Zumutungen: Das HR Management bei Fusionen' (Demands and impositions: the HR management of mergers), *Personalführung*, **2**, 30–39.

Jensen, M. (1986), 'Agency costs of free cash flow, corporate finance, and takeovers', *American Economic Review*, **76** (2), 323–9.

Jensen, M.C. (1988), 'Takeovers: their causes and consequences', *Journal of Economic Perspectives*, **2**, 21–48.

Jensen, M.C. (2003), *Agency Costs of Overvalued Equity Work in Progress*, Boston, MA: Harvard Business School Press.

Jensen, M. and R. Ruback (1983), 'The market for corporate control: the scientific evidence', *Journal of Financial Economics*, **11**, 5–50.

Keltner, D., D.H. Gruenfeld and C. Anderson (2003), 'Power, approach, and inhibition', *Psychological Review*, **110**, 265–84.

King, D.R., D.R. Dalton, C.M. Daily and J.G. Covin (2004), 'Meta-analyses of post-acquisition performance: indications of unidentified moderators', *Strategic Management Journal*, **25**, 187–200.

Krishnan, H.A., M.A. Hitt and D. Park (2007), 'Acquisition premiums, subsequent workforce reductions and post-acquisition performance', *Journal of Management Studies*, **44**, 709–32.

Lammers, J. and D.A. Stapel (2009), 'How power influences moral thinking', *Journal of Personality and Social Psychology*, **97** (2), 270–89.

Lasserre, P. (2007), *Global Strategic Management*, 2nd edn, New York: Palgrave Macmillan.

Lerner, J.S. and P.E. Tetlock (1999), 'Accounting for the effects of accountability', *Psychological Bulletin*, **125**, 255–75.

Magee, J.C., A.D. Galinsky and D.H. Gruenfeld (2007), 'Power, propensity to negotiate, and moving first in competitive interactions', *Personality and Social Psychology Bulletin*, **33**, 200–212.

Malmendier, U. and G. Tate (2005), 'CEO overconfidence and corporate investment', *Journal of Finance*, **60** (6), 2661–700.

Maner, J.K., M.T. Gailliot, D. Butz and B.M. Peruche (2007), 'Power, risk, and the status quo: does power promote riskier or more conservative decision-making?', *Personality and Social Psychology Bulletin*, **33**, 451–62.

Marris, R. (1964), *The Economic Theory of Managerial Capitalism*, Glenview, IL: Free Press of Glencoe.

Martynova, M. and L. Renneboog (2008), 'A century of corporate takeovers: what have we learned and where do we stand?', *Journal of Banking and Finance*, **32** (10), 2148–77.

McKinsey & Associates (1988), *Surviving Merger and Acquisition*, edited by Michael L. McManus and Michael Lee Hergert, Glenview, IL: Scott, Foresman & Co.

Mergerstat (2006), *Mergerstat Review*, computer program.

Milgram, S. (1963), 'Behavioral study of authority', *Journal of Abnormal and Social Psychology*, **67**, 371–8.

Moeller, S.B., F.P. Schlingemann and R.M. Stulz (2004), 'Firm size and the gains from acquisitions', *Journal of Financial Economics*, **73**, 201–28.

Moeller, S.B., F.P. Schlingemann and R.M. Stulz (2005), 'Wealth destruction on a massive scale? A study of acquiring-firm returns in the recent merger wave', *Journal of Finance*, **60** (2), 757–82.

Officer, M.S. (2007), 'The price of corporate liquidity: acquisition discounts for unlisted targets', *Journal of Financial Economics*, **83**, 571–98.

Overbeck, J.R. and B. Park (2006), 'Powerful perceivers, powerless objects: flexibility of powerholders' social attention', *Journal of Personality and Social Psychology*, **99**, 227–43.

Puranam, P. and H. Singh (1999), 'Rethinking M&A for the high technology sector', Wharton School Working Paper, University of Pennsylvania, Philadelphia, PA; presented at AOM 2000 meetings.

Rau, P.R. and T. Vermaelen (1998), 'Glamour, value and the post-acquisition performance of acquiring firms', *Journal of Financial Economics*, **49**, 223–53.

Ravenscraft, D.J. and F.M. Scherer (1987), *Mergers, Sell-offs and Economic Efficiency*, Washington, DC: Brookings Institution.

Ravenscraft, D.J. and F.M. Scherer (1989), 'The profitability of mergers', *International Journal of Industrial Organization*, **7**, 101–16.

Rhoades, S.A. (1998), 'The efficiency effects of bank mergers: an overview of case studies of nine mergers', *Journal of Banking and Finance*, **22**, 273–91.

Rockness, J.W., H.O. Rockness and S.H. Ivancevich (2001), 'The M&A game changes', *Financial Executive*, **17** (7), 22–5.

Roll, R. (1986), 'The Hubris hypothesis of corporate takeovers', *Journal of Business*, **59**, 197–216.

Roll, R. (1988), 'Empirical evidence on takeover activity and shareholder wealth', in J.C. Coffee, L. Lowenstein and S. Rose-Ackerman (eds), *Knights, Raiders and Targets: The Impact of the Hostile Takeover*, Oxford and New York: Oxford University Press, pp. 241–52.

Schenk, H. (2003), 'Organisational economics in an age of restructuring, or: how corporate strategies can harm your economy', in P. de Gijsel and H. Schenk (eds), *Multidisciplinary Economics: The Birth of a New Economics Faculty in the Netherlands*, Dordrecht: Springer, pp. 333–66.

Shleifer, A. and R.W. Vishny (1989), 'Management entrenchment: the case of manager-specific investments', *Journal of Financial Economics*, **25** (1), 123–39.

Simon, J.L., M. Mokhtari and D.H. Simon (1996), 'Are mergers beneficial or detrimental? Evidence from advertising agencies', *International Journal of Economics and Business*, **3** (1) 69–82.

Sirower, M. (1997), *The Synergy Trap*, New York: Free Press.

Smith, P.K. and Y. Trope (2006), 'You focus on the forest when you're in charge of the trees: power priming and abstract information processing', *Journal of Personality and Social Psychology*, **90**, 578–96.

Stulz, R., R.A. Walking and M.H. Song (1990), 'The distribution of target ownership and the division of gains in successful takeovers', *Journal of Finance*, **45** (3), 817–33.

Taylor, S.E. and J.D. Brown (1988), 'Illusion and well-being: a social psychological perspective on mental health', *Psychological Bulletin*, **103**, 193–210.

Tetlock, P.E. (1981), 'Pre- to post-election shifts in presidential rhetoric: impression management or cognitive adjustment?', *Journal of Personality and Social Psychology: Attitudes and Social Cognition*, **41**, 207–12.

Tetlock, P.E. (1992), 'The impact of accountability on judgment and choice: toward a social contingency model', *Advances in Experimental Social Psychology*, **25**, 331–76.

Tetlock, P.E., L. Skitka and R. Boettger (1989), 'Social and cognitive strategies for coping with accountability: conformity, complexity, and bolstering', *Journal of Personality and Social Psychology*, **57**, 632–40.

Trautwein, F. (1990), 'Merger motives and merger prescriptions', *Strategic Management Journal*, **11**, 283–95.

Van Kleef, G.A., C.K.W. De Dreu, D. Pietroni and A.S.R. Manstead (2006), 'Power and emotion in negotiation: power moderates the interpersonal effects of anger and happiness on concession making', *European Journal of Social Psychology*, **36**, 557–81.

Van Kleef, G.A., C. Oveis, I. Van der Löwe, A. LuoKogan, J. Goetz and D. Keltner (2008), 'Power, distress, and compassion: turning a blind eye to the suffering of others', *Psychological Science*, **19**, 1315–22.

Weitzel, U. and K.J. McCarthy (forthcoming), 'Theory and evidence on mergers and acquisitions by small and medium enterprises', *International Journal of Entrepreneurship and Innovation Management*.

Weston, J.F. and S.K. Mansinghka (1971), 'Tests of efficiency performance in conglomerate firms', *Journal of Finance*, **26**, 916–36.

Weston, J.F., M.L. Mitchell and H.J. Mulherin (2004), *Takeovers, Restructuring and Corporate Governance*, Upple Saddle River, NJ: Pearson Prentice-Hall.

WilmerHale (2009), 'Mergers and acquisitions', available at www.wilmerhale.com/files/upload/M8A__Deal__Flyer.pdf.

Zhong, C., A.D. Galinsky, J.C. Magee and W.W. Maddux (2008), 'The cultural contingency of power: conceptual associations and behavioral consequences', unpublished manuscript, University of Toronto.

2. Reinforcing ethical behavior through organizational architecture: a hypothesized relationship

Raymond O.S. Zaal

1 INTRODUCTION

In today's turbulent world, organizations can no longer assume that there is homogeneity of values, ethics and rules of thumb for appropriate behavior within their workforce (O'Brien, 2009). Many organizations actively pursue diversity (for example, gender, age, ethnicity), making their workforce no longer homogeneous. Additionally, falling trade barriers and increased international business have created opportunities for organizations to expand their operations internationally. This global economy has increased the complexity of dealing with ethical issues due to varying cultural perceptions of morality (Enderle, 1997). One potential source of confusion resides in the variability of ethical standards. What might have been acceptable behavior 10 or 15 years ago may not be so today. Social changes brought about by a broad spectrum of causes such as, for example, secularization, on the one hand, and corporate restructuring on the other, clearly have altered conceptions of socially accepted behavior. Moreover, the progressive globalization of corporations is increasingly forcing corporate employees to recognize and adapt to differences in national or regional cultural expectations. Given this large and, in some ways, growing uncertainty about what constitutes appropriate behavior within large organizations, corporate codes of ethics and training programs play a potentially important educational role by effectively communicating corporate expectations to employees and by demonstrating to them how certain kinds of behavior reduce the value of the firm. Moreover, in the process of globalizing and thus dealing with customers worldwide, companies might be forced to respond to increasing cultural differences – or an absence of shared expectations – among their managers and employees by providing more explicit communication of standards and expectations.

Research on business ethics suggests that ethical or unethical behavior in organizations is a function of both individual characteristics and contextual factors (Meyers, 2004). Therefore, in general, two approaches to promote ethical behavior are available to business managers. The first is to focus on the individual. According to this approach, managers assume that an individual's level of moral development and ethical sensitivity are the primary sources of motivation affecting the ethical behavior of employees. These sources are anchored to the internal drives and needs of the individual rather than triggered by situational forces. Under the individual approach, company policies and procedures reflect efforts to appeal to the employees' sense of right and wrong and to make employees sensible to ethical issues in the organization. Organizations do this in part by specifying and communicating ethical objectives through training and codes of ethics, instruments which were traditionally viewed by many managers as the most effective way of promoting ethical behavior within the firm (Metzger et al., 1993). Ample research has been done on the effectiveness of ethics programs and tools to manage ethical behavior. Kaptein and Schwartz (2008), for example, have thoroughly reviewed existing literature which reveals at least 79 empirical studies that examine the effectiveness of business codes. The results of these studies are clearly mixed: 35 percent have found that the codes are effective, 16 percent have found that the relationship is weak, 33 percent have shown that there is no relationship at all, and 14 percent have presented mixed results. Only one study has found that business codes could be counterproductive.

It seems therefore appropriate to focus on the second approach to promote ethical behavior, which emphasizes organizational aspects. Under this approach, individual behavior is assumed to be primarily affected by factors external to the individual, such as organizational structure, organizational culture, and other environmental conditions.

Brickley et al. (1995) propose to structure the firm's organizational architecture to encourage ethical behavior of employees. However, little is known about the effectiveness of dimensions of organizational architecture to reinforce ethical behavior of employees, as proposed by Brickley et al. There is much about how the formal organizational structure affects the ethical behavior of employees that is not yet fully understood. Specifically, very little research has been conducted into examining how decision-making assignments within firms affect the ethical behavior of employees.

This chapter takes up this challenge. The framework developed is an attempt to better understand how the organizational architecture of a firm relates to the ethical conduct of its employees. The primary purpose of this chapter is to generate more interest in advancing the theory of how ethical behavior is affected by dimensions of organizational architecture and to propose research questions which need further grounding in empirical research.

2 ETHICAL CULTURE

In addition to organizational architecture, corporate culture plays an important role in promoting or discouraging ethical conduct. An important characteristic shared by most conceptualizations of organizational culture is the expected relationship between culture and ethical conduct. Culture helps to establish what is considered legitimate or unacceptable in an organization and can exert a powerful influence on individual ethical behavior. Whether defined as an informal organizational control system (Deal and Kennedy, 1982; Martin and Siehl, 1983) or an instrument of domination, organizational culture is thought to provide direction for day-to-day behavior. In recent years, a number of research studies have attempted to link various attributes of organizational cultures to ethical behavior (Frederick, 1995; Treviño and Nelson, 2004).

Many researchers such as Hibbard (1998) and White (1998) have focused on values in defining organizational culture. Whereas values are important elements of organizational culture, research has demonstrated that organizations showed more differences in practices than in values (Wilderom and Van den Berg, 1999; Hofstede, 2001: 394). Organizational practices are therefore a common focus of culture measurement (Hofstede et al., 1990; Hofstede, 1998; Van den Berg and Wilderom, 2004). Van den Berg and Wilderom define organizational culture as shared perceptions of organizational work practices within organizational units that may differ from other organizational units. These practices reflect the shared knowledge and competence of the organization. By defining ethical culture as shared perceptions of ethical organizational practices within organizational units that may differ from other organizational units, the concept is similar to ethical (organizational) climate, which has typically been conceived as employees' perceptions of observable practices and procedures (Victor and Cullen, 1987; Denison, 1996). An important distinguishing feature, however, is that climate relates to the evaluation of a current state of affairs and culture relates to the registration of actual work behaviors (Denison, 1996).

Ethical culture represents a subset of the overall organizational culture, combining formal and informal systems of behavioral control that work together to guide employee moral reasoning and ethical behavior (Treviño and Weaver, 2003: 221). These systems have the potential to influence ethics and integrity to the degree that they are actually supportive. Therefore, ethical organizational culture helps to establish what is considered ethical or unethical in an organization and is thought to provide direction for daily employee behavior (ibid.: 235).

Thus, culture is an important organizational aspect which influences ethical behavior. It complements organizational structure by 'filling in the gaps' that exist in formal organizational structures (James, 2000).

In the remainder of this chapter, I shall emphasize the role of organizational architecture in reinforcing ethical behavior.

3   ETHICAL BEHAVIOR

According to Beauchamp and Bowie (2008), ethics pertains to good and evil, right and wrong, and thus what people are assumed to do or not. The domain of business ethics concerns the ethics of business organizations and of individuals and groups in business organizations. Lewis (1985) synthesized 38 different definitions and defines business ethics as comprising the rules, standards, principles or codes giving guidelines for morally sound behavior. Ethical behavior implies adherence to these moral norms, whereas unethical behavior implies the violation of these moral norms. Unethical behavior in and of business organizations is behavior which is morally unacceptable for the larger community (Jones, 1991). An essential feature of unethical behavior is that it concerns misbehaviors where fundamental interests are at stake. Contrary to rule breaking, criminal behavior and noncompliance, unethical behavior is not limited to violations of official and explicit standards, rules and laws, but includes violations of informal and implicit norms.

Business organizations and their employees bear ethical responsibilities. A much-used theory to ground these ethical responsibilities is stakeholder theory. Originally developed by Freeman (1984), this theory holds that business organizations have multiple relationships with all kinds of individuals, groups and organizations. These stakeholders enter into a relationship with business organizations to protect or promote their interests. Because a business organization and a stakeholder become interdependent, mutual expectations arise between both parties demanding that they engage with others' interests in an ethically responsible manner. Kaptein (2008) states that because of the existence of different ethical responsibilities to each stakeholder group, different types of unethical behavior exist toward the most important stakeholder groups: financiers, customers, employees, suppliers and society.

Thus, ethical behavior can be defined as employee behavior that is consistent with the norms and values, rules and obligations of the stakeholders of the organization.

4 ORGANIZATIONAL ARCHITECTURE AND ETHICAL BEHAVIOR

Jensen and Meckling (1976) and Brickley et al. (1995) developed organizational architecture out of a classical theory of the firm that has evolved from Coase (1937), Hayek (1945), Williamson (1964), and Alchian and Demsetz (1972), among others, and is rooted in the context of the 'traditional firm'.

Organizational architecture refers to three key dimensions of the firm: (a) the assignment of decision rights within the organization, (b) the structure of systems to evaluate the performance of both individuals and business units, and (c) the methods of rewarding individuals. Brickley et al. (1995) argue that successful corporations assign decision rights in ways that effectively link decision-making authority with necessary information for making value-enhancing decisions. When assigning these decision rights, however, senior executives must ensure that the company's performance evaluation and reward systems provide decision makers with appropriate incentives to undertake value-increasing decisions. They also state that the components of organizational architecture are fundamentally interdependent. The appropriate performance evaluation system depends on the allocation of decision rights and vice versa. Within a well-structured firm, the various components of organizational architecture are mutually consistent and reinforcing. They are like three legs of a stool: all three must be coordinated to ensure that the stool is functional.

Performance evaluation and compensation practices may create incentives or pressures for employees to behave unethically. How employees respond to such incentives or pressures depends in part on whether they have decision-making authority and control over the decision-making process. Business ethics and the organization's organizational architecture are therefore inextricably linked. The joining of organizational architecture and ethics research generates many interesting questions which have not yet been explored empirically.

How do employees respond to questions of ethics when they operate in a centralized or decentralized organizational structure? Do employees behave in an ethical manner if their performance is closely monitored, also with regard to integrity behavior? Can reward systems be designed to guide ethical behavior? Is there a difference in ethical behavior for those who work in an organization with a highly developed organizational architecture versus those who work in an organization with an organizational architecture that is less developed?

In the following subsections, I shall further elaborate on the three elements of organizational architecture and how they relate to ethical behavior.

Assignment of Decision Rights

In a hierarchical, vertically structured organization, authority for making critical organization-wide decisions is located or 'centralized' in the top apex of the organization among the executive officers. In contrast to centralized decision making, management's intent in decentralizing is to allocate responsibility more widely throughout the structure, both vertically and horizontally.

Decentralization leads to a shift in responsibilities. Employees in the lower echelons are given greater responsibilities. The corporation, thereby, has become more dependent on, and therefore vulnerable to, the intentions and intuitions of employees.

In general, the need to organize ethics is partly a consequence of the increased decentralization within many companies. The primary rationale for decentralization in today's complex and dynamic external environment is to equip the organization to respond more quickly to customers and rapidly changing competitive threats. Decentralization enables organizations to respond immediately to the situation, which can mean the difference between success and failure (for example, Pound, 1995; Hitt et al., 1998; Hankinson, 1999; Stanford, 2002).

The nature of decision-making rights and responsibilities affects the ethical sensitivities and behavior of employees. Compensation practices and performance evaluation may create incentives or pressures for employees to behave unethically. How employees respond to such incentives or pressures depends in part on whether they have decision-making authority and control over the decision-making process.

In a centralized structure, especially a highly centralized one, a positive relationship exists between the individual's level of authority and the potential for opportunistic action to increase one's personal interests: the higher the level, the higher the potential return when opportunistic actions are taken. The more decisions are shared, the fewer the opportunities to act independently in one's own interests. A decentralized structure therefore diminishes opportunities to further one's own interests. Considering the ethical ramifications of organizational decisions and providing opportunities for employees at all levels to participate in decision making can increase the likelihood that ethically suspect means of reaching institutional goals will be questioned before they result in damaging consequences (Cohen, 1993).

A number of theorists have stressed the relationship between decentralized decision making and ethical behavior (Yukl, 1989; Metzger and Schwenk, 1990; Ocasio, 1994; Daboub et al., 1995; Mayer and Davis, 1995). Among these theorists, the two who make the strongest plea are Collins (1997: 504), who speaks of the 'ethical superiority of participatory management', and Sashkin (1986: 74), who believes that 'participative management is an ethical imperative'.

Organizational structure may also serve to diffuse responsibility for the consequences of action by promoting external definitions of responsibility based upon formal role definitions, hierarchy, and authority jurisdictions. Individuals can avoid guilt by believing that they had no choice and, therefore, are not responsible for their actions or the consequences (Kelman and Hamilton, 1989). Employees who feel compelled to act unethically – either because a manager tells them to or because they lack the authority to propose or choose more ethical alternatives – are more likely to act unethically. Kanter (1983) argues that a culture dominated by restrictive vertical relationships, where duties are finely specified and honoring the chain of command is of utmost importance, is a culture that protects against individual action. In such a segmented structure, the isolated individual is encouraged to do as he or she is told, to work without troubling others, to see only local manifestations of a problem, and to take responsibility only for his/her limited, compartmentalized actions. It appears that the advantages of a flat hierarchy are counteracted by cultural messages that discourage upward communication about problem areas. Even well-intentioned organizational characteristics (for example, decision-making authority) can 'backfire' on the ethical front when the culture reinforces the belief that value conflicts experienced down the line are not a priority concern for top management (Kram et al., 1989).

Structure of Performance Evaluation

Agency theory states that broadening the scope of an agent's activities by delegating more decision rights provides the agent with substantial degrees of freedom to make trade-offs among these activities (Jensen, 2001; Prendergast, 2002). This creates a need for performance measures that allow for (more) discretion, but at the same time creates a need for constraining the agent's actions to prevent the extraction of private benefits.

Prendergast (2002) argues that this delegation-incentive problem can be addressed by tying pay to an aggregate measure of performance. The use of an aggregate measure provides incentives for the agent to make trade-offs among all available activities, supporting the delegation of decision rights. The aggregate measure also allows the principal to constrain the agent's actions to those in the principal's interest by tying this measure to pay. As a result, an aggregate performance measure can complement the delegation choice by allowing discretion to those with decision-relevant information (the agent) while also providing those lacking this information (the principal) with an instrument to constrain the extraction of private benefits. Comprehensive financial (accounting) measures, such as the net income or return on assets, represent the most aggregate performance measures because the full consequences of every action the agent takes ultimately flow through the financial statements.

In contrast, using specific measures for subsets of the agent's available actions reduces the ability to make trade-offs, which effectively reduces delegation (Jensen, 2001; Abernethy et al., 2004). Moreover, since the benefits of delegation are highest in settings where the principal has no idea what the agent should be doing, it is difficult to tie pay to multiple specific performance measures because the principal is unable to identify the specific actions the agent should take and, therefore, the specific measures and their weighting (Prendergast, 2002).

A number of authors have argued that broadening the set of performance measures enhances organizational performance (for example, Lingle and Schiemann, 1996; Edvinsson and Malone, 1997). The premise is that managers have an incentive to concentrate on those activities for which their performance is measured, often at the expense of other relevant but non-measured activities, and greater measurement diversity can reduce such dysfunctional effects (Lillis, 2002). Analytical studies have further identified potential benefits from using performance measures that are subjectively derived (for example, Baker et al., 1994; Baiman and Rajan, 1995).

However, the literature has also noted potential drawbacks from measurement diversity. It increases system complexity, thus taxing managers' cognitive abilities (Ghosh and Lusch, 2000; Lipe and Salterio, 2000, 2002). It also increases the burden of determining relative weights for different measures (Ittner and Larcker, 1998; Moers, 2005). Finally, multiple measures are also potentially conflicting (for example, manufacturing efficiency and customer responsiveness), leading to incongruence of goals, at least in the short run (Holmstrom and Milgrom, 1991; Baker, 1992), and organizational friction (Lillis, 2002).

Despite these potential drawbacks, there is considerable empirical support for increased measurement diversity. For example, Van der Stede et al. (2006) have found evidence that firms with more-extensive performance measurement systems, especially ones that include objective and subjective nonfinancial measures, have higher performance.

Performance monitoring processes are important determinants affecting the ethical sensitivities and behaviors of employees because they are the primary means of informing employees about what is expected of them. Ethics concerns can be made part of a firm's performance measurement system. Poorly designed and implemented performance and evaluation processes will not only fail to detect unethical behavior, but also inadvertently encourage such behavior by creating the expectation that unethical behavior is tolerated or necessary in order to achieve corporate goals. In effect, employees may misbehave because they believe that their superiors and the organization expect such behavior of them. Ethically sensitive performance and evaluation processes are increasingly important as organizations become larger and more complex, and as the interactions between individuals within organizations and organizational subunits become increasingly formal, complex, and impersonal (Vaughan, 1983).

Business managers can promote ethical behavior within firms by ensuring that the processes by which employees are monitored and evaluated do not create ethical tensions within the organization. Ethical tensions arise when managers, as well as stated policies and procedures, create pressures for workers to comply with decisions that they believe are ethically questionable (Carrol, 1975).

Evaluation of employee performance must reinforce the expectation that ethical behavior is desired and that unethical behavior will not be rewarded. This occurs when management establishes guidelines specifying how employees are to achieve stated corporate goals, when managers monitor the ethical performance of employees through feedback and other appropriate control processes (Treviño and Nelson, 2004), and when they remove obstacles impeding employees from making ethical decisions (Vidaver-Cohen, 1998).

Ethics programs can be developed as a form of organizational control based on the propagation of rules and the use of behavioral monitoring and discipline, affecting behavior through rewards for rule compliance and punishment for noncompliance (Adler and Borys, 1996; Weaver et al., 1999). Alternatively, ethical behavior can be achieved in more encouraging and noncoercive ways, appealing to employees' sense of obligation and their aspirations to act ethically (Weaver et al., 1999). These approaches, which in the literature are referred to as 'compliance' and 'values orientations', respectively, are not mutually exclusive. Research has found that many companies combine these approaches in some way. However, in most companies, an emphasis on a compliance orientation predominates (ibid.).

Weaver and Treviño (2001) state that if concern for ethical behavior is not incorporated into performance appraisal, an organization will be less able to articulate a values orientation that is integrated across the organization. If this happens, employees may suspect that some organizational processes and individuals are not accountable to the ethical ideas of the organization and they may be tempted to test the organization to see if they are among those who are excused from ethical behavior. To support a values-oriented, integrated ethics program, performance evaluation processes should incorporate concern for ethics and fairness, both in the evaluative criteria used and in the way that appraisal is conducted.

Individuals who have decision authority which is appropriately collocated with their knowledge and who feel that their performance is evaluated and linked to an appropriate reward system are likely to conform to the desires of the stakeholders of the organization. Role theory helps us to understand the way individuals behave ethically. Role theory posits that human behavior is guided by norms and expectations held both by the individual and by other people. The norms and expectations for functionally differentiated sets of behaviors among employees are referred to as 'roles', which add structure to interpersonal relationships at work (Katz and Kahn, 1978). Roles consist of a set of rules or norms that function as plans or blueprints to guide behavior, specifying what goals should be pursued, what tasks accomplished and what performances are required in a given situation. In a firm, these rules and norms are specified by the assignment of decision rights and the performance evaluation system. These elements of the organizational architecture provide a structure where employees are held responsible and need to justify their behaviors to managers with reward and sanction authority, where the rewards and sanctions are perceived to be contingent upon the evaluation of such conduct.

Reward Systems

Reinforcement theory states that employees are more likely to do what is rewarded and avoid doing what is punished (for example, Skinner, 1953; Paine, 1994; Kaptein and Wempe, 2002; Storr, 2004; Dunn and Schweitzer, 2005).

Francis (1990) argues that the dominance of financial rewards in the traditional workplace is a key obstacle to transforming business into a moral practice. If performance evaluation systems are solely based on financial measures and rewards, workers and managers are encouraged to take actions that lead to favorable individual evaluations, but that may be detrimental to the organization's overall goals. It is therefore important to incorporate ethical considerations into performance evaluation and reward systems.

However, ethical behavior may respond in a different manner to rewards. Treviño and Youngblood (1990) failed to find that providing indirect rewards for ethical behavior increased ethical decisions. From a practical point of view, it is not easy to reward ethical conduct in organizations. Most ethical conduct is simply expected, and employees do not expect to be rewarded for not cheating on their expense reports or not harassing co-workers. Rewards for normally expected behavior may conflict with some employees' beliefs that ethical behavior should be its own intrinsic reward, and that ethical behavior is diminished in stature if it is rewarded (Weaver and Treviño, 2001). Although people do not expect rewards for doing the right thing, they do not want to feel 'punished' for doing so because others get away with misconduct or are rewarded for it (Treviño and Ball, 1992).

Therefore, short of customizing rewards to the specific motivations of individual employees, rewards for ethical conduct might be best presented in the form of long-term rewards such as promotions, or as symbolic rewards (for example, recognition and praise) rather than pecuniary rewards (for example, bonuses), so as to not diminish the status of ethical behavior in the mind of the person who acts ethically. It is essential for employees to feel that, over time, people of integrity are the ones who get ahead in the organization.

Rewards and punishments can inadvertently increase unethical behavior when they positively reinforce unethical conduct or punish ethical behavior (Hegarty and Sims, 1978; Treviño, 1990). Conflicts between espoused ethical values and an organization's reward system, result in ethical ambivalence, increasing the potential to undermine management's ethical intentions (James, 2000). An ethical culture should include a reward system that supports ethical conduct and punishes unethical behavior. However, research suggests that employees' perceptions that ethical behavior is rewarded were more important than were perceptions that unethical behavior is punished (Treviño and Nelson, 2004).

It may be extremely difficult to formally measure and consequently reward how well employees follow appropriate standards of conduct, since typically, appropriate behavior reflects the absence of illegitimate practices (Treviño, 1990). However, some organizations have successfully linked performance appraisal to observance of company codes of conduct, while others reward ethical conduct by publicly recognizing employees who detect ethical problems in the organization or those who have made exceptional contributions to the community (Business Roundtable, 1988). Numerous suggestions have been made in the literature as to how effectively organizational preferences toward ethical actions have been enforced. Murphy (1989) calls for blunt and realistic sanctions to create an ethical business environment. Gellerman (1989) advocates unusually high rewards for good performance, unusually high punishments for bad performance, and an implicit sanctioning of explicitly forbidden acts. However, these suggestions suffer from a lack of empirical validation. In contrast, Baucus and Beck-Dudley (2005) state that the heavy reliance on rewards and punishments creates organizations that operate at the lowest levels of moral reasoning (Colby and Kohlberg, 1987), resulting in unethical behavior. Cohen (1993) argues that anomie in an organization is often directly related to the criteria used for administering punishment or reward. In organizations that operate exclusively on performance-outcome-based incentive systems, rewards in the form of compensation, power and status are administered in direct proportion to goals achieved. When performance goals are excessively demanding, the message conveyed to employees is that any means available may be used to achieve these goals, regardless of the legitimacy of those means, and anomie ensues (ibid.).

5   CONCLUSION

Over the past few decades, ethics programs have proliferated. These programs have proved useful in informing employees about legal requirements of the organization, addressing specific concerns and serving as guidelines for required practice within the organization. However, unethical conduct continues to occur as is evidenced by a variety of sources, varying from, for example, the regular survey results of the Ethics Resource Center (Arlington, VA) to frequent media attention which results from ethical incidents in the corporate world.

Organizations do not behave unethically, people sometimes do. An organization can only be as ethical as the people who own, manage and work for it. However, its organizational architecture can be more or less conducive to ethical conduct. One way to ensure that employees behave appropriately is for the organization to provide an effective organizational architecture. If employees at all levels are provided with opportunities to participate in decision making, realize that their performance is measured and embedded in an effective reward structure and know exactly what the organization expects from them in terms of ethical behavior, then there should be more ethical behavior on the part of these employees.

The three dimensions of organizational architecture presented in this chapter – assignment of decision rights, structure of performance evaluation, and reward systems – have significant research implications which need further grounding in empirical research.

By understanding how ethical behavior is affected by dimensions of organizational architecture, researchers can assist managers in creating a more ethical environment in organizations, ultimately allowing them to be more successful.

REFERENCES

Abernethy, M.A., J. Bouwens and L. Van Lent (2004), 'Determinants of control system design in divisionalized firms', *The Accounting Review*, **79** (3): 545–70.

Adler, P.S. and B. Borys (1996), 'Two types of bureaucracy: enabling and coercive', *Administrative Science Quarterly*, **41**: 61–90.

Alchian, A. and H. Demsetz (1972), 'Production, information costs, and economic organization', *American Economic Review*, **62** (5): 777–95.

Baiman, S. and M. Rajan (1995), 'Centralization, delegation, and shared responsibility in the assignment of capital investment decision rights', *Journal of Accounting Research*, **33** (Supplement): 135–64.

Baker, G. (1992), 'Incentive contracts and performance measurement', *Journal of Political Economy*, **100** (3): 598–614.

Baker, R., R. Gibbons and K.J. Murphy (1994), 'Subjective performance measures in optimal incentive contracts', *Quarterly Journal of Economics*, **109**: 1125–56.

Baucus, M.S. and C.L. Beck-Dudley (2005), 'Designing ethical organizations: avoiding the long-term negative effects of rewards and punishments', *Journal of Business Ethics*, **56**: 355–70.

Beauchamp, T.L. and N.E. Bowie (2008), *Ethical Theory and Business*, New York: Prentice-Hall.

Brickley, J.A., C.W. Smith and J.L. Zimmerman (1995), 'The economics of organizational architecture', *Journal of Applied Corporate Finance*, **8** (2): 19–31.

Business Roundtable (1988), *Corporate Ethics: A Prime Business Asset*, New York: Business Roundtable.

Carrol, A.A. (1975), 'Managerial ethics', *Business Horizons*, April: 4–11.

Coase, R. (1937), 'The nature of the firm', *Economica*, **4**: 386–405.

Cohen, D.V. (1993), 'Creating and maintaining ethical work climates: anomie in the workplace and implications for managing change', *Business Ethics Quarterly*, **3** (4): 343–58.

Colby, A. and L. Kohlberg (1987), *The Measurement of Moral Judgement, Theoretical Foundations and Research Validation*, Vol. I, Cambridge: Cambridge University Press.

Collins, D. (1997), 'The ethical superiority and inevitability of participatory management as an organizational system', *Organization Science*, **8** (5): 489–507.

Daboub, A.J., A.M.A. Rasheed, R.L. Priem and D.A. Gray (1995), 'Top management team characteristics and corporate illegal activity', *Academy of Management Review*, **20** (1): 138–70.

Deal, T.E. and A.A. Kennedy (1982), *Corporate Cultures*, Reading, MA: Addison-Wesley.

Denison, D. (1996), 'What is the difference between organizational culture and organizational climate? A native's point of view on a decade of paradigm wars', *Academy of Management Review*, **21** (3): 619–54.

Dunn, J. and M.E. Schweitzer (2005), 'Why good employees make unethical decisions: the role of reward systems, organizational culture, and material oversight', in R.E. Kidwell Jr. and C.L. Martin (eds), *Managing Organizational Deviance*, Thousand Oaks, CA, London and New Delhi: Sage, pp. 39–68.

Edvinsson, L. and M. Malone (1997), *Intellectual Capital: Realizing Your Company's True Value by Finding Its Hidden Brainpower*, New York: Harper Business.

Enderle, G. (1997), 'A worldwide survey of business ethics in the 1990s', *Journal of Business Ethics*, **16**: 1475–83.

Francis, J.R. (1990), 'After virtue? Accounting as a moral and discursive practice', *Accounting, Auditing and Accountability Journal*, **3** (3): 5–17.

Frederick, W.C. (1995), *Values, Nature, and Culture in the American Corporation*, Oxford and New York: Oxford University Press.

Freeman, R.E. (1984), *Strategic Management: A Stakeholder Approach*, Marshfield, MA: Pitman.

Gellerman, S. (1989), 'Managing ethics from the top down', *Sloan Management Review*, Winter, 73–9.

Ghosh, D. and R.F. Lusch (2000), 'Outcome effect, controllability and performance evaluation of managers: some evidence from multi-outlet businesses', *Accounting, Organizations and Society*, **25** (4/5): 411–25.

Hankinson, P. (1999), 'An empirical study which compares the organizational structures of companies managing the world's top 100 brands with those managing outsider brands', *Journal of Product and Brand Management*, **8** (5): 402–16.

Hayek, F. (1945), 'The use of knowledge in society', *American Economic Review*, **35**: 519–30.

Hegarty, W.H. and H.P. Sims (1978), 'Some determinants of unethical decision behavior: an experiment', *Journal of Applied Psychology*, **63** (4): 451–7.

Hibbard, J. (1998), 'Cultural breakthrough', *Informationweek*, **701** (21 September): 44–55.

Hitt, M.A., B.W. Keats and S.M. DeMarie (1998), 'Navigating in the new competitive landscape: building strategic flexibility and competitive advantage in the 21st century', *Academy of Management Executive*, **12** (4): 22–43.

Hofstede, G. (1998), 'Identifying organizational subcultures: an empirical approach', *Journal of Management Studies*, **35** (1): 1–12.

Hofstede, G. (2001), *Culture's Consequences: Comparing Values, Behaviors, Institutions, and Organizations across Nations*, Thousand Oaks, CA: Sage.

Hofstede, G., B. Neuijen, D.D. Ohayv and G. Sanders (1990), 'Measuring organizational cultures: a qualitative and quantitative study across twenty cases', *Administrative Science Quarterly*, **35** (2): 286–316.

Holmstrom, B. and P. Milgrom (1991), 'Multitask principal–agent analyses: incentive contracts, asset ownership, and job design', *Journal of Law, Economics, & Organization*, **7** (September): 24–52.

Ittner, C.D. and D.F. Larcker (1998), 'Innovations in performance measurement: trends and research implications', *Journal of Management Accounting Research*, **10**: 205–38.

James, H.S. (2000), 'Reinforcing ethical decision making through organizational structure', *Journal of Business Ethics*, **28**: 43–58.

Jensen, M. (2001), 'Value maximization, stakeholder theory, and the corporate objective function', *Journal of Applied Corporate Finance*, **14**: 8–21.

Jensen, M. and W. Meckling (1976), 'Theory of the firm: managerial behavior, agency costs and ownership structure', *Journal of Financial Economics*, **3**: 305–60.

Jones, T.M. (1991), 'Ethical decision making by individuals in organizations: an issue-contingent model', *Academy of Management Review*, **16** (2): 366–95.

Kanter, R.M. (1983), *The Changemasters*, New York: Simon & Schuster.

Kaptein, M. (2008), 'Development of a measure of unethical behavior in the workplace: a stakeholder perspective', *Journal of Management*, **34**: 978–1008.

Kaptein, M. and M. Schwartz (2008), 'The effectiveness of business codes: a critical examination of existing studies and the development of an integrated research model', *Journal of Business Ethics*, **77** (2): 111–27.

Kaptein, M. and J. Wempe (2002), *The Balanced Company: A Theory of Corporate Integrity*, Oxford: Oxford University Press.

Katz, D. and R.L. Kahn (1978), *The Social Psychology of Organizations*, 2nd edn, New York: John Wiley.

Kelman, H.C. and V.L. Hamilton (1989), *Crimes of Obedience: Toward a Social Psychology of Authority and Responsibility*. New Haven, CT: Yale University Press.

Kram, K.E., P.C. Yeager and G.E. Reed (1989), 'Decisions and dilemmas: the ethical dimension in the corporate context', in J.E. Post (ed.), *Research in Corporate Social Performance and Policy*, Vol. 11, Greenwich, CT: JAI Press, pp. 21–54.

Lewis, P.V. (1985), 'Defining "business ethics": like nailing jelly to a wall', *Journal of Business Ethics*, **4**: 377–85.

Lillis, A.M. (2002), 'Managing multiple dimensions of manufacturing performance: an exploratory study', *Accounting, Organizations and Society*, **27** (6): 497–529.

Lingle, J. and W. Schiemann (1996), 'From balanced scorecard to measurement', *Management Review*, March: 56–61.

Lipe, M.G. and S.E. Salterio (2000), 'The balanced scorecard: judgemental effects of common and unique performance measures', *Accounting Review*, **75** (3): 283–98.

Lipe, M.G. and S.E. Salterio (2002), 'A note on the judgement effects of the balanced scorecard's information organization', *Accounting, Organizations and Society*, **27** (6): 531–40.

Martin, J. and C. Siehl (1983), 'Organizational culture and counterculture: an uneasy symbiosis', *Organizational Dynamics*, Autumn: 52–64.

Mayer, R.C. and J.H. Davis (1995), 'An integrative model of organizational trust', *Academy of Management Review*, **20** (3): 709–34.

Metzger, M.B. and C.R. Schwenk (1990), 'Decision making models, devil's advocacy, and the control of corporate crime', *American Business Law Journal*, **28** (3): 323–78.

Metzger, M., D.R. Dalton and J.W. Hill (1993), 'The organization of ethics and the ethics of organizations: the case for expanded organizational ethics audits', *Business Ethics Quarterly*, **3** (1): 27–43.

Meyers, C. (2004), 'Institutional culture and individual behavior: creating an ethical environment', *Science and Engineering Ethics*, **10** (2): 269–76.

Moers, F. (2005), 'Discretion and bias in performance evaluation: the impact of diversity and subjectivity', *Accounting, Organizations and Society*, **30** (1): 67–80.

Murphy, P. (1989), 'Creating ethical corporate structures', *Sloan Management Review*, Winter, 81–7.

O'Brien, R. (2009), 'Global ethics: beyond local leadership', *Journal of International Business Ethics*, **1**: 102–6.

Ocasio, W. (1994), 'Political dynamics and the circulation of power: CEO succession in US industrial corporations', *Administrative Science Quarterly*, **39** (2): 285–313.

Paine, L.S. (1994), 'Managing for organizational integrity', *Harvard Business Review*, **72** (2): 106–17.

Pound, J. (1995), 'The promise of the governed corporation', *Harvard Business Review*, **73** (2): 89–99.

Prendergast, C. (2002), 'The tenuous trade-off between risk and incentives', *Journal of Political Economy*, **110** (5): 1071–102.

Sashkin, M. (1986), 'Participative management remains an ethical imperative', *Organizational Dynamics*, **14** (4): 62–75.

Skinner, B.F. (1953), *Science and Human Behavior*, New York: Free Press.

Stanford, J.H. (2002), 'Leadership and Bureaucracy: the 21st century oxymoron', Proceedings from the Society for Advanced Management (SAM) 2002 International Conference, Abstract and paper available from www.cob.tamucc.edu/sam.

Storr, L. (2004), 'Leading with integrity: a qualitative research study', *Journal of Health Organization and Management*, **18** (6): 23–30.

Treviño, L.K. (1990), 'A cultural perspective on changing and developing organizational ethics', in R. Woodman and W. Passmore (eds), *Research in Organizational Change and Development*, Greenwich, CT: JAI Press, pp. 195–230.

Treviño, L.K. and G.A. Ball (1992), 'The social implications of punishing unethical behavior: observers' cognitive and affective reactions', *Journal of Management*, **18** (4): 751–69.

Treviño, L.K. and K.A. Nelson (2004), *Managing Business Ethics: Straight Talk About How to Do It Right*, New York: John Wiley & Sons.

Treviño, L.K. and G.R. Weaver (2003), *Managing Ethics in Business Organizations: Social Scientific Perspectives*, Stanford, CA: Stanford University Press.

Treviño, L.K. and S.A. Youngblood (1990), 'Bad apples in bad barrels: a causal analysis of ethical decision making behavior', *Journal of Applied Psychology*, **75** (4): 378–85.

Van den Berg, P.T. and C.P.M. Wilderom (2004), 'Defining, measuring and comparing organizational cultures', *Applied Psychology: An International Review*, **53** (4): 570–82.

Van der Stede, W.A., C.W. Chow and T.W. Lin (2006), 'Strategy, choice of performance measures, and performance', *Behavioral Research in Accounting*, **18**: 185–205.

Vaughan, D. (1983), *Controlling Unlawful Organizational Behavior: Social Structure and Corporate Misconduct*, Chicago, IL: University of Chicago Press.

Victor, B. and J.B. Cullen (1987), 'A theory and measure of ethical climate in organizations', *Research in Corporate Social Performance and Policy*, **9**: 51–71.

Vidaver-Cohen, D. (1998), 'Motivational appeal in normative theories of enterprise', *Business Ethics Quarterly*, **8** (3): 385–407.

Weaver, G.R. and L.K. Treviño (2001), 'The role of human resources in ethics/compliance management: a fairness perspective', *Human Resource Management Review*, **11**: 113–34.

Weaver, G.R., L.K. Treviño and P.L. Cochran (1999), 'Corporate ethics practices in the mid-1990s: an empirical study', *Journal of Business Ethics*, **18**: 283–94.

White, J. (1998), 'Portrait of a winning corporate culture', *Benefits Canada*, **22** (11): 13–14.

Wilderom, C.P.M. and P.T. Van den Berg (1999), 'Firm culture and leadership as firm performance indicators: a resource based perspective', Discussion Paper 003, Center for Economic Research, Tilburg University, Tilburg, The Netherlands.

Williamson, O.E. (1964), *The Economics of Discretionary Behavior: Managerial Objectives in a Theory of the Firm*, Englewood Cliffs, NJ: Prentice-Hall.

Yukl, G. (1989), 'Managerial leadership: a review of theory and research', *Journal of Management*, **15** (2): 251–89.

3. Industry differences in strategic decision making of Dutch top management teams

**Alexander S. Alexiev, Justin J.P. Jansen,
Frans A.J. Van den Bosch and
Henk W. Volberda**

1 INTRODUCTION

A central question for strategy is the quality of the decision-making process undertaken by the top management team (TMT). Decision comprehensiveness, or the degree of rationality of decisions, has received a considerable amount of attention from scholars in reference to its influence on decision quality and firm performance under different environmental conditions (Fredrickson, 1984; Elbanna and Child, 2007; Forbes, 2007; Miller, 2008). Extensive research has been conducted in order to uncover which TMT characteristics or processes are able to stimulate comprehensive decision making. For example, Simons et al. (1999) argued that diversity in TMT composition and debate are precursors to extracting the benefits of decision comprehensiveness through elaboration and processing of task-relevant information, reflection and healthy disagreements on how the team works (Van Knippenberg and Schippers, 2007).

Interestingly, existing research on decision comprehensiveness overlooks how TMTs interact with their environment, namely with the extra-team sources that feed into the decision process. Studies have shown that sourcing divergent knowledge from the environment can be critical for the organizational ability to adapt and overcome the persistence of existing strategies (Zahra and George, 2002; Jansen et al., 2005). This gap is particularly striking, considering the amount of literature emphasizing the importance of understanding the nature of organizational environments, for example through the concepts of uncertainty and dynamism (Fredrickson and Mitchell, 1984; Huber and Daft, 1987; Gilbert, 2005; Forbes, 2007).

The assumption that we make for the argument in this chapter is that the immediate informational environment surrounding senior managers is predominantly social, that is, TMTs tend to rely on other people for information (Mintzberg, 1973; Kotter, 1986). TMTs gather information through advice seeking, and due to their unique position at the organizational boundary, advice seeking can be both internal with regard to the organization, that is, from lower-level managers in the same organization, or external, that is, from counselors and managers of other companies (Mintzberg, 1973; Elenkov, 1997; McDonald and Westphal, 2003; Arendt et al., 2005). Literature suggests that executive advice seeking has two independent dimensions based on whether the source of advice is external or internal. Each individual TMT member may exhibit preference for either external or internal advice, which can aggregate on a group level as a TMT-level external or internal advice-seeking behavior (Menon and Pfeffer, 2003; Alexiev et al., 2010). TMT advice seeking is the process that feeds information to decision making and allows new opportunities to be recognized or evidence to be gathered for selected courses of action (McGrath, 2001; Kaplan et al., 2003). Although research has postulated separate positive effects of external and internal advice seeking on organizational outcomes such as exploratory innovation and performance (McDonald and Westphal, 2003; McDonald et al., 2008; Alexiev et al., 2010), insufficient attention has been given to the process of strategic decision making and how external or internal advice seeking can contribute to it.

Studying decision-making processes has also been challenging from an empirical standpoint, and most of the studies in this area have relied on qualitative methods and laboratory experiments (Mintzberg et al., 1976; Eisenhardt and Zbaracki, 1992; Kerr and Tindale, 2004; Sniezek et al., 2004). Little research has been done on comparing strategy processes across organizations and across industries. Particularly interesting, but still underresearched, is the phenomenon of institutional influences on executive behaviors and processes (Meyer and Rowan, 1977; Pfeffer and Salancik, 1978; DiMaggio and Powell, 1983). While organizations change in an attempt to align better with their environment and gain legitimacy, senior managers are likely to mimic the behavior of relevant others (Greenwood and Hinings, 1996). Preferences towards external and internal advice (Menon and Pfeffer, 2003) may become institutionalized within the industry and fulfill industry norms and logics. This study investigates empirically the level of isomorphism with regard to the process of strategic decision making.

By exploring these effects, we aim to unravel the structure of the TMT information environment beyond the team itself. The main premise of this study's approach is that managers do not interact directly with the environment, but with information about the environment (Huber and Daft, 1987; Forbes, 2007). The key to understanding strategic decision-making processes is therefore focusing on the behaviors that link managers with their external and internal environment, and understand the forces that influence these behaviors.

In the next section, we present a literature overview and hypotheses. A comparative study of five industry sectors follows. We conclude with some theoretical and management implications and suggestions for future research.

2 LITERATURE AND HYPOTHESES

TMT Advice Seeking and Decision Comprehensiveness

Decision comprehensiveness is defined as 'the extent to which an organization attempts to be exhaustive or inclusive in making and integrating strategic decisions' (Fredrickson, 1984, p. 447), which are decisions that are 'important, in terms of the actions taken, the resources committed, or the precedents set' (Mintzberg et al., 1976, p. 246). The question of how comprehensive or rational strategic decisions are has belonged to synoptic views on strategy formulation (Eisenhardt and Zbaracki, 1992), which argue that analyzing and integrating a greater amount of information in decision making is beneficial to firms as it increases the strategic understanding of their environments (Forbes, 2007). Decision comprehensiveness can improve firm performance in turbulent environmental conditions as organizations need information about the dynamics of emerging opportunities and threats (Fredrickson, 1984; Fredrickson and Mitchell, 1984; Goll and Rasheed, 2005; Forbes, 2007; Miller, 2008). Thus, decision comprehensiveness has emerged as a defining characteristic of the strategic decision-making process and the functioning of TMTs (Miller et al., 1998; Simons et al., 1999).

Simons et al. (1999) argued that decision comprehensiveness can be enhanced if a TMT is composed of members with diverse backgrounds who debate multiple and divergent points of view. Subsequent studies have provided additional empirical evidence for that relationship and for that of several other TMT demographic variables, such as average tenure or educational level (for example, Goll and Rasheed, 2005; Talaulicar et al., 2005; Mitchell et al., 2009). Diverse teams may indeed have an advantage over homogeneous ones, but existing research remains silent about what determines the limits of decision comprehensiveness, or in other words, how do TMTs, diverse and non-diverse, source the information that they use in decision making. In fact, synoptic models of decision making have been criticized for ignoring the limits of rationality, an observation that organizations typically make noncomprehensive choices and 'satisfice' in their search for solutions (Cyert and March, 1963; Fredrickson and Mitchell, 1984; Winter, 2000). Moreover, choice sets are not available to decision makers from beforehand and interpretations of environmental information must be constructed first (Forbes, 2007; Knudsen and Levinthal, 2007).

In this sense, diversity of knowledge and opinions of top executives may be a function not only of their professional experience or education background, but also of specific prior occurrences of deliberate information exchange with their external and internal advisers. We propose that the degree to which TMTs connect to external and internal sources of information can pose limits to the comprehensiveness of the decision process. March and Simon (1958, p. 3) suggested that decision making is less about choice than it is about attention. Abundant literature suggests that one of the primary sources that directs senior managers' attention is their social environment – the way they interact with other people in their surroundings – often advisers from within or outside the firm, such as lower-level managers or managers from competitor, consultant, customer or supplier firms (Mintzberg, 1973; Elenkov, 1997; Ingram and Roberts, 2000; McDonald and Westphal, 2003). TMT advice-seeking behavior is aimed at task-related information exchange that can improve the probability of accurate decisions (Goldsmith and Fitch, 1997; McDonald and Westphal, 2003; Bonaccio and Dalal, 2006). Advisers also offer decision makers new alternatives that may not have been considered earlier and provide new perspectives on the problem at hand (Alexiev et al., 2010). Credible advice from external and internal sources can alter the choices TMT members make and may guide subsequent organizational action and behavior away from established patterns and routines (Druckman, 2001).

The influence of the degree to which TMTs tap into these social information sources on decision comprehensiveness has been elusive in the literature. Both types of TMT advice seeking can be related to decision comprehensiveness as connecting to more information sources leads to improvement in the quality of the decisions made (Forbes, 2007). External advice and knowledge is typically more costly to obtain (Menon and Pfeffer, 2003). Having multiple external advice connections reduces the cost due to benefits such as timing and suitable referrals (Burt, 1992). The lower cost to generating multiple options can allow for a more-comprehensive decision-making process (Fredrickson and Mitchell, 1984). Provided that the external advice linkages span structural holes, maintaining multiple external advisers allows the organization to sustain a comprehensive decision-making process even when the environment changes

(Burt, 1992, 2000). Firms that are less connected may miss important signals for environmental shifts. Fredrickson and Mitchell (1984) suggest that decision comprehensiveness in unstable environments is vulnerable and can break down in the face of turbulence. If TMTs are strong on external advice seeking, they are likely to be able to uphold also a comprehensive decision-making process. External advice seeking supports integrative comprehensiveness as well (Fredrickson, 1984). Integrative comprehensiveness ensures that strategic decisions reinforce each other and constitute a single whole. By sourcing external expert opinions or consulting the reactions of fellow managers, TMTs are able to check whether internal plans make sense (Miles and Snow, 1978). That can increase the congruence of the options that are deliberated and thus improve comprehensiveness. Following these arguments, we suggest the following hypothesis:

Hypothesis 1: TMT external advice seeking is positively related to decision comprehensiveness.

Increased advice seeking by the TMT from internal advisers can also have a positive relationship with decision comprehensiveness. Internal advice seeking ensures that TMTs stay in touch with the internal organizational environment. Lower-level managers can put forward initiatives that will enlarge the range of options available beyond those generated by the TMT itself (Bower, 1970; Burgelman, 1983). Internal advice is also useful when options are evaluated and the costs and risks are mapped out. The lower-level managers in a complex organization are more likely to possess critical knowledge about enablers or obstacles to a particular knowledge. Such knowledge can lead to a better assessment of the feasibility and fit of a deliberated option. Internal advice seeking can clear the way for a more rational decision-making process as managers whose input has been considered are less likely to engage in political behaviors that have been shown to be detrimental to the decision effectiveness (Elbanna and Child, 2007). Ensuring buy-in of lower-level managers reduces opposition and thus facilitates the authorization and implementation of strategic decisions. This gives rise to:

Hypothesis 2: TMT internal advice seeking is positively related to decision comprehensiveness.

Institutional Influences in Strategic Decision Making

External and internal advice seeking of TMTs can be seen as two distinctive behaviors, which are driven by competing mechanisms. Individual managers tend to manifest either one or the other behavior (Menon and Pfeffer, 2003; Menon et al., 2006). Externally oriented TMT members tend to criticize information obtained internally and venerate external knowledge, which is scarcer and more costly to obtain. Going to great lengths to obtain such information may drive such managers to become overcommitted to it and reject equally viable options generated internally (Menon and Pfeffer, 2003). Moreover, such managers can see internal lower-level managers as a competitive threat to their position and status (Salancik and Pfeffer, 1977). Internally oriented TMT members, on the other hand, often fall victim to the not-invented-here (NIH) syndrome (Katz and Allen, 1982). They may also overvalue internal knowledge at the expense of rejecting anything that is external and foreign.

As a result, depending on the prevalence of externally or internally oriented senior managers, TMTs will have an overall preference for one or another source of advice. Interestingly, there has been little research aimed at explaining the differences among TMTs with regard to their orientation towards external or internal advice seeking. In a series of qualitative studies, Menon and colleagues (Menon and Pfeffer, 2003; Menon et al., 2006) point to intraorganizational competition and characteristics of the knowledge itself, such as its scarcity, that can account for an increased valuation of external knowledge. On the other hand, social identity and social categorization mechanisms of in-group and out-group delineation are used to explain the NIH syndrome and the strong preference for internal knowledge and derogation of external knowledge (Katz and Allen, 1982; Tajfel and Turner, 1986; Hogg and Terry, 2000). Yet, extant literature has offered little evidence about the empirical prevalence of the two phenomena. Following from that, it is also relevant to investigate whether external or internal advice seeking can impact the process of strategic decision making depending on the institutional context in which an organization is situated.

In this chapter, we argue that the use of external or internal advice by TMTs to reach decision comprehensiveness is conditioned by institutional pressures on the industry level. Institutional pressures emerge as processes at the interorganizational level, the consequence of which is that firms in a given field become more homogeneous (DiMaggio and Powell, 1983). Institutional theorists have documented firm isomorphism with regard to organizational structures and forms (Meyer, 1983; Scott, 1987; Powell, 1990), operational practices (Westphal et al., 1997), and specific strategic responses (Davis, 1991; Haveman, 1993). We propose that homogeneity can also be sought with regard to the strategic decision-making process, such that isomorphism can be observed in the way decision comprehensiveness is associated with internal or external advice seeking. Industry fields can provide cognitive frames of reference for the scope of search in the decision-making process (Nutt, 1998). Advice seeking can be seen as a management practice performed by TMTs which can be exposed on legitimacy, mimetic and normative isomorphic forces (DiMaggio and Powell, 1983). Powerful stakeholders in a particular industry may be exerting political influence on the TMT to conform to a set of rules and expectations with regard to whom they consult for advice when strategies are created. Getting advice from external consultants may thus be considered inappropriate in some industries (Suchman, 1995). Strategic decision making is a practice that is highly complex and causally ambiguous, and uncertainty can drive TMT members towards mimetic behavior. TMTs observe other organizations in their industry and try to imitate them to reduce uncertainty (Porac et al., 1989). Choosing external or internal advice seeking is on the other hand quite a clear prescription, which suggests it may be adopted unchanged and unquestioned (Ansari et al., 2010). The professionalization of management may also be a source of normative isomorphism as more senior executives follow degree programs from a handful of top business schools. Business schools or other professional networks of which senior managers are part, may propagate one type of advice seeking as the 'best practice': as in the case of 'open innovation' made popular across the information-technology-driven industries (Abrahamson, 1996; Abrahamson and Fairchild, 1999; Chesbrough, 2003). Top management promotion and hiring practices can also contribute to isomorphic strategic processes across the industry. Externally or internally oriented managers may be given preferred consideration for promotion to the TMT. In sum, the following prediction is made:

Hypothesis 3: An organization's industry will influence whether or not TMT external and internal advice seeking are related to decision comprehensiveness.

3   METHODS

Sample and Data Collection

Empirical data for this study were gathered from firms with more than 20 employees across five industries in the Netherlands. A sample of 7,340 firms was drawn from the REACH electronic database, the largest information source about organizations registered in the Netherlands Chambers of Commerce. The database provided address and management team information, as well as publicly available characteristics such as number of employees and financial data. As a primary source for the analyses, we used a survey administered in a paper-based and a web form. To ensure that we were able to survey knowledgeable respondents for typically confidential information (Miller et al., 1998), we addressed the survey strictly to the CEO. Two weeks after the initial mailing, we followed up with reminder notes and telephone calls. We obtained fully completed surveys from 659 respondents (8.98 percent response rate). The final sample included firms from the manufacturing ($n = 177$), transport and trade ($n = 103$), construction ($n = 96$), business services ($n = 214$), and information and communication technology (ICT) ($n = 69$) industries.

To test for nonresponse bias, we examined differences between respondents and nonrespondents. A t-test showed no significant differences ($p > 0.05$) between the two groups based on the number of full-time employees, revenues, and years since the firm's founding. We also compared early and late respondents and paper and web respondents in terms of demographic characteristics and model variables. These comparisons did not reveal any significant differences ($p > 0.05$), indicating that differences between respondents were not related to nonresponse bias. To examine reliability issues associated with single-informant data, we surveyed an additional TMT member from each respondent firm. We received a total of 111 second-respondent surveys, or 13.7 percent of our final sample, from firms that were comparable in size, age, and revenues to our full sample. We calculated an interrater agreement score (r_{wg}) for each study variable (James et al., 1993). The median interrater agreement ranged from 0.88 to 0.98, which suggests high agreement. The examination of intraclass correlations also revealed a strong level of interrater reliability: correlations were consistently significant at the 0.001 level (Jones et al., 1983). We also tested for the possibility of interference of single-method bias. For each of the five industries, a Harman's one-factor test on the questionnaire items found multiple factors, and the first factor did not account for the majority of variance.

Measurement of Constructs

To measure our constructs we used scales from previous literature verified through various analyses.

Decision comprehensiveness
The dependent variable was measured by a six-item Likert scale, developed by Miller et al. (1998). Respondents were asked to rate the decision-making process of the TMT on the degree to which they: (i) developed multiple scenarios and alternatives to solve a problem, (ii) considered

many diverse criteria for eliminating possible courses of action, (iii) thoroughly examined multiple explanations for the problem or opportunity, (iv) conducted various analyses on suggested courses of action, (v) investigated multiple responses in depth, and (vi) based their decisions on factual information ($\alpha = 0.85$).

External and internal advice seeking

We asked the respondents to rate (i) the TMT's frequency of their advice seeking, (ii) the extent to which they gathered knowledge with regard to their current strategy, and (iii) the extent to which they sought advice with regard to future strategy (Alexiev et al., 2010). We repeated the questions twice, first about advice sought from managers from other organizations (*external advice seeking*) and second, about advice sought from within their own organization (*internal advice seeking*). Cronbach's α was 0.92 and 0.94 for external and internal advice seeking, respectively.

Control variables

We controlled for various factors identified in previous literature as determinants to decision comprehensiveness (Miller et al., 1998; Simons et al., 1999; Goll and Rasheed, 2005). We accounted for *firm size*, measured by the natural logarithm of the number of full-time employees within organizations, as larger organizations may possess more resources which can allow them to invest in a comprehensive strategic decision-making process. We also measured *firm age*, by the number of years since founding, to capture the effect of formalization of organizational practices. Third, TMT size might affect dynamics in decision-making processes and therefore we included *TMT size* by measuring the number of senior executives who are responsible for strategy formulation and implementation (Siegel and Hambrick, 2005). Fourth, TMT composition may influence the extent to which the comprehensive decision-making process is adopted. We measured *TMT heterogeneity* (Miller et al., 1998; Simons et al., 1999) with a scale adopted from Campion et al. (1993). This is a five-item composite measure that asked respondents to assess the degree of heterogeneity on both demographic and functional attributes, namely expertise, background, experience, complementary skills, and education ($\alpha = 0.77$). Research has shown that composite team heterogeneity constructs are good predictors of team outcomes (Van Knippenberg and Schippers, 2007). Fifth, environmental attributes such as dynamism tend to relate to the degree of decision comprehensiveness. We therefore included a four-item measure for *environmental dynamism* (see Dill, 1958; Jansen et al., 2006). The scale for environmental dynamism ($\alpha = 0.85$) tapped into the rate of change and the instability of the external environment.

Validation of Measures

For all multi-item scales, we constructed an integrated confirmatory factor analysis (CFA) in order to test for convergent and discriminant validity. Each item was constrained to load only on its respective latent variable. The results showed a good fit within the model (χ^2/df = 2.836, CFI (confirmatory fit index) = 0.959, RMSEA (root mean square error of approximation) = 0.048). All loadings were significant ($p < 0.001$), which showed the convergent validity of the scales. The factor correlation matrix had moderate values (between 0.080 and 0.478), and we tested whether each correlation differed significantly from unity. We constructed models where this correlation was constrained to one and compared them with the unconstrained model. The results from each of the 15 pairwise comparisons showed that constraining to unity worsens the models' fit in each case (rho values between 0.041 and 0.212), which attested to the discriminant validity of the latent variables.

4   ANALYSIS AND RESULTS

We analyzed the relationship between external and internal advice seeking and decision comprehensiveness in each of the five studied industries separately. Table 3.1 contains the descriptive statistics of decision comprehensiveness across the five industries. An ANOVA test showed no significant differences between the means of decision comprehensiveness across the five industries ($p > 0.05$). The variable had significant variation within each industry. We constructed linear regression models for the total sample and for each industry and reported the standardized coefficients in Table 3.2. The F-statistic (Table 3.2) shows the change from a baseline model, which includes only the control variables. All models showed significant differences, with the exception of the model for the ICT industry.

Table 3.1   Descriptive statistics of decision comprehensiveness across the studied industries

Industry	N	Mean	SD
1. Manufacturing	177	4.75	1.02
2. Transport & trade	103	4.66	1.05
3. Construction	96	4.52	1.00
4. Business services	214	4.62	1.04
5. ICT	69	4.87	0.96

Table 3.2   Results of hierarchical regression analyses:[a] decision comprehensiveness

	Total sample ß	Manufacturing ß	Transport & trade ß	Construction ß	Business services ß	ICT ß
Firm size[b]	−0.009	−0.077	−0.107	−0.054	0.030	0.002
Firm age	0.066†	0.151*	0.005	0.114	0.029	−0.045
TMT size	0.027	0.021	0.231**	−0.089	0.062	0.058
TMT heterogeneity	0.207***	0.170*	0.288***	0.191†	0.145*	0.235*
Environmental dynamism	0.171***	0.312***	0.030	0.013***	0.157*	0.278*
Transport & trade[c]	−0.037					
Construction	−0.023					
Business services	−0.009					
ICT	−0.015					
External advice	0.128**	0.103	0.344***	0.023	0.040	0.234*
Internal advice	0.274***	0.262***	0.124	0.387**	0.339***	0.020
N	659	177	103	96	214	69
R^2	27.4 %	36.3 %	47.7 %	26.3 %	24.1 %	23.7 %
F change	47.30***	11.58***	14.20 ***	8.10 **	15.27***	2.06

Notes:

[a]   Standardized coefficients.

[b]   Logarithm of the number of full-time employees.

[c]   Manufacturing is the baseline category.

†$p < 0.10$; *$p < 0.05$; **$p < 0.01$; ***$p < 0.001$.

The required conditions for the regression method were satisfied. We used variance inflation factors (VIFs) to judge the presence of multicollinearity in the models. Across all models, the highest VIF was 1.45, which is well below the cut-off point of 10 (Neter et al., 1990). The models explained between 23.7 and 47.7 percent shown by the R^2 on Table 3.2. Of the control variables, firm age was positively associated with decision comprehensiveness in the total sample ($p < 0.10$) and in the manufacturing industry ($p < 0.05$). TMT size had a positive association with decision comprehensiveness in the transport and trade industry ($p < 0.01$). Environmental dynamism and TMT heterogeneity both had positive relationships ($p < 0.10$ to $p < 0.001$) with decision comprehensiveness, thus confirming existing theories. An exception to this is the relationship between environmental dynamism and decision comprehensiveness in the transport and trade sector. External and internal advice seeking were positive and significant with decision comprehensiveness in the overall sample ($\beta = 0.128$, $p < 0.01$; $\beta = 0.262$, $p < 0.001$, respectively), thus confirming Hypotheses 1 and 2. External advice seeking had positive association with decision comprehensiveness in the transport and trade ($\beta = 0.344$, $p < 0.001$) and ICT ($\beta = 0.234$, $p < 0.05$) industries. Internal advice seeking was positive and significant in the manufacturing ($\beta = 0.262$, $p < 0.001$), construction ($\beta = 0.387$, $p < 0.01$) and business services ($\beta = 0.339$, $p < 0.001$) industries. These results provide strong support for Hypothesis 3.

5   DISCUSSION

This chapter aimed to unravel patterns in the boundary-spanning roles of TMTs. The focus was on the strategic decision-making process and specifically on the role of TMT advice seeking on decision comprehensiveness. We also investigated industry differences in these relationships in the context of TMTs from a five-industry sample of Dutch firms.

The first main finding of this study is that both internal and external advice seeking can contribute to a comprehensive decision-making process. With this, we contribute to studies on strategy process that aim at uncovering the antecedents of decision comprehensiveness and the quality of strategic decision making (Fredrickson, 1984; Fredrickson and Mitchell, 1984; Elbanna and Child, 2007). Our study shows that TMTs can source critical and valuable information both from across an organization's boundary and from within its lower hierarchical ranks. Existing research has investigated what aspects of TMT composition and behavior can contribute to a comprehensive strategic decision-making process (Simons et al., 1999; Goll and Rasheed, 2005; Talaulicar et al., 2005; Mitchell et al., 2009). We extended this literature by probing into the information sources of TMTs – their internal and external advisers. Internal advice seeking had a stronger association with decision comprehensiveness, indicating that across industries, relying on internal advice more often supports decision comprehensiveness. In essence, this can be seen as evidence for a bottom-up strategy process with the TMT as a resource allocator to lower-level employee initiatives (Bower, 1970; Burgelman, 1983). Yet, TMTs can contribute significantly to the process by utilizing their external social capital and source advice from outside.

Our second finding is that the contribution of advice seeking to decision comprehensiveness varies across industries. The data demonstrated clear patterns of significant association of only one type of advice seeking per industry subsample. From the five studied sectors, internal advice seeking was significantly related to decision comprehensiveness in manufacturing, construction and business services industries. External advice seeking was linked significantly in the transport and trade and ICT industries. To explain this result which confirms our Hypothesis 3, we involve an institutional theoretical argumentation (DiMaggio and Powell, 1983). The use of TMT advice seeking was conceptualized as a strategic management practice that is subject to legitimacy, mimetic and normative isomorphic forces on an industry level. Future studies need to explore the process of diffusion of that practice in order to rule out alternative explanations. By using qualitative and social network methodologies, such studies can probe into the dynamics and diffusion patterns of external versus internal TMT advice seeking. One such possible explanation may be related to the task environment and the nature of technological knowledge. For instance, for some industries the locus of new knowledge may be embedded in networks of interorganizational relationships which may explain a TMT's preference for external advisers (Powell et al., 1996).

A structural and relational network approach may be appropriate for future multilevel research investigating the emergence of industry norms and logics. Research should look into the information exchange across industries as well. The structure and patterns of relationships may determine how industry norms and logics emerge, and advice seeking might have a role in those processes too (Abrahamson and Rosenkopf, 1997; Abrahamson and Fairchild, 1999). Industries may vary in the degree of interconnectedness, which is a factor that determines whether or not firms are likely to conform to or resist institutional pressures (Oliver, 1991). In that sense, more connected TMTs are likely to be not only more rational in their strategic decision-making process but also more resistant to iso-morphic tendencies.

Industry norms and logics may influence the practice of strategic decision making of TMTs, but other studies need to test whether that has an impact on organizational outcomes, such as performance and innovation. Although some studies have suggested a positive role for decision comprehensiveness in particular environments (Fredrickson, 1984; Fredrickson and Mitchell, 1984), comparing conformist and non-conformist firms with regard to performance may be a worthwhile avenue for future research.

Several limitations of this study deserve discussion. Although our survey technique attempted to achieve aggregated measurements for the TMT, not all TMT members in the responding organizations completed our survey. This may affect construct validity even though we have attempted to reduce such issues by validating our scales through inter-rater agreement scores and interclass correlations. Another limitation is the cross-sectional design of the study, which prevents us from drawing a firm conclusion about the direction of causality between the variables we have studied. Future research could address this shortcoming through a longitudinal setup.

Future studies can also explore the quality of relationships when TMT members seek advice, and thus open the black box of TMT advice-seeking behaviors. Previous research has indicated that managers tend to seek more advice from friends and similar others and less from acquaintances and dissimilar others (McDonald and Westphal, 2003). The quality of relationships may be underlying executive biases and breakdown of the comprehensive decision-making process. Social capital, particularly with the relational and cognitive dimensions, can be used in explaining the occurrence of such behaviors (for example, Nahapiet and Ghoshal, 1998). Researchers can also concentrate on identifying organizational policies and conditions that stimulate advice-seeking behaviors of managers.

Although designed to complement existing studies on TMT processes, this study can be extended in the future by focusing more attention on other TMT processes. The structure of the strategic decision-making process includes the phases of issue identification, option development and option selection (Mintzberg et al., 1976). Besides juxtaposing teamcentric with leadercentric integration mechanisms (Smith and Tushman, 2005), future research can also explore the dynamics of executive roles related to involvement in the identification and development phases of the decision-making process.

REFERENCES

Abrahamson, E. (1996), 'Management fashion', *Academy of Management Review*, **21**: 254–85.

Abrahamson, E. and G. Fairchild (1999), 'Management fashion: lifecycles, triggers and collective learning processes', *Administrative Science Quarterly*, **44**: 708–40.

Abrahamson, E. and L. Rosenkopf (1997), 'Social network effects on the extent of innovation diffusion: a computer simulation', *Organization Science*, **8**: 289–309.

Alexiev, A.S., J.J.P. Jansen, F.A.J. Van den Bosch and H.W. Volberda (2010), 'Top management team advice seeking and exploratory innovation: the moderating role of TMT heterogeneity', *Journal of Management Studies*, **47**: 1343–64.

Ansari, S.M., P.C. Fiss and E.J. Zajac (2010), 'Made to fit: how practices vary as they diffuse', *Academy of Managament Review*, **35**: 67–92.

Arendt, L.A., R.L. Priem and H.A. Ndofor (2005), 'A CEO–adviser model of strategic decision making', *Journal of Management*, **31**: 680–99.

Bonaccio, S. and R.S. Dalal (2006), 'Advice taking and decision-making: an integrative literature review, and implications for the organizational sciences', *Organizational Behavior and Human Decision Processes*, **101**: 127–51.

Bower, J.L. (1970), *Managing the Resource Allocation Process: A Study of Corporate Planning and Investment*, Boston, MA: Harvard Business School Press.

Burgelman, R.A. (1983), 'A process model of internal corporate venturing in the diversified major firm', *Administrative Science Quarterly*, **28**: 223–44.

Burt, R.S. (1992), *Structural Holes: The Social Structure of Competition*, Cambridge, MA: Harvard University Press.

Burt, R.S. (2000), 'The network structure of social capital', in R.I. Sutton and B.M. Staw (eds), *Research in Organizational Behavior*, Vol. 22, Greenwich, CT: JAI Press, pp. 345–423.

Campion, M.A., G.J. Medsker and A.C. Higgs (1993), 'Relations between work group characteristics and effectiveness: implications for designing effective work groups', *Personnel Psychology*, **46**: 823–47.

Chesbrough, H. (2003), *Open Innovation: The New Imperative for Creating and Profiting from Technology*, Boston, MA: Harvard Business School Press.

Cyert, R. and J. March (1963), *A Behavioral Theory of the Firm*, Englewood Cliffs, NJ: Prentice-Hall.

Davis, G.F. (1991), 'Agents without principles? The spread of the poison pill through the intercorporate network', *Administrative Science Quarterly*, **36**: 583–613.

Dill, W.R. (1958), 'Environment as an influence on managerial autonomy', *Administrative Science Quarterly*, **2**: 409–43.

DiMaggio, P. and W. Powell (1983), 'The iron cage revisited: institutional isomorphism, and collective rationality in organization fields', *American Sociological Review*, **48** (2): 147–60.

Druckman, J.N. (2001), 'Using credible advice to overcome framing effects', *Journal of Law, Economics, and Organization*, **17** (1): 62–82.

Eisenhardt, K.M. and M.J. Zbaracki (1992), 'Strategic decision making', *Strategic Management Journal*, **13**: 17–37.

Elbanna, S. and J. Child (2007), 'Influences on strategic decision effectiveness: development and test of an integrative model', *Strategic Management Journal*, **28**: 431–53.

Elenkov, D.S. (1997), 'Strategic uncertainty and environmental scanning: the case for institutional influences on scanning behaviour', *Strategic Management Journal*, **18**: 287–303.

Forbes, D.P. (2007), 'Reconsidering the strategic implications of decision comprehensiveness', *Academy of Management Review*, **32**: 361–76.

Fredrickson, J.W. (1984), 'The comprehensiveness of strategic decision processes: extension, observations, future directions', *Academy of Management Journal*, **27**: 445–66.

Fredrickson, J.W. and T.R. Mitchell (1984), 'Strategic decision processes: comprehensiveness and performance in an industry with an unstable environment', *Academy of Management Journal*, **27**: 399–423.

Gilbert, C.G. (2005), 'Unbundling the structure of inertia: resource versus routine rigidity', *Academy of Management Journal*, **48**: 741–63.

Goldsmith, D.J. and K. Fitch (1997), 'The normative context of advice as social support', *Human Communication Research*, **23**: 454–76.

Goll, I. and A.A. Rasheed (2005), 'The relationships between top management demographic characteristics, rational decision making, environmental munificence, and firm performance', *Organization Studies*, **26**: 999–1023.

Greenwood, R. and C.R. Hinings (1996), 'Understanding radical organizational change: bringing together the old and the new institutionalism', *Academy of Management Review*, **21**: 1022–54.

Haveman, H.A. (1993), 'Follow the leader: mimetic isomorphism and entry into new markets', *Administrative Science Quarterly*, **38**: 593–627.

Hogg, M.A. and D.J. Terry (2000), 'Social identity and self-categorization processes in organizational contexts', *Academy of Management Review*, **25**: 121–40.

Huber, G.P. and R.L. Daft (1987), 'The information environments of organizations', in F. Jablin, L. Putnam, K. Roberts and L. Porter (eds), *Handbook of Organization Communication*, Beverly Hills, CA: Sage, pp. 130–64.

Ingram, P. and P. Roberts (2000), 'Friendships among competitors in the Sydney hotel industry', *American Journal of Sociology*, **106**: 387–423.

James, L.R., R.G. Demaree and G. Wolf (1993), 'r_{wg}: an assessment of within-group interrater agreement', *Journal of Applied Psychology*, **78**: 306–9.

Jansen, J.J.P., F.A.J. Van den Bosch and H.W. Volberda (2005), 'Managing potential and realized absorptive capacity: how do organizational antecedents matter?', *Academy of Management Journal*, **48**: 999–1015.

Jansen, J.J.P., F.A.J. Van den Bosch and H.W. Volberda (2006), 'Exploratory innovation, and performance effects of organizational antecedents and environmental moderators', *Management Science*, **52**: 1661–74.

Jones, A.P., L.A. Johnson, M.C. Butler and D.S. Main (1983), 'Apples and oranges: an empirical comparison of commonly used indices of interrater agreement', *Academy of Management Journal*, **26**: 507–19.

Kaplan, S., F. Murray and R. Henderson (2003), 'Discontinuities and senior management: assessing the role of recognition in pharmaceutical firm response to biotechnology', *Industrial and Corporate Change*, **12**: 203–33.

Katz, R. and T.J. Allen (1982), 'Investigating the not-invented-here (NIH) syndrome: a look at performance, tenure and communication patterns of 50 R&D project groups', *R&D Management*, **12**: 7–19.

Kerr, N.L. and R.S. Tindale (2004), 'Group performance and decision making', *Annual Review of Psychology*, **55**: 623–55.

Knudsen, T. and D.A. Levinthal (2007), 'Two faces of search: alternative generation and alternative evaluation', *Organization Science*, **18**: 39–54.

Kotter, J.P. (1986), *The General Managers*, New York: Free Press.

March, J.G. and H.A. Simon (1958), *Organizations*, New York: Wiley.

McDonald, M., P. Khanna and J. Westphal (2008), 'Getting them to think outside the circle: corporate governance, CEO's external advice networks, and firm performance', *Academy of Management Journal*, **51** (3): 453–75.

McDonald, M.L. and J.D. Westphal (2003), 'Getting by with the advice of their friends: CEOs' advice networks and firms' strategic responses to poor performance', *Administrative Science Quarterly*, **48**: 1–32.

McGrath, R.G. (2001), 'Exploratory learning, innovative capacity, and managerial oversight', *Academy of Management Journal*, **44**: 118–31.

Menon, T. and J. Pfeffer (2003), 'Valuing internal versus external knowledge: explaining the preference for outsiders', *Management Science*, **49**: 497–513.

Menon, T., L. Thompson and H.S. Choi (2006), 'Tainted knowledge versus tempting knowledge: people avoid knowledge from internal rivals and seek knowledge from external rivals', *Management Science*, **52**: 1129–44.

Meyer, J.W. (1983), 'Institutionalization and the rationality of formal organizational structure', in J.W. Meyer and W.R. Scott (eds), *Organizational Environments: Ritual and Rationality*, rev. edn, Beverly Hills, CA: Sage, pp. 261–82.

Meyer, J.W. and B. Rowan (1977), 'Institutionalized organizations: formal structure as myth and ceremony', *American Journal of Sociology*, **83** (2): 340–63.

Miles, R.E. and C.C. Snow (1978), *Organizational Strategy, Structure and Process*, New York: McGraw-Hill.

Miller, C.C. (2008), 'Decisional comprehensiveness and firm performance: towards a more complete understanding', *Journal of Behavioral Decision Making*, **21**: 598–620.

Miller, C.C., L.M. Burke and W.H. Glick (1998), 'Cognitive diversity among upper-echelon executives: implications for strategic decision processes', *Strategic Management Journal*, **19**: 39–58.

Mintzberg, H. (1973), *The Nature of Managerial Work*, New York: Harper & Row.

Mintzberg, H., D. Raisinghani and A. Theoret (1976), 'The structure of "unstructured" decision processes', *Administrative Science Quarterly*, **21**: 246–75.

Mitchell, R., S. Nicholas and B. Boyle (2009), 'The role of openness to cognitive diversity and group processes in knowledge creation', *Small Group Research*, **40**: 535–54.

Nahapiet, J. and S. Ghoshal (1998), 'Social capital, intellectual capital, and the organizational advantage', *Academy of Management Review*, **23**: 242–66.

Neter, J., W. Wasserman and M.H. Kutner (1990), *Applied Linear Statistical Models*, 3rd edn, Homewood, IL: Irwin.

Nutt, P.C. (1998), 'Framing strategic decisions', *Organization Science*, **9**: 195–216.

Oliver, C. (1991), 'Strategic responses to institutional processes', *Academy of Management Review*, **16**: 145–79.

Pfeffer, J. and G.R. Salancik (1978), *The External Control of Organizations: A Resource Dependence Perspective*, New York: Harper & Row.

Porac, J.F., H. Thomas and C. Baden-Fuller (1989), 'Competitive groups as cognitive communities', *Journal of Management Studies*, **26**: 397–416.

Powell, W.W. (1990), 'Neither market nor hierarchy: network forms of organization', *Research in Organizational Behavior*, **12**: 295–336.

Powell, W.W., K.W. Koput and L. Smith-Doer (1996), 'Interorganizational collaboration and the locus of innovation: networks of learning in biotechnology', *Administrative Science Quarterly*, **41**: 116–45.

Salancik, G.R. and J. Pfeffer (1977), 'Who gets power – and how they hold on to it: a strategic-contingency model of power', *Organizational Dynamics*, **5** (3): 3–21.

Scott, W.R. (1987), 'The adolescence of institutional theory', *Administrative Science Quarterly*, **32**: 493–511.

Siegel, P.A. and D.C. Hambrick (2005), 'Pay disparities within top management groups: evidence of harmful effects on performance of high-technology firms', *Organization Science*, **16**: 259–74.

Simons, T., L.H. Pelled and K.A. Smith (1999), 'Making use of difference: diversity, debate, and decision comprehensiveness in top management teams', *Academy of Management Journal*, **42**: 662–73.

Smith, W.K. and M.L. Tushman (2005), 'Managing strategic contradictions: a top management model for managing innovation streams', *Organization Science*, **16**: 522–36.

Sniezek, J.A., G.E. Schrah and R.S. Dalal (2004), 'Improving judgement with prepaid expert advice', *Journal of Behavioral Decision Making*, **17**: 173–90.

Suchman, M.C. (1995), 'Managing legitimacy: strategic and institutional responses', *Academy of Management Review*, **20**: 571–610.

Tajfel, H. and J. Turner (1986), 'Social identity theory of intergroup behavior', in S. Worschel and W.G. Austin (eds), *Psychology of Inter-group Relations*, Chicago, IL: Nelson-Hall, pp. 2–24.

Talaulicar, T., J. Grundei and A.V. Werder (2005), 'Strategic decision making in start-ups: the effect of top management team organization and processes on speed and comprehensiveness', *Journal of Business Venturing*, **20**: 519–41.

Van Knippenberg, D. and M.C. Schippers (2007), 'Work group diversity', *Annual Review of Psychology*, **58**: 515–41.

Westphal, J.D., R. Gulati and S.M. Shortell (1997), 'Customization or conformity? An institutional and network perspective on the content and consequences of TQM adoption', *Administrative Science Quarterly*, **42**: 366–94.

Winter, S.G. (2000), 'The satisficing principle in capability learning', *Strategic Management Journal*, **21**: 981–96.

Zahra, S.A. and G. George (2002), 'Absorptive capacity: a review, reconceptualization, and extension', *Academy of Management Review*, **27**: 185–203.

PART II

Between firms

Introduction to Part II: New firms interacting

Wilfred Dolfsma and Geert Duysters

Just as relations between agents and groupings within a firm change in the newly emerging economic reality, so are relations between firms subject to much experimentation. Institutional environments are changing rapidly, as Michael Hitt has argued in previous work and forcefully again in his contribution to this volume with Tiago Ratinho (Chapter 4). This partly reflects developments in what some would call the economic base. The strategic challenges this poses to firms is also clearly shown in their contribution (see Sirmon et al., 2011). Firms need to get themselves organized if they aim to maintain competitive and appropriate rents from their investments and innovative activities (Coff, 2010).

Some would argue that if key capabilities are required to maintain a position in an industry, or even strengthen it, a firm needs to develop (Barney, 1991). As such, there will be a juggling for position in a value chain where most of the benefits are to be found (Mol et al., 2005), and in the process, capabilities necessary to appropriate benefits will be developed. In Chapter 5, Rietveld shows how choosing a position in a chain is not self-evident, even for established players in a chain. Despite clear incentives, VRIN (*V*aluable, *R*are, *I*mperfectly imitable and *N*on-substitutable) capabilities are exceedingly difficult to develop. VRIN resources, emphasized in the resource based view of the firm, can sometimes offer competitive shelter over an extended period, enabling a firm to maintain a strong competitive position over a longer timeframe. Rather than developing these key capabilities itself, a firm may be forced to seek cooperation with another firm, thereby relinquishing a large part of the proceeds to that other firm. While in such a situation as David Teece's (1986) logic of boundaries of the firm, emphasizing strategic considerations rather than immediate cost-minimizing ones as transaction cost economics would, integration into a single firm would be recommended; in fact it makes creative sense to keep firms separate to focus more fully on key capabilities. Core strengths with a twist. The resulting agreement between two or more firms is of a kind in-between that of a stereotypical market and a stereotypical hierarchy (Dolfsma and van der Eijk, 2010).

Some connections between formerly separate firms take the form of alliances. Creating and maintaining successful alliances is, however, in itself a capability that is in need of separate appreciation (Heimeriks and Duysters, 2007). Accumulating experience in collaborating with other firms does not unequivocally contribute to a firm's competitive position, as ter Wiel and Vlaar point out in Chapter 7. Amiryany, Cloodt, de Man and Huysman (Chapter 6) strongly suggest that knowledge transfer across boundaries of firms that are intimately cooperating to the extent that they integrate is a crucial issue. Even firms that do not undergo the strenuous merger or acquisition phase find it difficult to stimulate adequate knowledge transfer within their relatively stable boundaries, however (Szulanski, 1996). What facilitates the process is a shared conceptual framework for understanding the outside and the possibilities (Daft and Weick, 1984).

These developments strongly suggest that it makes quite a bit of sense to start exploring more seriously other notions of what a firm is and what a firm does. An emphasis, at the macro level, on the role of knowledge in an economy, is now drawing scholars increasingly to the realization that what firms do may include gathering information and attracting attention (Ocasio, 1997). Insights from behavioral sciences will have a noticeable impact on the theory of the firm and our understanding of industrial organization in the future. The contributions to Part III indicate where that impact is likely to be most visible.

REFERENCES

Barney, J.B. (1991), 'Firm resources and sustained competitive advantage', *Journal of Management*, **17**: 99–120.

Coff, R.W. (2010), 'The coevolution of rent appropriation and capability development', *Strategic Management Journal*, **31**: 711–33.

Daft, R.L. and K.E. Weick (1984), 'Toward a model of organizations as interpretation systems' *Academy of Management Review*, **9** (2): 284–95.

Dolfsma, W. and R. van der Eijk (2010), 'Knowledge development and coordination via market, hierarchy and gift exchange', in J. Davis (ed.), *Global Social Economy: Development, Work and Policy*, London & New York: Routledge, pp. 58–78.

Heimeriks, K. and G. Duysters (2007), 'Alliance capability as mediator between experience and alliance performance: an empirical investigation into the alliance capability development process', *Journal of Management Studies*, **44** (1): 25–49.

Mol, J.M., N.M. Wijnberg and C. Carroll (2005), 'Value chain envy: explaining new entry and vertical integration in popular music', *Journal of Management Studies*, **42** (2): 251–76.

Ocasio, W. (1997), 'Towards an attention-based view of the firm', *Strategic Management Journal*, **18**: 187–206.

Sirmon, D.G., M.A. Hitt, R.D. Ireland and B.A. Gilbert (2011), 'Managing resources to create competitive advantage: breadth, life cycle, and depth effects', *Journal of Management*, in press.

Szulanski, G. (1996), 'Exploring internal stickiness: impediments to the transfer of best practice within the firm', *Strategic Management Journal*, **17**: 27–43.

Teece, D. (1986), 'Profiting from technological innovation: implications for integration, collaboration, licensing and public policy', *Research Policy*, **15**: 285–305.

4. The multifaceted effects of institutions on firm strategies and entrepreneurial actions

Michael A. Hitt and Tiago Ratinho

1 INTRODUCTION

Globalization has changed the way businesses operate in the twenty-first century. All firms must compete in a global competitive landscape, and be knowledgeable of, and sensitive to it even if they operate only in a local market. For example, some of their competitors may be foreign companies competing in multiple markets. Further, emerging markets have become increasingly important in the global economy. In fact, much of the recent growth in the world's economy has come from emerging market countries. Several emerging market countries have increased their competitiveness, a few to the extent that they are now among the top countries in international benchmark reports (IMD, 2010; Schwab et al., 2010). These and other changes heighten the importance of country institutional environments and their influence on firm strategies.

Institutions refer to the formal and informal rules and norms that provide order and structure in society and thereby guide individual and organizational actions (North, 1990; Scott, 1995). While there has been considerable research on the effects of specific institutions (for example, political risk, intellectual property protection), the concept of national institutions is complex (for example, formal and informal institutions (Kogut and Ragin, 2006) and polycentric (Ostrom, 2005; Batjargal, 2010). Furthermore, institutions are partly interdependent and thus have collective influences on managerial decisions (Hitt et al., 2004; Delmas and Toffel, 2008). These collective influences include shaping the resources available to firms and how those resources can be accessed (Oliver, 1997).

Because of their importance to firm strategies and success, this chapter focuses on institutional environments and their influences. We identify the most important types of formal institutions, regulatory, economic and political, along with the most representative type of informal institution, culture. We then explore some of the important influences of these institutions on firm strategies. In addition, we examine the effects of specific institutions on the outcomes of firm strategies and the influences of institutional deficits on the strategic behavior of firms.

2   WHICH INSTITUTIONS ARE RELEVANT?

The core tenets of institutional theory (for example, Meyer and Rowan, 1977; North, 1990) suggest that institutional environments influence organizations by establishing the 'rules of the game' and the context under which organizations operate. Institutions provide constraints that shape human interaction and, in consequence, can affect the performance of national economies (North, 1990, p. 3). From an organizational behavior perspective, it is interesting to note that investment in resources, variations in normative patterns, and incentives based on regulations affect the content and amount of organizational learning by firms. For example, Henisz and Delios (2001) found that political instability has an effect on international plant location decisions. Also, North (1990) had already emphasized that country-level institutions produce constraints that provide stability, reduce uncertainty, and alleviate information complexity in economic exchange. North argued that the constraints of formal institutions occur through legal, regulatory, and economic structures.

The institutional environment is composed of three main pillars: regulative, normative, and cognitive (Scott, 1995, p. 34). The regulative pillar constrains behavior through rule-setting, monitoring, and sanctions. These institutions are perhaps the most conventional and moderate ones. The normative pillar is composed of the values and norms that exist in society. They are morally governed and individuals comply with them as a social obligation. Finally, the cognitive pillar is culturally supported, reflecting how symbols are used and understood to provide guidelines for action. However, this derived taxonomy of institutions neglects key economic components and was originally conceptualized at the organization level (Peng, 2002). Furthermore, the institutional environment includes both the formal and informal institutions.

Countries' institutional environments are complex and are composed of several formal institutions reflecting polycentricism (Ostrom, 2005). Therefore, we examine specifically three types of formal institutions that are more likely to shape the context in which organizations operate. The idea that 'institutions are commonly state-linked' (Zucker, 1987, p. 446) implies that the primary force driving their establishment and operation are governments. In fact, sovereign authorities often delegate to formal institutions the task of defining rules through legal systems and the adequate control systems to enforce their adherence and conformity (Covaleski and Dirsmith, 1988). Building on the work of North (1990) and others (for example, Holmes et al., 2011), formal institutions may be defined as the regulatory, political, and economic structures of a country. Taken together, these three types of formal institutions constitute and define the context within which businesses operate. Given the importance of these institutions for government policy, along with the supply and the demand of multinational enterprises' (MNEs') products and services, management decisions about foreign direct investment (FDI) are likely to be related to these three major types of institutions.

Regulatory Institutions

Government is typically responsible for the regulation of the activities of organizations within a country. Regulatory institutions establish rules set out to reduce the uncertainty of organizations' activities as well as to standardize their practices. Also, regulatory institutions are responsible for the maintenance of such rules and often monitor their conformity too. Society's normative expectations pertaining to the influence and degree of autonomy of organizations are encoded within these rules, regardless of the specific content of regulations (North, 1990; Scott, 1995). Property rights and their enforcement are an example of specific laws enacted with the purpose of restraining and protecting the activities of organizations, particularly the foreign ones (Spicer et al., 2000; Bekaert et al., 2005).

Political Institutions

Besides regulatory institutions, governments are also responsible for defining the standards for institutional change. The basis for change is the political process (Hillman and Keim, 1995) and the rules of power distribution among society's members and across governmental sectors. This set of rules typically defines individuals' participation in the political process as well as how societal rights are used (Persson, 2002). Political institutions are therefore characterized by the collection of rules and practices allowing governments and citizens to devise new institutions as well as reform existing ones. Their function is critical since it impacts on the stability of the institutional environment (DiMaggio and Powell, 1983). Political institutions allow several specific arrangements: best-known configurations range from autocratic regimes with a few individuals concentrating power to democratic settings in which citizens are encouraged to participate actively (Fearon, 1994; de Mesquita and Siverson, 1995; Ross, 2001).

Economic Institutions

Some other formal institutions are responsible for the establishment of rules and standards to regulate production, consumption and capital investments. These institutions basically regulate society's access to financial resources as well as their value and availability. The best-known example of these economic institutions are national monetary and fiscal policies (Beck et al., 2000; Lucas, 2003). As financial factors are vital in the growth process of countries (Levine and Zervos, 1998), these institutions play a vital role in the growth and development of a country's economy.

Informal Institutions: Culture

Alongside formal institutions, informal institutions are also important and specifically influence managerial decisions. Informal institutions are pervasive collections of non-codified shared meanings and collective understandings that shape social cohesion and coordination among individuals (Scott, 1995). The best-known example of this kind of institution is national culture (North, 1990; Scott, 1995). Fu et al. define a country's culture as the 'created and learned standards for perception, cognition, judgment, or behavior shared by members of a certain group' (2004, p. 288). Further, culture encompasses what society considers to be ethical, desirable and acceptable (Reed, 1996). One of its defining characteristics is that it remains unchangeable for long periods of time and changes, if they do occur, are extremely slow (McGrath et al., 1992; Reed, 1996; Brett et al., 1997). Despite being tacitly understood by all society, cultural knowledge is most likely to be acquired through socialization processes (Greif, 1994).

3   EFFECTS OF FORMAL INSTITUTIONS ON FIRM STRATEGIES

Foreign Direct Investment: Placement of International Activities

The decision to internationalize is one of the most important strategic decisions that MNE managers execute. The determinants of location choice and the number of international activities are key features in the understanding of international strategy (Hitt et al., 1997; Goerzen and Beamish, 2003). Several theoretical perspectives have been used to study firm internationalization and FDI. On the one hand, research has emphasized ownership advantages and the influence of firm resources on international strategies; on the other, some authors posit that an improved picture of country-level explanations is necessary before cross-national FDI differences can be fully understood (for example, Gomes-Casseres, 1997; Meyer, 2001). Further, the recognition of the importance that institutional environments have in internationalization processes has added yet another dimension to the study of this phenomenon. For instance, it is well known that MNEs' foreign performance and FDI decisions are strongly influenced by the host-country institutional context (for example, Delios and Beamish, 1999; Gaur et al., 2007; Chan et al., 2008; Meyer et al., 2009).

In recent years, a different stream of research has concentrated on FDI and international strategies of MNEs in a new context: 'semi-globalization' (Ghemawat, 2003; Rugman and Verbeke, 2004). Semi-globalization describes a context in which firms are not completely integrated (or globalized) while, at the same time, their activities are not necessarily circumscribed to an insulated national market. According to these authors, MNEs are changing their international strategies, increasingly starting foreign activities in regions rather than in whole countries. These results highlight the need to rethink the importance of regions in order to fully understand MNEs' international strategy (Rugman and Verbeke, 2001, 2004; Ghemawat, 2003; Buckley and Ghauri, 2004). Rugman and Verbeke (2005) note that today's MNEs expand their activities across regions, thus limiting their geographical scope, to maintain local responsiveness and build on their location-specific advantages.

These perspectives on internationalization in a context of semi-globalization and the influence on the institutional environment on MNEs' strategies have developed independently. This creates large gaps in our understanding of the role that regions play in international strategies. For example, Chan et al. (2008) call for further research on the impact of institutions on MNE performance, suggesting that the correct level of analysis should be identified (country or region). Furthermore, it is necessary to understand which and how institutional dimensions affect internationalization decisions at the country and regional levels. Adopting the semi-globalization perspective is likely to have a great impact on these relationships.

The first important finding on this topic is that regulatory control, political democracy and capital availability affect the inward FDIs made in a given country (Holmes et al., 2011). This means that those institutions have an influence on foreign firms' managers, affecting their decision on where they place their international efforts. This is not surprising but it shows the collective effect of institutions on firms' strategies. Previous work has shown that multinational firms focus their international strategies in geographic regions and therefore exploit regional advantages (Rugman and Verbeke, 2004). Arregle et al.'s (2009) recent work expands this finding, showing that within a certain region, firms specifically choose countries with relatively more favorable institutional environments to place their investments.

Also, Zhu et al. (2009) examined almost 10,000 cross-border mergers and acquisitions (M&As) in both developed and developing countries to understand firm strategies in terms of location choices, activities and how institutions affect these decisions. Their findings suggest that regulatory and economic institutions directly influence post-acquisition returns, and political institutions moderate these relationships. Formal regulatory and economic institutions derive directly from governments; these are mostly legal mechanisms, regulations or they govern issues such as money supply. The political system affects how these institutions are shaped. For instance, the USA enacted the Sherman Anti-trust Act more than 100 years ago but its implementation and enforcement has varied over the years. Interpretations of the act have changed with different presidential administrations; for example, during the 1980s there was a big change in how it was interpreted. Therefore, the political institutions moderate the relationship between the regulatory institutions and merged firm performance.

Alliances

Strategic alliances are an increasingly popular mechanism used by firms willing to expand into international markets (Lane and Beamish, 1990; Osborn and Hagedoorn, 1997; Kim and Parkhe, 2009). Typically, this kind of alliance is established by allowing partners to freely exchange technical capabilities, managerial skills and marketing practices while sharing risk to a certain degree (Lyles and Salk, 1996; Fahy et al., 2000; Hitt et al., 2000).The goal of such alliances is to establish formal relationships aimed at competing more efficiently with other firms outside the alliance (Gulati, 1998; Jarillo, 1988). While the benefits of strategic alliances are appealing to firms, a high level of dissatisfaction is often reported with the actual outcomes when expectations are not met (Park and Russo, 1996; Madhok and Tallman, 1998). Particularly in the context of international strategic alliances, high rates of dissolution have been reported (Hennart et al., 1998). There are two main factors affecting the likelihood of success of each strategic alliance: partner selection (Hitt et al., 2000) and institutional factors of the countries involved (Li et al., 2009). The next subsections analyze these factors in turn.

Partner selection

Drawing on the resource-based theory of the firm (Barney, 1991), it is reasonable to assume that firms search for partners that have specific resources they can leverage. The firms can leverage resources that are complementary through integration that creates synergies. The integration allows firms to bundle the resources to build capabilities and skills that provide greater value to customers and create or sustain a competitive advantage. The underlying assumption is that firms often need specific additional resources to be competitive in particular markets (Hitt et al., 1999). In the context of internationalization, particularly important resources are, for example, financial capital, technical capabilities, managerial skills, and other intangible assets, such as firm reputation or knowledge of particular markets.

Developed market firms with large resource endowments try to leverage their resources by seeking to form alliances with partners with complementary capabilities and unique competencies in local markets. Firms with smaller resource endowments (for example, partners in developing markets) often wish to acquire new technical and managerial capabilities, while firms with larger resource endowments (for example, partners from developed markets) want to build relationships that provide access to unknown markets (Khanna et al., 1998). Partner selection is therefore a critical factor for the overall effectiveness of the alliance.

Several factors influence the choice of partners for alliances in emerging and developed markets. Hitt et al. (2000) conducted a cross-country study of alliance partner selection involving firms based in three developed markets and three emerging markets. They found that emerging market firms more strongly emphasized financial assets, technical capabilities, intangible assets and willingness to share expertise than their developed market counterparts. The emerging market firms also emphasized capability for quality more strongly than did the developed market firms (Hitt et al., 2000).

Developed market firms emphasized partners' unique competencies and market knowledge and access more strongly than did emerging market firms. Interestingly, the developed market firms also emphasized partners' previous alliance experience, the cost of alternatives, and industry attractiveness, along with special skills to learn from a partner, more strongly than did emerging market firms. Partners' complementary and managerial capabilities were important and of similar priority to both emerging and developed market firms. The cost of alternatives was unimportant to emerging market firms, and partners' technical capabilities were unimportant to developed market firms. A partner's ability to acquire skills was unimportant to firms from both contexts (ibid.). More recently, these relationships have been found to be moderated by the set of criteria that managers use to select partners (Shah and Swaminathan, 2008). Both partners' characteristics have varied effects on partner selection and attractiveness; this is mostly dependent on the degree of complexity of each alliance and the degree to which the outcomes can be clearly identified (ibid.). We now turn our attention to the specific case of value creation for emerging market partners in the context of different institutional factors.

The influence of the rule of law
International strategic alliances help emerging market firms to acquire technical knowledge, develop managerial skills and marketing practices and, as a result, increase their probability of survival and overall performance (Lyles and Salk, 1996; Fahy et al., 2000; Hitt et al., 2000). There are, however, some shortcomings. Knowledge transfer is sometimes time consuming and difficult and its success depends heavily on the motivations of both parties involved (Szulanski, 1996, 2000). More specifically, difficulties emerge if the foreign partner intentionally conceals knowledge from the local partner to maintain its local and international competitiveness (Kale et al., 2000; Oxley and Sampson, 2004; Li et al., 2008). Firms seeking to start activities in emerging markets might see this difficulty amplified since their weak rule of law promotes knowledge dissipation (Porta et al., 1997; Hoskisson et al., 2000).

Emerging markets have enjoyed strong economic growth in recent years (see, for instance, IMD, 2010). Yet in many of these countries, the institutional environment is still largely uncertain (Williamson, 1991; Newman, 2000) as there has been no parallel development of regulatory institutions (Meyer, 2001). Firms need financial, organizational and technological resources; the poor institutional environment populated with weak institutions does not provide an appropriate setting for these firms to compete (Hitt et al., 2000). This alone provides a motivation for emerging market firms to form alliances with foreign partners coming from more developed markets. This kind of alliance is at first sight symbiotical: emerging market firms gain access to a set of resources that allows them to compete more effectively locally and abroad; developed market firms accelerate their understanding of local conditions and therefore are more able to leverage their set of existing competencies to operate in those specific markets.

Differences between formal institutions across emerging and developed markets impact negatively on the relationship of both alliance partners, namely with regard to knowledge sharing (ibid.). Further, a poor institutional environment might allow firms and encourage individuals to pursue opportunistic behaviors illegal in other stronger institutional settings (Miller et al., 2008). For instance, a weaker rule of law can trigger local partners to abuse proprietary technology (Teece, 1986) or free ride brand reputation, certain in the knowledge that such actions are not likely to be punished. Foreign firms therefore exercise caution in any knowledge transfer with local partners and, as a result, reduce the access of important resources to the local emerging market partner. Even if resources are indeed transferred, the emerging market partner does not fully enjoy the expected value creation.

When the rule of law is weak, the developed market partner is less motivated to engage in knowledge-transfer activities with emerging market partners (Szulanski, 1996). Empirical evidence confirms this premise. In a study involving Brazil, Russia, India and China – the so-called BRIC countries – Li et al. (2009) found that investors do not assume that emerging partners will unambiguously gain access to the new technologies or knowledge residing with foreign partners. Moreover, the results suggest that investors expect, when the rule of law is weak, that the foreign partner will be less motivated to share knowledge, or at least will implement more safeguards to prevent knowledge leakages. These overprotective actions of the foreign partner inhibit, rather than help, the emerging market partner's ability to acquire the requisite knowledge resources to develop its own capabilities (ibid.). Further results posit that the knowledge transfer and value creation for the local partner within alliances is dependent on the rule of law and the level of state ownership of the local partner.

4 EFFECTS OF INFORMAL INSTITUTIONS ON FIRM STRATEGIES

Formal institutions are stable once established, since their basis is the shared cognitive understanding and acceptance of individuals in the society (Zucker, 1987). Therefore, society's culture determines the creation and maintenance of formal institutions (Reed, 1996; Redding, 2005; Jackson and Deeg, 2008). Formal institutions embody the set of rules and standards devised to solve problems obstructing the society's ability to reach important goals (DiMaggio, 1988). Culture can be seen as the 'tool kit' of institutionalized solutions to solve those societal problems (DiMaggio and Powell, 1991, p. 28). Culture is a shared understanding among individuals in a society and has an undeniable effect on its beliefs (Schooler, 1996), norms (Sirmon and Lane, 2004), values (Hofstede, 1980) and assumptions (Huang and Harris, 1973).

North (1990) emphasized the importance of the history of institutions of a given country to understand institutions themselves and their change through time. Indeed, we see that formal and informal institutions are inextricably linked through a society's culture. Culture provides a foundation from which people see the world (Chui et al., 2002) and helps individuals to interpret events (Witt and Redding, 2009). It follows that a society's culture influences what problems are identified and which are deemed as most important to be solved and regulated by institutions. We can therefore assume that culture is also expressed by the resulting formal institutions (Redding, 2005). Further, if culture leads to different institutional settings, it also provides a good basis to identify systematic differences across countries and regions (Hofstede, 1980; Greif, 1994).

Hofstede pioneered cultural studies analyzing different cultures in a considerable number of countries (Hofstede, 1980). Two of Hofstede's cultural dimensions are more likely to influence national formal institutions: collectivism and long-term orientation. Collectivism is related to the value given by society's members to be integrated in cohesive units and the extent to which they prioritize the group's interest above their own; conversely, in an individualistic context, society's members are expected to display their individual interests above the group's. Policies are often a result of the conflicting interests of groups of citizens, politicians and other organizations (Persson, 2002). The extent to which a given society values the collective versus individuals is therefore very likely to influence its formal institutions. The long-term orientation dimension is related to the value society places in long-term outcomes compared to short-term ones. A common illustration of long-term or future orientation is planning and investing aiming at long-term gratification (Brodbeck et al., 2002; Ashkanasy et al., 2004). The accumulation of financial resources is commonly achieved by withholding current spending. The resulting savings and accumulated capital can constitute the means to invest in longer-term growth opportunities (Baxter and Crucini, 1993; Beck et al., 2000). These behaviors are influenced by society's norms and therefore future orientation shapes the economic institutions that manage financial resources.

Formal and Informal Institutions' Impact on Inward FDI

Holmes et al. (2011) analyzed the extent to which informal institutions influence formal institutions and, in turn, the overall effect of these institutions in managerial decisions such as inward FDI. A linkage between a country's informal institutions (that is, its culture) and its formal institutions (that is, regulatory, political, and economic institutions) is shown to exist. This relationship between national culture and formal institutions implies that, in fact, formal institutions mirror society's collective values and actions (Powell, 1991; Tolbert and Zucker, 1996).

The same study also found that in-group collectivism positively influences the level of regulatory control and negatively influences the use of democratic political institutions (Holmes et al., 2011). Collectivism is associated with promoting society's interest above the individual's. As a result, the highest-valued businesses will be most likely the ones acting in beneficial ways to society. At the same time, the focus on collectivism will limit the value granted to democratic institutions, which give voice to individuals. Some evidence was also found for the positive relationship between future orientation and economic institutions promoting capital investments. A society oriented towards the future values long-term outcomes and thus invests in mechanisms to facilitate such results. This translates into monetary and fiscal policies to stimulate savings and investment.

The study of the joint impact of formal and informal institutions on FDI leads to one principal conclusion: formal institutions affect inward FDI beyond the influence of culture (ibid.). Regulatory institutions controlling organizational behavior discourage inward FDI since MNE managers tend to avoid any restrictions to their activities. Political institutions, on the other hand, encourage inward FDI the more autocratic they are. The main reason behind this might be the fact that less-democratic regimes enable firms to leverage their investments in a less-constrained context. Also, certain MNEs might enjoy special treatment by the authorities in less-transparent and -accountable institutional settings.

5   EFFECTS OF INSTITUTIONAL DEFICITS

Institutions are not homogeneous across regions or countries. This means that both the presence and absence of formal institutions can influence entrepreneurs' actions and firm strategies. But what happens when institutions are absent is seldom studied. Batjargal et al. (2009) provide evidence about how entrepreneurs cope with the absence of institutions, sometimes referred to as 'institutional deficits'. Relationships are an important cultural attribute in a number of emerging market countries and are critical for business transactions (Xin and Pearce, 1996; Batjargal, 2007; Redding, 2008). Given the rapid increase in new ventures in emerging economies (Langowitz and Minniti, 2007), informal institutions such as social networks and associated relationships are likely to be especially important for new venture success. Therefore, do social networks provide different rates of return for new ventures across national contexts with varying importance of social relationships? Furthermore, are there differences among men and women in terms of their ventures' performance?

Batjargal et al. (2009) found that women have larger social networks, female-owned ventures have lower revenue growth, and social network size generally has a positive effect on revenue growth. Basically, entrepreneurs in emerging markets used their social networks to access resources that were unavailable through formal institutions. Thus, the informal institutions (for example, culture) served as a substitute for formal institutions. Also, men benefited more than women from their social networks. Women had to build larger networks because they likely had even less access to resources than did male entrepreneurs. The results varied across countries with different cultures, especially those in which the norms for the importance of relationships varied. The results supported their argument that the effects of social networks on new ventures' revenue growth are contingent upon gender and national culture.

6 CONCLUSION

The global competitive landscape has changed dramatically in the last decade. Some emerging market countries are becoming strong, developing valuable capabilities, thereby enhancing their competitiveness in world markets (for example, IMD, 2010; Schwab et al., 2010). Among those are China, India, Brazil, Malaysia, Thailand and the Czech Republic (Hitt and He, 2008). Because of these changes in the international landscape, there are greater economic opportunities but also increased competitive strength and rivalry in global markets. In addition, the institutional environments of these emerging market countries are also changing. Thus, we need to understand the institutional environments, their influences on firm strategies and the effects of changes in institutional environments. This brief foray into the complex world of institutions and institutional environments represents a step in this direction.

Research has shown that regulatory, economic and political institutions affect the amount of inward FDI in countries. Specific institutions such as the rule of law and intellectual property protection influence the strategic behaviors of firms in local markets, especially foreign competitors. For example, they affect the formation of strategic alliances and especially influence the manner in which the alliances are governed. Further, in environments where the rule of law and intellectual property protection are weak, the foreign partner in alliances formed commonly insists on an equity alliance in order to have greater control over the operations and outcomes (Li et al., 2008). In addition, these institutions affect the amount and type of competitive rivalry in these markets.

Institutions also affect entrepreneurial behavior in a country. For example, in countries with institutional voids or deficits, entrepreneurs develop larger social networks to overcome these deficits. In particular, these larger networks help the entrepreneur to access resources needed that are not available due to the institutional voids (Batjargal et al., 2009). Informal institutions tend to be more influential when formal institutions are weak and in the face of institutional deficits. For example, informal institutions have a greater effect on firms' strategic behaviors in mainland China and Taiwan than in Hong Kong (Ahlstrom et al., 2010). Recent research also suggests that informal institutions influence the evolution of formal institutions (Holmes et al., 2011).

Also demonstrating the complexity of institutional environments and their polycentricity (Ostrom, 2005), Batjargal (2010), found that there are different levels of institutions including country- and industry-level institutions. Furthermore, industry norms and standards influence entrepreneurial behaviors (for example, their social networks used in their businesses), and industry norms were influenced by both formal and informal country-level institutions.

Much more research is needed to understand the complex effects of institutional environments, suggesting the need for substantial research in developing institutions. We hope that this effort serves as a catalyst for such future efforts.

REFERENCES

Ahlstrom, D., E. Levitas, M. Hitt, M.T. Dacin and H. Zhu (2010), 'The three faces of China: strategic alliance partner selection in greater China', working paper, Chinese University of Hong Kong.

Arregle, J.-L., S. Miller, M.A. Hitt and P.W. Beamish (2009), 'How regions matter? An integrated institutional and semiglobalization perspective on MNEs' internationalization decisions', paper presented at the Academy of Management Meeting, Chicago, IL, August.

Ashkanasy, N., V. Gupta, M.S. Mayfield and E. Trevor-Roberts (2004), 'Future orientation', in R.J. House, P.J. Hanges, M. Javidan, P.W. Dorfman and V. Gupta (eds), *Culture, Leadership, and Organizations: The GLOBE Study of 62 Societies*, Thousand Oaks, CA: Sage, pp. 282–342.

Barney, J. (1991). 'Firm resources and sustained competitive advantage', *Journal of Management*, **17** (1), 99–120.

Batjargal, B. (2007), 'Network triads: transitivity, referral and venture capital decisions in China and Russia', *Journal of International Business Studies*, **38** (6), 998–1012.

Batjargal, B. (2010), 'The effects of network's structural holes: polycentric institutions, product portfolio, and new venture growth in China and Russia', *Strategic Entrepreneurship Journal*, **4** (2), 146–63.

Batjargal, B., M.A. Hitt, J. Webb, J.-L. Arregle and T. Miller (2009), 'Women and men entrepreneurs' social networks and new venture performance across cultures', paper presented at the Academy of Management Meeting, Chicago, IL, August.

Baxter, M. and M.J. Crucini (1993), 'Explaining saving–investment correlations', *American Economic Review*, **83** (3), 416–36.

Beck, T., R. Levine and N.V. Loayza (2000), 'Finance and the sources of growth', *Journal of Financial Economics*, **58**, 261–300.

Bekaert, G., C.R. Harvey and C. Lundblad (2005), 'Does financial liberalization spur growth?', *Journal of Financial Economics*, **77** (1), 3–55.

Brett, J.M., C.H. Tinsley, M. Janssens, Z.I. Barsness and A.L. Lytle (1997), 'New approaches to the study of culture in I/O psychology', in P.C. Earley and M. Erez (eds), *New Perspective on International/Organizational Psychology*, San Francisco, CA: Jossey-Bass, pp. 75–129.

Brodbeck, F.C., M. Frese and M. Javidan (2002), 'Leadership made in Germany: low on compassion, high on performance', *Academy of Management Executive*, **16** (1), 16–29.

Buckley, P.J., and P.N. Ghauri (2004), 'Globalisation, economic geography and the strategy of multinational enterprises', *Journal of International Business Studies*, **35** (2), 81–98.

Chan, C.M., T. Isobe and S. Makino (2008), 'Which country matters? Institutional development and foreign affiliate performance', *Strategic Management Journal*, **29** (11), 1179–205.

Chui, A.C.W., E.L. Alison, and C.C.Y. Kwok (2002), 'The determination of capital structure: is national culture a missing piece to the puzzle?', *Journal of International Business Studies*, **33** (1), 99–127.

Covaleski, M.A. and M.W. Dirsmith (1988), 'An institutional perspective on the rise, social transformation, and fall of a university budget category', *Administrative Science Quarterly*, **33** (4), 562–87.

de Mesquita, B.B. and R.M. Siverson (1995), 'War and the survival of political leaders: a comparative study of regime types and political accountability', *American Political Science Review*, **89** (4), 841–55.

Delios, A. and P.W. Beamish (1999), 'Ownership strategy of Japanese firms: transactional, institutional, and experience influences', *Strategic Management Journal*, **20** (10), 915–33.

Delmas, M.A. and M.W. Toffel, (2008), 'Organizational responses to environmental demands: opening the black box', *Strategic Management Journal*, **29** (10), 1027–55.

DiMaggio, P.J. (1988), 'Interest and agency in institutional theory', in L.G. Zucker (ed.), *Institutional Patterns and Organizations: Culture and Environment*, Cambridge, MA: Ballinger, pp. 3–21.

DiMaggio, P.J. and W.W. Powell (1983), 'The iron cage revisited: institutional isomorphism and collective rationality in organizational fields', *American Sociological Review*, **48** (2), 147–60.

DiMaggio, P.J. and W.W. Powell (1991), 'Introduction', in Powell and DiMaggio (eds), *The New Institutionalism in Organizational Analysis*, Chicago, IL: University of Chicago Press, pp. 1–38.

Fahy, J., G. Hooley, T. Cox, J. Beracs, F. Krzysztof and B. Snoj (2000), 'The development and impact of marketing capabilities in Central Europe', *Journal of International Business Studies*, **31** (1), 63–81.

Fearon, J.D. (1994), 'Domestic political audiences and the escalation of international disputes', *American Political Science Review*, **88** (3), 577–92.

Fu, P.P., J. Kennedy, J. Tata, G. Yukl, M.H. Bond and T.-K. Peng (2004), 'The impact of societal cultural values and individual social beliefs on the perceived effectiveness of managerial influence strategies: a meso approach', *Journal of International Business Studies*, **35** (4), 284–305.

Gaur, A.S., A. Delios and K. Singh (2007), 'Institutional environments, staffing strategies, and subsidiary performance', *Journal of Management*, **33** (4), 611–36.

Ghemawat, P. (2003), 'Semiglobalization and international business strategy', *Journal of International Business Studies*, **34**, 138–52.

Goerzen, A. and P.W. Beamish (2003), 'Geographic scope and multinational enterprise performance', *Strategic Management Journal*, **24** (13), 1289–306.

Gomes-Casseres, B. (1997), 'Alliance strategies of small firms', *Small Business Economics*, **9** (1), 33–44.

Greif, A. (1994), 'Cultural beliefs and the organization of society: a historical and theoretical reflection on collectivist and individualist societies', *Journal of Political Economy*, **102** (5), 912–50.

Gulati, R. (1998), 'Alliances and networks', *Strategic Management Journal*, **19** (4), 293–317.

Henisz, W.J. and A. Delios (2001), 'Uncertainty, imitation, and plant location: Japanese multinational corporations, 1990–1996', *Administrative Science Quarterly*, **46** (3), 443–75.

Hennart, J.-F., D.-J. Kim and M. Zeng (1998), 'The impact of joint venture status on the longevity of Japanese stakes in U.S. manufacturing affiliates', *Organization Science*, **9** (3), 382–95.

Hillman, A. and G. Keim (1995), 'International variation in the business-government interface: institutional and organizational considerations', *Academy of Management Review*, **20** (1), 193–214.

Hitt, M.A., D. Ahlstrom, M.T. Dacin, E. Levitas and L. Svobodina (2004), 'The institutional effects on strategic alliance partner selection in transition economies: China versus Russia', *Organization Science*, **15** (2), 173–85.

Hitt, M.A., M.T. Dacin, E. Levitas, J.L. Arregle and A. Borza (2000), 'Partner selection in emerging and developed market contexts: resource-based and organizational learning perspectives', *Academy of Management Journal*, **43** (3), 449–67.

Hitt, M.A. and X. He (2008), 'Firm strategies in a changing global competitive landscape', *Business Horizons*, **51** (5), 363–9.

Hitt, M.A., R.E. Hoskisson and K. Hicheon (1997), 'International diversification: effects on innovation and firm performance in product-diversified firms', *Academy of Management Journal*, **40** (4), 767–98.

Hitt, M.A., R.D. Nixon, P.G. Clifford and K.P. Coyne (1999), 'The development and use of strategic resources', in Hitt, Clifford, Nixon and Coyne (eds), *Dynamic Strategic Resources: Development, Diffusion and Integration*, Chichester, UK: Wiley, pp. 1–14.

Hofstede, G. (1980), *Culture's Consequences: International Differences in Work-related Values*, Beverly Hills, CA: Sage.

Holmes, R.M., T. Miller, M.A. Hitt and M. Salmador (2011), 'The interrelationships among informal institutions, formal institutions and foreign direct investment', *Journal of Management*, in press.

Hoskisson, R.E., L. Eden, C.M. Lau and M. Wright (2000), 'Strategy in emerging economies', *Academy of Management Journal*, **43** (3), 249–67.

Huang, L.C. and M.B. Harris (1973), 'Conformity in Chinese and Americans', *Journal of Cross-Cultural Psychology*, **4** (4), 427–34.

IMD (2010), *World Competitiveness Yearbook*, Online Version, accessed 22 November, 2010.

Jackson, G. and R. Deeg (2008), 'Comparing capitalisms: understanding institutional diversity and its implications for international business', *Journal of International Business Studies*, **39** (4), 540–61.

Jarillo, J.C. (1988), 'On strategic networks', *Strategic Management Journal*, **9** (1), 31–41.

Kale, P., H. Singh and H. Perlmutter (2000), 'Learning and protection of proprietary assets in strategic alliances: building relational capital', *Strategic Management Journal*, **21** (3), 217–37.

Khanna, T., R. Gulati and N. Nohria (1998), 'The dynamics of learning alliances: competition, cooperation, and relative scope', *Strategic Management Journal*, **19** (3), 193–210.

Kim, J. and A. Parkhe (2009), 'Competing and cooperating similarity in global strategic alliances: an exploratory examination', *British Journal of Management*, **20** (3), 363–76.

Kogut, B. and C. Ragin (2006), 'Exploring complexity when diversity is limited: institutional complementarity in theories of rule of law and national systems revisited', *European Management Review*, **3** (1), 44–59.

Lane, H.W. and P.W. Beamish (1990), 'Cross-cultural cooperative behavior in joint ventures in LDCs', *Management International Review*, **30** (special issue), 87–102.

Langowitz, N. and M. Minniti (2007), 'The entrepreneurial propensity of women', *Entrepreneurship: Theory and Practice*, **31** (3), 341–64.

Levine, R. and S. Zervos (1998), 'Stock markets, banks, and economic growth', *American Economic Review*, **88** (3), 537–58.

Li, D.A.N., L. Eden, M.A. Hitt and R.D. Ireland, (2008), 'Friends, acquaintances, or strangers? Partner selection in R&D alliances', *Academy of Management Journal*, **51** (2), 315–34.

Li, D.A.N., S. Miller, L. Eden and M.A. Hitt (2009), 'Rule of law and value creation through strategic alliances in emerging markets', paper presented at the Academy of International Business, San Diego, CA, June.

Lucas, R.E. (2003), 'Macroeconomic priorities', *American Economic Review*, **93**, 1–14.

Lyles, M.A. and J.E. Salk (1996), 'Knowledge acquisition from foreign parents in international joint ventures: an empirical examination in the Hungarian context', *Journal of International Business Studies*, **27** (5), 877–903.

Madhok, A. and S.B. Tallman (1998), 'Resources, transactions and rents: managing value through interfirm collaborative relationships', *Organization Science*, **9** (3), 326–39.

McGrath, R.G., I.C. MacMillan, E.A.-Y. Yang and W. Tsai (1992), 'Does culture endure, or is it malleable? Issues for entrepreneurial economic development', *Journal of Business Venturing*, **7** (6), 441–58.

Meyer, J.W. and B. Rowan (1977), 'Institutionalized organizations: formal structure as myth and ceremony', *American Journal of Sociology*, **83** (2), 340–63.

Meyer, K.E. (2001), 'Institutions, transaction costs, and entry mode choice in Eastern Europe', *Journal of International Business Studies*, **32** (2), 357–67.

Meyer, K.E., S. Estrin, S.K. Bhaumik and M.W. Peng (2009), 'Institutions, resources, and entry strategies in emerging economies', *Strategic Management Journal*, **30** (1), 61–80.

Miller, S.R., D. Li, L. Eden and M.A. Hitt (2008), 'Insider trading and the valuation of international strategic alliances in emerging stock markets', *Journal of International Business Studies*, **39** (1), 102–17.

Newman, K.L. (2000), 'Organizational transformation during institutional upheaval', *Academy of Management Review*, **25** (3), 602–19.

North, D.C. (1990), *Institutions, Institutional Change and Economic Performance*, Cambridge: Cambridge University Press.

Oliver, C. (1997), 'Sustainable competitive advantage: combining institutional and resource-based views', *Strategic Management Journal*, **18** (9), 697–713.

Osborn, R.N. and J. Hagedoorn (1997), 'The institutionalization and evolutionary dynamics of interorganizational alliances and networks', *Academy of Management Journal*, **40** (2), 261–78.

Ostrom, E. (2005), *Understanding Institutional Diversity*, Princeton, NJ: Princeton University Press.

Oxley, J.E. and R.C. Sampson (2004), 'The scope and governance of international R&D alliances', *Strategic Management Journal*, **25** (8/9), 723–49.

Park, S.H. and M.V. Russo (1996), 'When competition eclipses cooperation: an event history analysis of joint venture failure', *Management Science*, **42** (6), 875–90.

Peng, M.W. (2002), 'Towards an institution-based view of business strategy', *Asia Pacific Journal of Management*, **19** (2), 251–67.

Persson, T. (2002), 'Do political institutions shape economic policy?', *Econometrica*, **70** (3), 883–905.

Porta, R.L., F. Lopez-de-Silanes, A. Shleifer and R.W. Vishny (1997), 'Legal determinants of external finance', *Journal of Finance*, **52** (3), 1131–50.

Powell, W.W. (1991), 'Expanding the scope of institutional analysis', in W.W. Powell and P.J. DiMaggio (eds), *The New Institutionalism in Organizational Analysis*, Chicago, IL: University of Chicago Press, pp. 183–203.

Redding, G. (2005), 'The thick description and comparison of societal systems of capitalism', *Journal of International Business Studies*, **36** (2), 123–55.

Redding, G. (2008), 'Separating culture from institutions: the use of semantic spaces as a conceptual domain and the case of China', *Management and Organization Review*, **4** (2), 257–89.

Reed, M.I. (1996), 'Rediscovering Hegel: the "new historicism" in organization and management studies', *Journal of Management Studies*, **33** (2), 139–58.

Ross, M.L. (2001), 'Does oil hinder democracy?', *World Politics*, **53**, 325–61.

Rugman, A.M. and A. Verbeke (2001), 'Subsidiary-specific advantages in multinational enterprises', *Strategic Management Journal*, **22** (3), 237–50.

Rugman, A.M. and A. Verbeke (2004), 'A perspective on regional and global strategies of multinational enterprises', *Journal of International Business Studies*, **35** (1), 3–18.

Rugman, A.M. and A. Verbeke (2005), 'Towards a theory of regional multinationals: a transaction cost economics approach', *Management International Review*, **45** (1), 3–18.

Schooler, C. (1996), 'Cultural and social-structural explanations of cross-national psychological differences', *Annual Review of Sociology*, **22**, 323–49.

Schwab, K., X. Sala-i-Martin and R. Greenhill (2010), *The Global Competitiveness Report 2010–2011*, Geneva: World Economic Forum.

Scott, W.R. (1995), *Institutions and Organizations*, Thousand Oaks, CA: Sage.

Shah, R.H. and V. Swaminathan (2008), 'Factors influencing partner selection in strategic alliances: the moderating role of alliance context', *Strategic Management Journal*, **29** (5), 471–94.

Sirmon, D.G. and P.J. Lane (2004), 'A model of cultural differences and international alliance performance', *Journal of International Business Studies*, **35** (4), 306–19.

Spicer, A., G.A. McDermott and B. Kogut (2000), 'Entrepreneurship and privatization in Central Europe: the tenuous balance between destruction and creation', *Academy of Management Review*, **25** (3), 630–49.

Szulanski, G. (1996), 'Exploring internal stickiness: impediments to the transfer of best practice within the firm', *Strategic Management Journal*, **17**, 27–43.

Szulanski, G. (2000), 'The process of knowledge transfer: a diachronic analysis of stickiness', *Organizational Behavior and Human Decision Processes*, **82** (1), 9–27.

Teece, D.J. (1986), 'Transactions cost economics and the multinational enterprise: an assessment', *Journal of Economic Behavior and Organization*, **7** (1), 21–45.

Tolbert, P.S. and L.G. Zucker (1996), 'The institutionalization of institutional theory', in S.R. Clegg, C. Hardy and W. Nord (eds), *Handbook of Organizational Studies*, London: Sage, pp. 75–190.

Williamson, O.E. (1991), 'Comparative economic organization: the analysis of discrete structural alternatives', *Administrative Science Quarterly*, **36** (2), 269–96.

Witt, M.A. and G. Redding (2009), 'Culture, meaning, and institutions: executive rationale in Germany and Japan', *Journal of International Business Studies*, **40** (5), 859–85.

Xin, K.R. and J.L. Pearce (1996), 'Guanxi: connections as substitutes for formal institutional support', *Academy of Management Journal*, **39** (6), 1641–58.

Zhu, H., M.A. Hitt, L. Eden and L. Tihanyi (2009), 'Cross border mergers and acquisitions', paper presented at the Academy of Management Meeting, Chicago, IL, August.

Zucker, L.G. (1987), 'Institutional theories of organization', *Annual Review of Sociology*, **13**, 443–64.

5. Profiting from digitally distributed cultural products: the case of content producers in the video games industry

G.J. (Joost) Rietveld[1]

1 INTRODUCTION

With the advent of digital distribution in cultural industries, pure information goods such as books, music, films and video games no longer have to be tied to a physical information carrier to be distributed. The effects of the emergence of digital distribution channels are noticeable throughout the entire value chain as value propositions evolve and power positions change (Bockstedt et al., 2006). The most significant consequence for actors creating the cultural goods is the ability to independently publish their products onto digital distribution channels.

One significant entry barrier to the stage of publishing has been lowered as complex and capital-intensive logistics of an international distribution network for physical goods are no longer necessary (Kretschmer et al., 2001). However, two other entry barriers for the publishing business have remained intact: (i) huge marketing costs involved in bringing a cultural good into the market; and (ii) the need for overproduction in a winner-takes-all market where the reasons for success are unknown beforehand (Caves, 2000; Kretschmer et al., 2001).

Although content producers within cultural industries can – with the help of online digital channels – publish their products themselves, they often lack complementary assets as relationships with relevant gatekeepers in order to overcome the remaining entry barriers (Mol et al., 2005). Mol et al. looked at the role of vertical competition within the Dutch music industry and the influences of digital distribution on value distribution among different actors in the value system. They conclude that content producers did not have the necessary contacts with relevant gatekeepers to market their innovations successfully.

This study investigates whether and how video game developers can profit from their innovations with the advent of the online channel. Teece (1986) pointed out that several factors are relevant in determining who profits from innovations. In many cases, innovating companies have to rely on complementary assets, such as marketing and competitive manufacturing, to make the innovation a success. In certain cases, the innovator (for example, content producer) does not have the complementary assets in-house, and it has to rely on third parties (for example, publishers). Hirsch (1972) investigated commonly deployed strategies in cultural industries to enhance chances for pre-selection and market success by publishing organizations.

The purpose of this study is twofold: (i) to develop theory for successful commercialization of digitally distributed cultural products; and (ii) to illustrate it through practical case study analysis. The theory is illustrated by conducting a case study analysis of the video games industry. The study investigates a video game developer that released one of its focal products on two comparable online platforms through different commercialization strategies. Empirical data were collected using sales-tracking databases, interviews with employees and management, field notes, company documentation, and observations to determine the relative success of each strategy.

The results of this study indicate that vertical integration in the stage of publishing will lead to successful commercialization only when content producers have specialized complementary assets in-house or have sufficient cash to buy these assets. Content producers are more likely to commercialize their innovations successfully by forming strategic alliances with incumbent publishing houses, as these actors are in the possession of specialized complementary assets that enable them to deploy strategies for successful commercialization

2   VIDEO GAMES INDUSTRY[2] OVERVIEW

The Emergence of Digital Distribution within the Video Games Industry

The current generation of video game consoles launched in 2005 with Microsoft's Xbox 360. Sony and Nintendo followed suit in 2006 by launching their competing systems PlayStation 3 and Wii. In September 2009, over 267 million units of current generation video game consoles were sold (VGChartz, 2009). New in this generation of video game consoles is the possibility of digital distribution.

All three consoles possess the ability, next to physical distribution through discs, to distribute video games bought at an online web shop

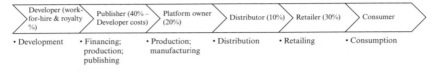

Figure 5.1   Physical distribution value system

directly to the consumer. The video games offered on these channels are smaller in size and lower in price compared to their physical counterparts. The larger part of these video games are developed and published by third-party developers, outside organizations unaffiliated with the platform owner (Williams, 2002). The digital character of the distribution channels allows for virtually unlimited shelf space as opposed to the physical retail channel.

Between 2006 and 2009 the digital distribution channels gained enormous popularity and grew substantially in terms of number of games available for download and additional services offered. John Riccitiello, CEO of EA, the world's leading video games publisher, said that the digital video games market would overtake the physical market in 2010, and has acted accordingly by changing the focus of the company's business strategy (Gamasutra, 2009; Gamesindustry, 2009). Within the video games industry, equal to the music and book publishing industries, digital distribution has been established as a legitimized way of doing business.

The Consequences of Digital Distribution on Video Game Developers

Physical distribution value system
The production network of physically distributed video games consists of seven production stages and a consumption stage: financing, development, production, publishing, manufacturing, distribution, retailing, and consumption (Williams, 2002; Johns, 2006). These stages are generally performed by six industry actors: developers, publishers, platform owners, distributors, retailers, and consumers. The production stages of the video games industry should not be seen as independent production entities as many organizations integrate several stages to obtain economies of scale and scope (Williams, 2002). The physical distribution value system with estimated percentages of value captured from one unit sold by each actor is depicted in Figure 5.1. Percentages are based on research conducted by Johns (2006).

In the value system as depicted in Figure 5.1, video game developers are to a large degree dependent on publishers as these actors provide financing for video game development projects. Video game developers traditionally suffer from a lack of financial resources. Publishers can be seen as the developers' buyers and act as a gateway to the end-users (Readman and Grantham, 2006). In return for the monetary means, publishers retain the intellectual property (IP) rights to the game, maintain decision-making power over the game until it reaches the customer, and carry the financial risks involved in the development stage (ibid.). Publishers have control over characters and franchise licences (IP rights) which are the industry's key resources (Readman and Grantham, 2006).

Due to their dependency on external financing, video game developers are often in a weak negotiation position. Publishers have far-reaching termination rights for development projects at almost any point in the development process (Charne, 2006). After the video game has been completed, it is adjusted to the various local markets on which the game is released, a process known as 'localization'. Thereafter, the video game is sent to the platform manufacturer for technical approval, after which the physical product is manufactured. Due to obligatory licensing agreements with platform manufacturers, publishers outsource the video game manufacturing activities to these actors.

Early in the evolution of the video games industry, hardware manufacturers realized that software sales would be far more profitable than the sale of hardware (Schilling, 2003; Johns, 2006). Furthermore, by controlling this stage of the production process and by granting video game developers development kits, hardware manufacturers can guarantee a degree of quality control and act as the industry's gatekeepers. After production, the products progress through a distribution and retailing stage before they reach the consumer. Distributors are responsible for the physical storage, delivery of the product, and the sales effort (Williams, 2002; Johns, 2006). The distribution stage is a low margin stage of the value system; publishers sometimes vertically integrate into the stage of distribution. The retail stage comprises powerful actors, so-called 'super stores', who determine which video games will reach the consumer.

Digital distribution value system
The advent of digital distribution has several consequences for video game developer business models and the industry's value system. The largest implication for the value system is the fact that physical good distributors and brick-and-mortar retailers are no longer a necessity since there are no physical goods to be distributed or sold at retail outlets. In a setting of digital distribution where the video game developer takes over the role of publisher, the video games industry's value system resembles the image depicted in Figure 5.2. Percentages of value captured from one digitally distributed video game by each actor are based on case study analysis.

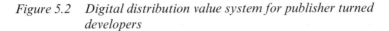

Figure 5.2   Digital distribution value system for publisher turned developers

Video game developers can now enter the stage of publishing as one of three of its most significant entry barriers have eroded: complex and capital-intensive logistics that require scale and scope advantages of an international distribution network. Independent video game developers are able to bypass the existing publishing oligopoly and sell directly to the customer (Johns, 2006). Two other entry barriers for the publishing business have nevertheless remained intact: (i) huge marketing costs involved with bringing a cultural good into the market; and (ii) the need for overproduction in a winner-takes-all market where the reasons for success are unknown beforehand (Caves, 2000; Kretschmer et al., 2001).

The role of publishers in digital distribution
In digital distribution, video game developers receive a larger share of revenue per unit sold and retain ownership over their internally developed IP rights, leading to greater freedom and creativity in determining the content of their video games. However, a major consequence of self-publishing video games on digital distribution channels for video game developers is that these actors have to become more network oriented in order to either acquire the skills needed for successful publishing or outsource them.

Traditionally, developers have been relatively isolated in terms of network connectivity compared to platform manufacturers and publishers, occupying a more peripheral position (Johns, 2006). Such a position would be problematic in overcoming the remaining entry barriers to the stage of publishing; huge marketing costs and the need for overproduction. In order to overcome these entry barriers, video game developers could still opt to commercialize their innovations by forming strategic alliances with publishing organizations. Figure 5.3 illustrates the value system of a video game developer forming a strategic alliance with a publisher in a setting of digital distribution. Percentages of value appropriated from each unit sold by each actor are based on results of the study at hand.

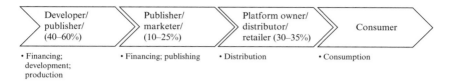

Developer/ publisher/ (40–60%)	Publisher/ marketer/ (10–25%)	Platform owner/ distributor/ retailer (30–35%)	Consumer
• Financing; development; production	• Financing; publishing	• Distribution	• Consumption

Figure 5.3   Digital distribution value system for developers forming strategic alliances with publishers

3   PROFITING FROM DIGITALLY DISTRIBUTED CULTURAL PRODUCTS[3]

Value Distribution and Value Chain Envy in Cultural Industries

The distribution of value within an industry largely depends on the bargaining power an actor has *vis-à-vis* other stages directly upstream and downstream within the value chain (Priem, 2007). The amount of profit an actor obtains is determined by the vertical dynamics of the value system. When the amount of captured value disproportionally exceeds the amount of value created at a particular stage of the value chain, new entrants and other actors within the value chain want to vertically integrate into that favourable stage – a phenomenon Mol et al. (2005) call 'value chain envy'.

Over the years, the role of publishers within cultural industries has diminished from a situation of scale advantages in printing, distributing, and later reproducing and distributing physical information carriers and collecting royalties, to a role where almost anyone can be a publisher (Caves, 2000; Mol et al., 2005). Nevertheless, publishers still capture a large part of the value being created; the term 'value chain envy' is applicable to this particular stage of cultural industries' value chains (ibid.). In the Dutch music industry nearly all new entrants in the stage of publishing were found to have difficulties with capturing value (ibid.).

In conjunction with literature on this topic (Peterson and Berger, 1975; Burnett, 1996; Kretschmer et al., 1999) Mol et al. conclude that the competitive advantages incumbent publishing houses have over new entrants can be attributed to their possession of certain complementary assets, namely strong relationships with relevant selectors or gatekeepers.

Cultural Industry Properties

Hirsch (1972) states that the production and distribution of both fine arts and popular culture entail relationships among a complex network of organizations which both facilitate and regulate the innovation process. Organizations that can both facilitate and regulate innovation have a gate-keeping role as an institutional regulator of innovation and can be defined as 'gatekeepers' (ibid.; Caves, 2000). For digitally distributed video games, this system of organizations consists of mass media actors and the plat-form owner for technical approval and promotional activities.

Cultural industries are characterized by 'cheap' technology, enabling organizations to compete by producing a surplus of products on relatively small capital investments (Hirsch, 1972). There are low marginal costs for (re-)production, whereas there are disproportionally large profit margins when a product becomes a 'hit'. Another trait of cultural industries is a high degree of demand uncertainty or 'nobody knows' (ibid.; Caves, 2000). Demand uncertainty exists as consumer reactions to a product are neither known in advance of product release, nor easily understood after (ibid.).

The distribution sector of cultural industries is more heavily concen-trated than the content-producing sector. Heavy marketing expenditures for differential promotional and marketing activities are a necessity to pass favourably through this stage of the value system (Hirsch, 1972). The advent of digital technologies has lowered value protection mechan-isms and consequently entry barriers to this stage of the value chain (Kretschmer et at., 2001; Clemons et al., 2003; Mol et al., 2005; Bockstedt et al., 2006).

In a setting of digital distribution, certain entry barriers for potential entrants disappear, and hence, the supply of cultural goods will grow. Recent research shows, however, that the demand curve of cultural goods will not be affected by online distribution channels. In contrast to the long-tail assumption which argues that online or digital channels will favour the sales of niche products, empirical research shows that the winner-takes-all principle still applies (Anderson, 2006; Elberse, 2008). Light consumers still concentrate heavily on hit products, whereas some heavy consumers are more likely to choose a mix of hit and niche products (ibid.). Knowledgeable heavy consumers tend to prefer hit products to niche products, leading them to eventually favour the hit products (ibid.).

More evidence that digital distribution channels enhance diversity in supply but reduce diversity in sales is given by a study on the impact of recommender systems on sales diversity. Fleder and Hosanagar (2009) conclude that recommender systems reduce diversity in sales due to a lock-in on popular products. Recommender systems cannot recommend products with limited historical data, even if they were viewed favourably; thus, recommender systems will stimulate the success of hits (ibid.). The increase in supply diversity and decrease in sales diversity further increase the importance of gatekeepers as selectors of cultural innovations within cultural industries.

Strategies for Successful Commercialization of Cultural Products

In order to maximize economic returns and minimize the dependence on elements of their task environments, publishing organizations in cultural industries have developed three proactive strategies (Hirsch, 1972):

1. *The allocation of numerous personnel to boundary-spanning roles*   Publishers allocate contact personnel to actively monitor the market, and use them as talent scouts. More importantly, contact personnel link the organization to distribution platforms and surrogate consumers (for example, video game magazines, relevant online portals and distribution platform owners) that act as independent gatekeepers.
2. *Overproduction and differential promotion of new items*   In an environment of low capital investments and demand uncertainty, publishers are wise to overproduce. Under these conditions it is more efficient to produce many 'failures' rather than to focus on fewer items that are pretested on a large scale. Publishers do not allocate their advertising budgets equally, but heavily advertise the most promising items.
3. *Cooptation of mass media gatekeepers*   Publishers often co-opt institutional gatekeepers to stimulate the chances of success of their products. Consumers' awareness of the products hinges almost exclusively on coverage by these independent and credible sources.

Other sources (Granovetter, 1982; Burt, 1992; Noria and Eccles, 1992) agree with Hirsch that 'for a cultural product to succeed, networks of relationships must be mobilized, coordinated and managed to get the job done' (Hirsch, 2000, p. 358). Since the advent of digitization, distribution channel concentration has further increased and costs for producing cultural products continue to decrease, making these strategies even more relevant in a setting of digital distribution.

Hypotheses

Linkages between strategy formulation and a firm's complementary assets position can be seen as a logical step, as strategy is contingent on these concepts (Pisano, 2006). Christmann (2000) states that complementary assets are required to capture the benefits associated with strategies. This study argues that access to specialized complementary assets as defined by Teece (1986) determines to what degree publishing actors are able to effectively deploy Hirsch's (1972) strategies for successful commercialization of cultural products.

Teece (1986) argues that marketing and competitive manufacturing are specialized complementary assets which help determine who profits from innovations. In addition, Mol et al. (2005) posit that relationships with relevant gatekeepers can be distinguished as a critical specialized complementary asset necessary for publishing actors in cultural industries. Marketing assets are needed to effectively deploy the 'overproduction and differential promotion of new items' strategy and the 'allocation of numerous personnel to boundary-spanning roles' strategy. In addition, in order to adequately fulfil the 'overproduction and differential promotion of new items' strategy, organizations must also be capable of rapidly producing a surplus of marginally differentiated products, that is, one needs competitive manufacturing assets. Finally, relationships with relevant gatekeepers are needed for effective deployment of the 'cooptation of mass media gatekeepers' strategy.

When content producers desire to vertically integrate into the stage of publishing and are not in possession of these specialized complementary assets, nor have sufficient financial means to buy them (Teece, 1986; Mol et al., 2005), these actors would be best positioned by forming strategic alliances with incumbent publishers who do have access to these assets (Teece, 1986, 2006; Mitchell et al., 2002).

This study hypothesizes that forming a strategic alliance with incumbent publishers will lead to greater value capturing for content producers compared with the strategy of independently publishing video games on digital channels. In a setting of digital distribution, incumbent publishing houses will thus remain important in successfully commercializing cultural products as of their complementary asset positions.

Hypothesis 1   Cultural content producers that integrate vertically into the stage of publishing and do not have access to complementary assets will be less successful in commercializing their cultural products compared to content producers forming strategic alliances with incumbent publishers to access complementary assets.

4   METHODOLOGY

A case study analysis with multiple aggregation levels was executed at a Dutch video game developer active across multiple video game platforms on a global scale. Special attention is given to one of its focal products which has been released on two comparable digital distribution platforms using two alternative strategies: the independent strategy and the strategic alliance strategy (see Section 2). The deployment of commercialization strategies and the organization's access to complementary assets differ per distribution channel.

Empirical data were collected using sales-tracking databases, interviews with employees and management, field notes, company documentation and observations. The tracking period for both products was 125 days from release. At the time of release, the distribution channels onto which the products have been released were comparable in terms of installed base, phase in the channel's lifecycle and to a large degree geographical scope. Some noticeable differences between both channels are not neglected. This study determines the success of a new game based on the relative market success (that is, the product's relative sales according to the channel onto which the product has been released) and on financial performance (that is, the product's profitability).

This study gathers data on the industry and firm levels, and triangulates the data using multiple data collection methods (Eisenhardt, 1989). Within the case study design, an event study methodology is deployed. Event studies can be seen as a powerful tool to judge the effects of endogenous events such as managerial decision making on the financial performance of a firm (McWilliams and Siegel, 1997).

Dutch Video Game Developer

The case study organization is a video game developer based in the Netherlands, hereafter called Dutch Video Game Developer (DVGD). DVGD has been operative for over a decade and has traditionally focused on the physical work-for-hire business model (see Section 2). With the advent of digital distribution, DVGD saw opportunities for operating autonomously and producing its internally developed IP. The company is 'platform agnostic', meaning that it is licensed to develop video games for multiple video game platforms.

The company's first internally developed IP, labelled *Chicken's Tale* (fictional), has been released onto two comparable digital distribution channels. The first time *Chicken's Tale* was released, in May 2008, DVGD integrated vertically into the stage of publishing regarding this release. However, in May 2009, when DVGD released *Chicken's Tale* onto a comparable distribution channel, a publisher was contracted. The first time *Chicken's Tale* was released will be labelled '*Independent Chicken's Tale*', whereas the game's second release will be labelled '*Strategic Chicken's Tale*'. Both products received generally favourable reviews during their

Table 5.1　Channel comparisons and success measures

Distribution channel data		Channel: *Independent Chicken's Tale*		Channel: *Strategic Chicken's Tale*	
Success indicators[1] (estimations / units sold)	Low end	6,000–25,000	60% of all products	100–1,500	85% of all products
	Mid end	25,000–50,000	30% of all products	1,500–5,000	10% of all products
	High end	50,000–350,000	10% of all products	5,000–1,500,000	5% of all products
Installed base		42,500,000[2]		37,000,000[3]	
Average selling price (€)		9.54[4]		1.32[5]	

Notes:
1. The classification of products that fall into the low-end category (unsuccessful product) and high-end category (successful product) are based on the relative sales figures per channel and are derived from Careless (2009).
2. The number of units sold per platform, 85 per cent of global market. US, EU and Australia included, Japan (approximately 15 per cent of global market) excluded (BBC News, 2009).
3. Apple Insider, 2009.
4. DVGD internal research.
5. Average selling price of Top 10 games converted from US dollars (Pocket Gamer, 2009).

release and are considered to be among the better titles available for the platforms onto which they were released (Table 5.1).

DVGD's Complementary Assets Position

DVGD lacks specialized complementary assets. The organization develops on average two video games a year, and has been told by publishers that the development costs of its products are above industry standards (indicating a lack of competitive manufacturing assets). Second, during the time of investigation, the company had no personnel responsible for marketing purposes. Nor did the company's founders have much expertise in marketing or promotional activities (indicating a lack of marketing assets). Lastly, DVGD did not have strong relationships with either platform owners or mass media actors (indicating a lack of relationships with relevant gatekeepers).

As the complementary assets are not in-house it was suggested that the company should look at its cash position to decide whether to vertically integrate or to form strategic alliances. DVGD has limited financial resources. In order to access complementary assets, DVGD should form a strategic alliance with an incumbent publisher (Teece, 1986, 2006). In commercializing Strategic Chicken's Tale, DVGD formed a strategic alliance with a publisher to have access to specialized complementary assets needed to deploy the strategies for successful commercialization of cultural products.

5 RESULTS

Independent Chicken's Tale Commercialization Analysis

Sales analysis
The product's sales curve is a typical downward linear curve, representative of cultural products. Sales follow demand. *Independent Chicken's Tale* sold for €9.00 throughout its entire release. The product's revenue curve follows the product's sales curve. The product's selling price was just below the channel's average selling price of €9.54. In the last 25 days of the sales tracking period, *Independent Chicken's Tale* sold on average 46 units each day (Figure 5.4).

The most apparent surge in sales occurred at day 14, or 2 June, when sales jumped from 296 to 1,265 units per day. This spike can be attributed to the launch of the product in the United States. There are also a number of smaller sales spikes noticeable in the product's sales curve. At day 5 or 24 May, sales jumped from 331 units per day to 409 units per day. Exactly one week later sales surged again, and after the US launch the pattern repeated itself more significantly. These sales spikes represent increased

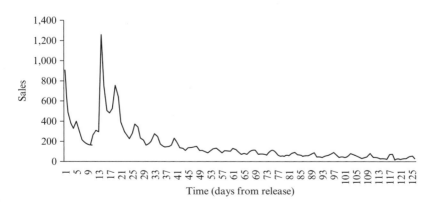

Figure 5.4   Sales per day Independent Chicken's Tale

weekend traffic on the online shop channel. Users of the online distribution channel generate more shopping activity during weekends compared to working day shopping activity. These repeated increases in sales can thus be attributed to exogenous influences.

Market performance and financial results

In total, *Independent Chicken's Tale* sold 20,845 units during the 125 days sales tracking period. According to Careless (2009), which provides an analysis of relative success in terms of units sold per digital distribution platform, the product is not successful as it resides in the 60 per cent lower end of products released onto the channel in terms of cumulative sales. Market performance of *Independent Chicken's Tale* can be considered unsuccessful.

Financial performance for the product follows its market performance. After deduction of currency conversions, platform owner value-added taxes, and a fixed percentage for every unit sold transferred to the platform owner, *Independent Chicken's Tale* generated €97,690 revenue. Development costs for *Independent Chicken's Tale* were €147,878. The product's earnings before interest, taxes, depreciation and amortization (EBITDA) are –€50,180. *Independent Chicken's Tale* is financially unsuccessful, as it generated a loss for DVGD.

Strategic Chicken's Tale Commercialization Analysis

Strategic Chicken's Tale shows a much more volatile sales curve with greater shocks in demand (Figure 5.5). Both during its pre-release and during the commercialization, the publisher effectively put its complementary assets to use in order to deploy Hirsch's (1972) strategies for successful commercialization, with significant effect:

● *Relationships with relevant gatekeepers* Pre-release promotional activities made possible due to the publisher's relationships with relevant gatekeepers include distributing press releases and securing product reviews by relevant media. During commercialization, one promotional activity resulting in a large boost in sales and revenue was the publisher's effort towards the platform owner. When the publisher visited the platform owner to promote *Strategic Chicken's Tale*, the platform owner decided to 'feature' the product in its online store. It is due to the publisher's relationship with the gatekeeper that *Strategic Chicken's Tale* was actively promoted by the platform owner, resulting in high visibility of the game. Without these relationships, the promotional activities would have lacked

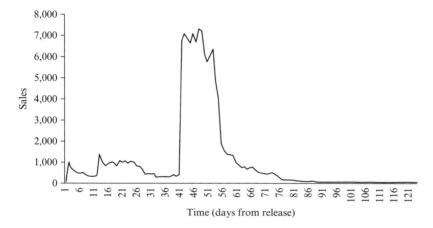

Time (days from release)

Figure 5.5   Sales per day Strategic Chicken's Tale

a platform for exposure and ultimately missed their purpose. The feature by the platform owner occurred at day 13, or 2 June, when sales jumped from 390 to 1,385 units sold per day. The number of units sold per day hovered around 1,000 during the period the game was featured by the platform owner, after which it dropped to approximately 400 units sold per day.

- *Marketing assets*   A pre-release marketing activity resulting in a noticeable 'buzz' for *Strategic Chicken's Tale* was organizing a promotional contest in which contestants could win channel store credit upon thinking of and realizing original ways to promote the game. Securing product reviews, developer interviews and various other forms of exposure in relevant media were other pre-release marketing activities performed by the publisher. Plotting out and realizing the product's price policy was a large part of the publisher's marketing expertise during release. In the first 41 days from release the product was sold for €3.99. Thereafter, from day 42 until day 55, the product went on sale, selling for €0.79. The result of this price reduction is immediately noticeable. The effect of the lowered price on sales was further boosted by the product's listing in several nations in shop Top 100 lists. Sales jumped from an average of 400 units per day to 6,400 units sold per day on average during the time the product was on sale. The sale period was followed by a transition price of €1.59 for the 20 days thereafter. Average units sold per day dropped to 1,700. Finally, in the remainder of the sales tracking period, the product was sold for its original price of €3.99.

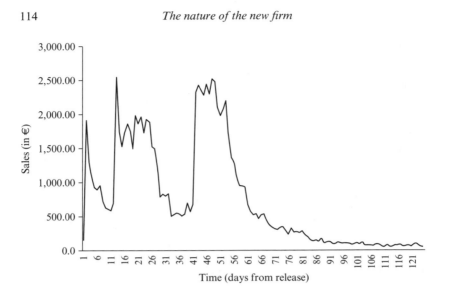

Figure 5.6   Revenue per day Strategic Chicken's Tale

- *Competitive manufacturing assets*   Less obviously related to spikes in the product's sales curve, but nonetheless important in realizing Hirsch's (1972) strategies for successful commercialization, is the publisher's ability for competitive manufacturing. It is thanks to the publisher's large portfolio of successful video games on the specific distribution channel that the company is of significant meaning to the platform owner. These competitive manufacturing assets pose leverage in negotiations with the platform owner and other media gatekeepers and have contributed to getting *Strategic Chicken's Tale* featured and reviewed on a large scale, resulting in higher sales. Furthermore, in conversations with both DVGD and the publisher it has been implied that a significant share of *Strategic Chicken's Tale* sales has been generated by customers of other games from the publisher's portfolio in which *Strategic Chicken's Tale* is marketed as being another game of high quality within the publisher's portfolio. Finally, employment of numerous boundary-spanning marketing personnel can only be financially viable when a company releases numerous products per year. Something an independent developer such as DVGD is unable to do.

Market performance and financial results
Strategic Chicken's Tale sold 135,288 units during the 125 days sales tracking period with an average price of €1.45 (Figure 5.6). According

Table 5.2   Comparison of results in the DVGD case study analysis

	Independent Chicken's Tale	Strategic Chicken's Tale
Sales (units)	20,845	135,288
Relative market performance	60% low end of market	5% high end of market
Revenue (in €)	97,690	104,441
Development costs (in €)	147,878	73,354
EBITDA (in €)	(50,180)	31,087

to Careless (2009) the number of units sold can be considered successful for the platform as it resides in the 5 per cent high-end range of games available for the platform. In addition, the average selling price of €1.45 is above the average selling price for the Top 10 bestselling video games on the platform (Pocket Gamer, 2009). In the last 25 days of the sales tracking period, *Strategic Chicken's Tale* sold on average 45 units per day. The product's market performance can be considered successful.

After deduction of currency conversions, platform owner value-added taxes, publisher fees, and a fixed percentage for every unit sold transferred to the platform owner, *Strategic Chicken's Tale* generated €104,441 revenue. The publisher was paid a 10 per cent fee per unit sold in the first month from release and a 15 per cent fee thereafter. The development costs for *Strategic Chicken's Tale* were €73,354. The product's financial performance can be considered successful, *Strategic Chicken's Tale* earned DVGD €31,087 before EBITDA.

Results: Conclusion

Table 5.2 shows a comparison of results for the case study analysis of DVGD in terms of sales (units sold), relative market performance based on Careless's (2009) indications of success within both distribution channels, revenue and EBITDA. Projected revenue for *Strategic Chicken's Tale* is the amount of money after deduction of publisher fees. Based on internal reports, development costs are divided between actual development costs for each project, and shared IP development costs. *Independent Chicken's Tale* required slightly higher actual development costs as the platform onto which the game has been released was more demanding.

In support of Hypothesis 1, the results show that the strategy of forming a strategic alliance with an incumbent publisher for DVGD was more successful in terms of both market and financial performance compared to independently publishing the game. Furthermore, the success of the strategic alliance strategy can be attributed to the performance of the publisher, which effectively maintains relationships with gatekeepers, grants access to specialized marketing assets, and uses its competitive manufacturing skills to improve its bargaining power over the platform owner. These complementary assets enabled the publisher to better commercialize DVGD's product than DVGD was independently able to do.

6 DISCUSSION AND CONCLUSIONS

Conclusion

In a digital distribution setting where innovators can vertically integrate into the stage of publishing, incumbent publishers remain value adding due to their complementary asset positions. These actors retain an important role in digitally distributing cultural products by effectively deploying strategies for successful commercialization of cultural products, whereas their access to critical specialized complementary assets serves as facilitator and value protection mechanism. Those content producers forming strategic alliances with incumbent publishers will be more successful in commercializing their products and capture a larger share of value compared to those producers integrating vertically into the stage of publishing. Incumbent publishers have added value and play an important role in achieving success even in an era of digital distribution of cultural products.

A case study of a video game developer releasing an identical product onto two comparable digital distribution channels through different commercialization strategies illustrates the theory and tests the hypothesis. In commercializing *Strategic Chicken's Tale*, DVGD formed a strategic alliance with a publisher to have access to specialized complementary assets needed to deploy strategies for successful commercialization of cultural products. When comparing both products' financial performances, it can be concluded that *Strategic Chicken's Tale* performed better in terms of units sold and EBITDA. Taking into account the differences of both distribution channels, *Strategic Chicken's Tale* can be considered more successful than *Independent Chicken's Tale* in terms of market performance. The publisher's promotional activities towards the platform owner resulting in the platform owner actively promoting the product, and the publisher's decision to temporarily lower the price contributed most significantly to the product's sales and earnings.

Implications

This study contributes to the literature by tying together Teece's (1986) complementary assets and strategy formulation for successful commercialization of cultural products (Hirsch, 1972). The study further illustrates the theoretical relevance and practical applicability of both theories. In addition, this study contributes by updating Hirsch's strategies to apply in a setting of digital distribution of cultural goods. The advent of the digital distribution channels has removed entry barriers and leads to more potential entrants. The difficulty of getting selected in these digital markets makes Hirsch's strategies for commercializing cultural products even more relevant than before.

Whereas previous studies, taking the perspective of resource-based retention and newly vulnerable markets, questioned the power and relevance of publishing actors in the music industry in a setting of digital distribution (Clemons et al., 2003; Bockstedt et al., 2006), this study illustrates that incumbent publishers will remain powerful actors in cultural industries. Value protection mechanisms in the form of specialized complementary assets critical for the success of cultural products make it difficult for content producers to break away from incumbent publishers. Therefore, although the digitization makes the publisher stage easier to enter, and it already was attractive to attack because of *value chain envy* (Mol et al., 2005), incumbent publishers can still defend their positions from new entrants as opposed to what Bockstedt et al. (2006) state.

The results of the study indicate that with the advent of digital distribution channels, incumbent publishing houses will remain a 'necessary evil' for the successful commercialization of cultural innovations, a topic of debate within the video games industry. The advent of digital distribution channels will lead to enhanced creative freedom for content producers. This freedom has added value as artists often produce 'art-for-art's-sake' (Caves, 2000). Digital distribution channels will likely alter the balance between creativity and rationalization in favour of creativity (Tschang, 2007). The number of new IPs in video game development has increased, as has competition among video game developers (Industry Gamers, 2010).

Limitations and Further Research

The study has some limitations. First, a 'thicker description' of the case could be provided. Second, although the in-depth analysis of the case study is suited for theory-building research (Eisenhardt, 1989), it is the design of such an approach that makes it difficult to test the proposed theory quantitatively. The developed theory should be tested in more depth and across other cultural industries to further generalize the research findings.

Despite the case being illustrative for most content producers, it would be interesting to see whether producers of 'hit' products are able to independently publish their succeeding products successfully onto digital distribution channels. Another limitation is that the effect of price fluctuations on consumer behaviour cannot be determined from one study; additional research needs to address this issue in greater detail. Future research should deploy a longer-term perspective on the effects of different commercialization strategies on financial success and IP management, that is, market performance of sequels.

From the data, two other suggestions for further research arise. Despite the publisher's involvement, both products sold an equal amount of units in the latter part of the sales tracking period. From a long-tail perspective of overproducing publishers, validating such an effect has added theoretical and practical value. Furthermore, the inclusion in Top 100 lists has boosted the effect of marketing activities. Further research should elaborate on the implications of such market-selection types of recommender systems and their practical implications on value distribution.

NOTES

1. The author acknowledges mentor and friend Dr. Thijs Broekhuizen for his continuous stream of helpful suggestions and constructive input.
2. Here, video games are referred to as those games played either on a home video game console connected to a television such as Nintendo's Wii, Sony's PlayStation 3 or Microsoft's Xbox 360, or on a handheld such as Nintendo's DS(i), Sony's PSP(go) or Apple's iPhone. PC Games are excluded from this study as these deploy different business models and value systems.
3. Hirsch (1972) defines cultural products as '"nonmaterial" goods directed at a public of consumers, for whom they generally serve an esthetic or expressive, rather than a clearly utilitarian function' (pp. 641–2).

REFERENCES

Academic Sources

Anderson, C. (2006), *The Long Tail: Why the Future of Business Is Selling Less of More*, New York: Hyperion.

Bockstedt, J.C., J. Kauffman and F.J. Riggins (2006), 'The move to artist-led on-line music distribution: a theory-based assessment and prospects for structural changes in the digital music market', *International Journal of Electronic Commerce*, **10** (3), 7–38.

Burnett, R. (1996), *The Global Jukebox*, London: Routledge.

Burt, R. (1992), *Structural Holes: The Social Structure of Competition*, Cambridge, MA: Harvard University Press.

Caves, R.E. (2000), *Creative Industries: Contracts between Arts and Commerce*, Cambridge, MA: Harvard University Press.

Charne, J. (2006), 'Understanding and negotiating termination issues in video game development contracts', *The Computer & Internet Lawyer*, **23** (9), 27–33.

Christmann, P. (2000), 'Effects of "best practices" of environmental management on cost advantage: the role of complementary assets', *Academy of Management Journal*, **43** (4), 663–80.

Clemons, E.K., B. Gu and K.R. Lang (2003), 'Newly vulnerable markets in an age of pure information products: an analysis of online music and online news', *Journal of Management Information Systems*, **19** (3), 17–41.

Eisenhardt, K.M. (1989), 'Building theories from case study research', *Academy of Management Review*, **14** (4), 532–50.

Elberse, A. (2008), 'Should you invest in the long tail?', *Harvard Business Review*, July–August, 88–96.

Fleder, D. and K. Hosanagar (2009), 'Blockbuster culture's next rise or fall: the impact of recommender systems on sales diversity', *Management Science*, **55** (8), 697–712.

Granovetter, M. (1982), 'The strength of weak ties: a network theory revisited', in P. Marsden and N. Lin (eds), *Social Structure and Network Analysis*, Newbury Park, CA: Sage, pp. 105–30.

Hirsch, P.M. (1972), 'Processing fads and fashions: an organization-set of cultural industry systems', *American Journal of Sociology*, **77** (4), 639–59.

Hirsch, P.M. (2000), 'Cultural industries revisited', *Organization Science*, **11** (3), 356–61.

Johns, J. (2006), 'Video games production networks: value capture, power relations and embeddedness', *Journal of Economic Geography*, **6**, 151–80.

Kretschmer, M., G.M. Klimis and C. Choi (1999), 'Increasing returns and social contagion in cultural industries', *British Journal of Management*, **10**, 561–72.

Kretschmer, M., G.M. Klimis and R. Wallis (2001), 'Music in electronic markets', *New Media & Society*, **3** (4), 417–41.

McWilliams, A. and D. Siegel (1997), 'Event studies in management research: theoretical and empirical issues', *Academy of Management Journal*, **40** (3), 626–57.

Mitchell, W., P. Dussauge and B. Garrette (2002), 'Alliances with competitors: how to combine and protect key resources?', *Creativity and Innovation Management*, **11** (3), 203–23.

Mol, J.M., N.M. Wijnberg and C. Charroll (2005), 'Value chain envy: explaining new entry and vertical integration in popular music', *Journal of Management Studies*, **42** (2), 251–76.

Noria, N. and R. Eccles (1992), *Networks and Organizations: Structure Form and Action*, Boston, MA: Harvard Business School Press.

Peterson, R. and D. Berger (1975), 'Cycles in symbol production: the case of popular music', *American Sociological Review*, **40**, 158–73.

Pisano, G. (2006), 'Profiting from innovation and the intellectual property revolution', *Research Policy*, **35**, 1122–30.

Priem, R.L. (2007), 'A consumer perspective on value creation', *Academy of Management Review*, **32** (1), 219–35.

Readman, J. and A. Grantham (2006), 'Shopping for buyers of product development expertise: how video game developers stay ahead', *European Management Journal*, **24** (4), 256–69.

Schilling, M.A. (2003), 'Technological leapfrogging: lessons from the U.S. video game console industry', *California Management Review*, **45** (3), 6–31.

Teece, D.J. (1986), 'Profiting from technological innovation: implications for integration, collaboration, licensing and public policy', *Research Policy*, **15**, 285–305.

Teece, D.J. (2006), 'Reflections on "Profiting from innovations"', *Research Policy*, **35**, 1131–46.

Tschang, F.T. (2007), 'Balancing the tensions between rationalization and creativity in the video games industry', *Organization Science*, **18** (6), 989–1005.

Williams, D. (2002), 'Structure and competition in the U.S. home video game industry', *International Journal on Media Management*, **4** (1), 41–54.

Informational Sources

Apple Insider (2009), 'Notes of interest from Apple's Q209 quarterly conference call', available at: http://www.appleinsider.com/articles/09/04/22/notes_of_interest_from_apples_q209_quarterly_conference_call.html (accessed 24 December 2009).

BBC News (2009), 'Nintendo Wii sales hit 50 million', available at: http://news.bbc.co.uk/2/hi/technology/7964459.stm (accessed 17 November 2009).

Careless, S. (2009), 'Rules for indie game success: the metrics', Digital distribution summit, conference presentation, Melbourne, Australia, September.

Gamasutra (2009), 'EA: "No Coincidence" that layoffs, PlayFish buy emerged simultaneously', available at: http://www.gamasutra.com/phpbin/news_index.php?story=26058&utm_source=feedburner&utm_medium=feed&utm_campaign=Feed%3A+GamasutraNews+%28Gamasutra+News%29 (accessed 22 December 2009).

Gamesindustry (2009), 'Ricciitiello: digital market will overtake consoles next year', available at: http://www.gamesindustry.biz/articles/riccitiello-digital-market-will-overtake-consoles-next-year (accessed 22 December 2009).

Industry Gamers (2010), 'The Divnich Debrief: new IP up 106% since 2007', available at: http://www.industrygamers.com/news/the-divnich-debrief-new-ip-up-106-since-2007/ (accessed 24 February 2010).

Pocket Gamer (2009), 'Analysing the App store paid games chart: 99-cent titles not (quite) as dominant as you'd think', available at: http://www.pocketgamer.biz/r/PG.Biz/App+Store/feature.asp?c=14291 (accessed 17 November 2009).

VGChartz (2009), 'Front page', available at: http://vgchartz.com/ (accessed 15 September 2009).

6. Serial acquirers' reconfiguration capability: moving beyond existing knowledge boundaries

Nima Amiryany, Marleen Huysman, Ard-Pieter de Man and Myriam Cloodt

1 INTRODUCTION

Increasing competition among high-technology firms has shifted the source of competitive advantage for these firms from tangible resources and market power to intangible resources such as knowledge (Collins and Smith, 2006). Thus, knowledge has become the most strategically important resource that firms possess (Grant, 1996). Acquiring knowledge-intensive firms and thus knowledge acquisition, therefore, has become an increasingly important strategic activity for high-tech companies to gain access to new knowledge and capabilities. Knowledge acquisition can be seen as an organizational learning process through 'grafting' (Huber, 1991). When knowledge that is meant to be acquired is complex, grafting seems to be faster and more complete than acquiring knowledge through, respectively, experience and imitation (ibid.). Technological complexity, the importance of specialized skills and expertise, fast-paced technological change, and knowledge-based resources' breadth and depth, trigger firms in high-tech industries to engage in knowledge acquisitions with the primary objective of sharing knowledge, in order to innovate (Ranft and Lord, 2002). Thus, innovation has become an important motive for high-technology companies engaging in knowledge acquisitions (de Man and Duysters, 2005).

Acquiring knowledge-intensive firms in order to innovate, however, is not always a successful strategy. Firms involved in knowledge acquisitions usually need to overcome various knowledge-specific boundaries (that is, boundaries that exist because of the nature of the firms' knowledge) such as syntactic (for example, not having a common language), semantic (for example, the existence of different interpretations), and pragmatic (for example, absence of a shared contextual framework) knowledge boundaries (Carlile, 2002). Since firms involved have to deal with so many different barriers, it is, therefore, probably not surprising that acquisitions usually have implementation and post-acquisition performance problems (Vermeulen and Barkema, 2001). In fact, Puranam et al. (2003) have argued that failure rates in knowledge acquisitions may reach between 60 and 80 percent; figures which would indicate an absence of organizational acumen. Apparently, acquiring a knowledge-intensive firm does not guarantee that firms involved are able to move beyond their existing knowledge boundaries and thus be able to share valuable knowledge successfully.

This chapter argues that an acquisition-based dynamic reconfiguration capability is needed in order for organizations to be successful in acquiring knowledge-intensive firms. Acquisition-based dynamic reconfiguration capability involves 'the capacity to combine resources from the target and the acquirer in order to create new resources, whether at the target or within the acquirer's original business unit or in some new organizational unit' (Capron and Anand, 2007, p. 82). Developing such capability, however, requires firms to have multiple acquisition experiences and thus be serial acquirers, that is, have at least carried out four acquisitions in a period of 10 years (Laamanen and Keil, 2008). Thus, acquisition-based dynamic reconfiguration capability is an ability that serial acquirers possess.

Given that most valuable resources within knowledge acquisitions are knowledge related, being able to combine these resources is of the utmost importance (for example, Teece, 2007) and thus is the essence of an acquisition-based dynamic reconfiguration capability of serial acquirers of knowledge-intensive firms. Knowledge-based resources can be combined through post-acquisition knowledge sharing, which involves bilateral and multilateral interfirm knowledge-sharing routines (Dyer and Nobeoka, 2000; Faems et al., 2007). In line with Dyer and Singh (1998) such interfirm knowledge-sharing routines are defined as regular patterns of interfirm interactions enabling the transfer, recombination, or creation of knowledge. These routines are institutionalized interfirm processes, which are explicitly designed to facilitate knowledge exchange (ibid.), between the acquired and the acquiring firm. These routines could be seen as the micro-foundations – the underlying individual and group-level microcomponents and interactional dynamics (Teece, 2007; Felin and Foss, 2009) – of acquisition-based dynamic reconfiguration capability since they enable the combining of knowledge-based resources through knowledge sharing, which is the essence of such reconfiguration capability.

Since acquisition-based dynamic reconfiguration capability involves the capacity to combine knowledge-based resources through knowledge sharing with the acquired firm, this capability could be seen as an acquirer's ability to move beyond its own existing knowledge boundaries in order to share knowledge and thus to innovate. Moving beyond existing knowledge boundaries involves using boundary-spanning activities. Such activities contain the use of objects and practices that are shared and shareable across different problem-solving areas, in order to overcome a certain knowledge boundary (Star, 1989; Wenger, 1998; Carlile, 2002). The knowledge-sharing routines that act as micro-foundations of such acquisition-based dynamic reconfiguration capability also act as boundary-spanning activities (Levina and Vaast, 2005).

Regardless of the contributions made until now, however, an understanding of post-acquisition boundary-spanning activities and thus the micro-foundations of acquisition-based dynamic reconfiguration capabilities, has remained absent in acquisition literature. Taking into account high failure rates of acquisitions and the importance of having an acquisition-based capability in order to have successful acquisitions, creating greater clarity regarding the micro-foundations of acquisition-based dynamic reconfiguration capability would not only be vital for academia, but would also make a significant contribution to practice. The purpose of this chapter, therefore, is to unravel the underlying micro-foundations of acquisition-based dynamic reconfiguration capability. Two questions are addressed: which boundary-spanning activities enable post-acquisition knowledge sharing, and how can these boundary-spanning activities enable the creation of an acquisition-based dynamic reconfiguration capability? This chapter aims to contribute to the literature of the knowledge-based and dynamic capabilities views of the firm by creating an understanding regarding the way serial acquirers enhance post-acquisition knowledge sharing beyond their existing knowledge boundaries and thus create an acquisition-based dynamic reconfiguration capability, in order to have more successful knowledge acquisitions.

In order to explain the framework within which this research takes place, in the next sections, dynamic capabilities and knowledge boundaries will be discussed. Subsequently, most appropriate boundary-spanning activities for enhancing post-acquisition cross-boundary knowledge sharing, which act as the micro-foundations of an acquisition-based dynamic reconfiguration capability will be discussed, along with a number of propositions. Finally, some concluding remarks are made.

2   DYNAMIC CAPABILITIES AND KNOWLEDGE BOUNDARIES

In dynamically competitive environments such as the high-technology industries, maintaining superior performance requires constantly renewing competitive advantage through innovation and development of new capabilities (Grant, 1996). In order to explore dynamic aspects of knowledge creation and application, Kogut and Zander (1992) have introduced the concept of 'combinative capability' which emphasizes the importance of synthesizing and applying current and acquired knowledge for enhancing innovation. Extending the idea of combinative capability, Grant (1996) states that deploying and extending a continuing core of capabilities is what leads to continuous innovation in dynamically competitive environments. Thus, according to Grant, dynamic capabilities are the solution to the problem of sustaining competitive advantage in dynamically competitive environments. Dynamic capabilities are 'the firm's ability to integrate, build, and reconfigure internal and external competences to address rapidly changing environments' (Teece et al., 1997, p. 516). Taking into account that sustaining competitive advantage in dynamically competitive markets has been seen as unlikely (Eisenhardt and Martin, 2000), having dynamic capabilities could enable firms to sustain their competitive advantage through constantly reconfiguring their resources and thus being successful (Teece et al., 1997).

One important type of dynamic capabilities that enhances a firm's potential for growth is acquisition-based dynamic capability (Capron and Anand, 2007). Acquisition-based dynamic capability is 'the capacity of the firm to purposefully create, extend, or modify the firm's augmented resource base, which includes the resources of partners' (ibid., p. 80). According to Capron and Anand, acquisition-based dynamic capabilities consist of three main elements: selection, identification, and reconfiguration. Selection is the capacity to recognize when an acquisition would be the most suitable activity for gaining new resources; identification is the capacity to find and negotiate with, the most suitable targets; and reconfiguration capability is 'the capacity to reshape resources within the target and acquiring firms' (p. 82) and involves the capacity for combining resources from the acquired and the acquiring firm in order to create new resources.

As stated earlier, in the context of knowledge acquisitions, given that most valuable resources are knowledge related, being able to combine these resources is extremely important and is the essence of an acquisition-based dynamic reconfiguration capability of serial acquirers of knowledge-intensive firms. Knowledge-based resources can be combined through post-acquisition knowledge sharing among the employees of the acquired and the acquiring firm. Thus, an acquisition-based dynamic reconfiguration capability of serial acquirers is concerned with the ability of the acquiring firm to act beyond existing knowledge boundaries in order to be able to share knowledge with the acquired firm. The knowledge boundaries beyond which the acquiring company must be able to act are the syntactic, semantic, and pragmatic knowledge boundaries (Carlile, 2002, 2004, see Figure 6.1).

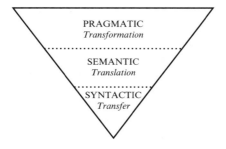

Source: Adapted from Carlile (2004).

Figure 6.1   Knowledge boundaries

The syntactic knowledge boundary is concerned with the need for a common syntax or language in order to be able to share knowledge (Carlile, 2002). This common language or syntax refers to a certain context in which the knowledge in question is known. For example, when collaborating, employees of the acquired and acquiring company may be confronted with a syntactic knowledge boundary if they use different terminologies, codes, or protocols in order to express what they know and explain how they accomplish their tasks (Kotlarsky et al., 2009). The problem that creates the boundary in this case is being able to process information or transfer knowledge and thus understand each other (Carlile, 2004). This boundary can be overcome if a common lexicon and information artifacts such as standards and repositories are developed (Kotlarsky et al., 2009).

The semantic knowledge boundary involves the existence of different interpretations regarding the same event (Carlile, 2002). The context-specific nature of knowledge means that individuals from different functional areas interpret events differently. Knowledge embedded in a certain practice requires deeper understanding than just having a common syntax or language (Kotlarsky et al., 2009). When collaborating, the employees of the acquiring and the acquired firms may make assumptions based on the way they are accustomed to carry out their tasks and interpret events. These assumptions, however, could be contradictory (ibid.). The problem, therefore, is no longer one of transferring knowledge but learning about the differences that exist and thus being able to translate knowledge (Carlile, 2004). It is about being able to translate others' and own knowledge in a given context in order to be able to share knowledge. This boundary can be bridged through the use of, for example, collective stories and cross-functional teams (Kotlarsky et al., 2009).

The pragmatic knowledge boundary is a result of an absence of a shared contextual framework when facing novelty. The existence of novelty (Carlile, 2002) questions existing key principles, rules, and assumptions (Kotlarsky et al., 2009). Therefore, the usual way of operating becomes insufficient since employees cannot operate on the basis of existing key principles, rules, and assumptions. Thus, new key principles, rules and assumptions must be created which help deal with new challenges in order to be able to further existing knowledge and thus to innovate. This requires from individuals involved in such settings a willingness to alter their own knowledge in order to be able to understand the differences that exist (Carlile, 2002). This also requires from such individuals an ability to transform others' knowledge (Carlile, 2004) in order to create a shared contextual framework which helps them understand each other's activities and the consequences of their actions. Without having a shared contextual framework, individuals involved in such settings will not be able to understand each other's differences and therefore will also be less willing and capable in altering each other's knowledge in order to innovate. Hence, sharing knowledge and learning from each other in order to innovate requires employees involved in such settings to create new shared activities in order to transform knowledge. Bridging this boundary can be done through the use of, for example, trial-and-error problem-solving activities or interacting in order to discuss problems regarding a given prototype (Kotlarsky et al., 2009).

In sum, the boundary-spanning activities that an acquisition-based dynamic reconfiguration capability must contain should be able to transfer, translate, and transform knowledge, in order to innovate. Understanding which boundary-spanning activities serial acquirers apply in the post-acquisition phase for sharing knowledge across different boundaries, could help us understand how firms involved in knowledge acquisitions can move beyond their existing knowledge boundaries and thus be able to build an acquisition-based dynamic reconfiguration capability. The next section will introduce a conceptual model that can be used to study in detail the potential for organizations to intervene in processes of boundary-spanning activities at both the operational as well as the managerial level.

3 MICRO-FOUNDATIONS OF ACQUISITION-BASED DYNAMIC RECONFIGURATION CAPABILITIES

Based on the literature of mergers and acquisitions (M&As), alliances, knowledge management, and human resources, we discern various

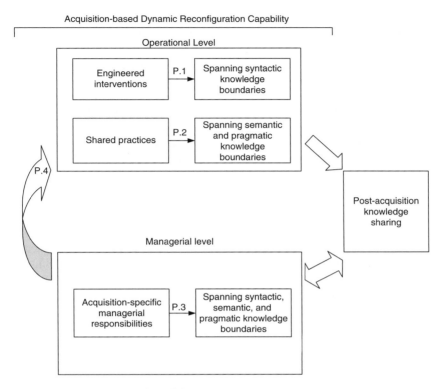

Figure 6.2   Conceptual model

boundary-spanning activities which could enhance post-acquisition cross-boundary knowledge sharing and thus act as micro-foundations of an acquisition-based dynamic reconfiguration capability. Figure 6.2 provides a conceptual model with these possible organizational interventions at both the operational and managerial levels.

Below we shall elaborate on this model, arguing that organizations can intervene at both the operational and the managerial level in order to move beyond the given knowledge boundaries, thereby developing an acquisition-based dynamic reconfiguration capability. Figure 6.2 primarily illustrates how the micro-foundations of acquisition-based dynamic reconfiguration capability enable organizations to move beyond their given knowledge boundaries. First, on an operational level, the use of engineered interventions enables organizations to transfer knowledge and thus be able to overcome the syntactic knowledge boundaries through the creation of a common language or a shared reference point of, for example, information or codes. Second, again on an operational level, shared practices based on frequent interaction among the employees of the acquired and acquiring firms enable organizations to translate and transform knowledge and thus to move beyond the existing semantic and pragmatic knowledge boundaries. Third, on a managerial level, the existence of acquisition-specific responsibilities (for example, M&A teams or an acquisition officer) enables organizations to move beyond their syntactic, semantic, and pragmatic knowledge boundaries through the creation of a common language, an understanding regarding the context, shared interpretations, and the creation of novel ideas regarding post-acquisition knowledge-sharing activities.

At the operational level, as mentioned above, we discern two interventions that cross knowledge boundaries: engineered interventions, which are concerned with sharing explicit knowledge, and shared practices, which are concerned with sharing tacit knowledge. These two interventions also need to be managed, therefore, on a managerial level, acquisition-specific responsibilities take this task into account. In the following subsections these three types of boundary-spanning activities will be discussed along with the existence of an organizational learning loop, and some propositions will be given.

Engineered Interventions

Serial acquirers accumulate their experience through the development of acquisition programs which enhance their subsequent acquisition performance. Such acquisition programs can be developed, partly, through codifying experience and creating standard documents and procedures regarding post-acquisition knowledge integration, which can be used in order to enhance the sharing of explicit knowledge. By using this approach, knowledge sharing usually takes place through the use of IT-based mechanisms. This approach of sharing explicit knowledge could be seen as a type of engineered intervention (Van den Hooff and Huysman, 2009). Firms that have acquisition experience will usually rely on their experience when developing such engineered interventions. Engineered interventions, therefore, contain the codified acquisition experience of organizations. Some examples of such interventions are the use of intranets, decision support systems, and manuals (Zollo and Singh, 2004; Heimeriks, 2008).

Through codifying past experience and creating engineered interventions to share explicit knowledge, the acquirer might be able to enhance knowledge sharing and thus improve the acquisition performance. The use of engineered interventions will help firms to overcome their syntactic knowledge boundaries. Engineered interventions facilitate the processing of information by the creation of a shared language or a common reference point of, for example, information or codes at an operational level. Thus, these interventions enhance the transfer of explicit knowledge among, for example, core knowledge workers such as R&D personnel. These arguments lead to the following proposition:

Proposition 1:   Engineered interventions will help firms at the operational level to overcome their syntactic knowledge boundaries in the post-acquisition phase and thus enhance post-acquisition knowledge sharing.

Shared Practices

In acquiring knowledge-intensive firms, knowledge that is meant to be shared is usually of a highly ambiguous and tacit nature, therefore, personal interactions are extremely important in the post-acquisition phase in order to share knowledge (Ranft, 1997). By using routines that are based on personal interactions there is no need to transform tacit knowledge into an explicit form, since knowledge sharing through the use of such routines takes place in coordinated work arrangements based on informal procedures and commonly understood roles and interactions among specialists (Grant, 1996). For example, having core knowledge workers (for example, R&D personnel) of the acquired and the acquiring firm working together face to face based on certain routines, could enhance the sharing of tacit knowledge among them (Levina and Vaast, 2005).

Such routines are repetitive activities such as practices, developed through the usage of firm's resources which enable knowledge sharing within the firm (Heimeriks, 2008). 'Practice refers to the organization's routine use of knowledge and often has a tacit component, embedded partly in individual skills and partly in collaborative social arrangements' (Szulanski, 1996, p. 28). Consequently, developing shared practices such as the use of cross-functional teams, brainstorming sessions, and solving problems together, have been mentioned as being important for the development of certain dynamic capabilities (Eisenhardt and Martin, 2000). This is because collective learning occurs when employees engage in constructive interactions (for example, collective discussions, workshops, debriefing sessions and so on) in order to exchange their ideas (Zollo and Singh, 2004).

Human resource scholars argue that commitment-based human resource practices such as job rotation and team-based work design aimed at creating mutual long-term exchange relations can enhance knowledge sharing through facilitating social climates of trust, cooperation, and shared codes and language (Collins and Smith, 2006). Another example of collective learning is the creation of knowledge connections. By creating the opportunity for knowledge connections, social interactions between the acquired and the acquiring company provide the foundation for evolving communities of practice (Von Krogh and Slocum, 1994). Knowledge connections are formed through formal and informal relationships between individuals and groups, and are driven by the belief that sharing tacit knowledge is best achieved through 'mutual adaptation among members with common knowledge and shared implicit coding schemes accumulated through group interactions' (Lam, 1997, p. 978). Examples of such knowledge connections are team buddy situations where a new employee is paired with the acquirer's personnel on a one-to-one basis, or site visit tours.

Since individual knowledge and perspectives remain personal unless they are amplified and articulated through social interaction (Nonaka, 1994) organizations should stimulate the occurrence and need for such interactions. On the one hand, on an operational level, through using shared practices that enhance social interactions among core knowledge workers, the acquirer enables employees to learn from each other and understand why the knowledge workers of the other firm interpret events differently. This will help core knowledge workers to overcome their given semantic knowledge boundaries by learning from each other and thus translating knowledge. On the other hand, again on an operational level, these shared practices enable core knowledge workers to understand the consequences of each other's actions and be able to see things from the viewpoint of their colleagues. The use of shared practices such as solving problems together, workshops, or team buddy situations, through the creation of constructive discussions, therefore, enhances the core knowledge workers' ability and willingness to alter their own knowledge and transform others' knowledge in order to create a shared contextual framework and thus overcome their pragmatic knowledge boundaries. Hence, shared practices could be seen as boundary-spanning activities which help firms to overcome their semantic and pragmatic knowledge boundaries on an operational level (Levina and Vaast, 2005). These arguments lead to the following proposition:

Proposition 2: Practices on the operational level which are based on frequent interaction among the employees of the acquiring and the acquired firm will help firms overcome their semantic and pragmatic knowledge boundaries and thus have a greater positive effect on post-acquisition knowledge sharing than engineered interventions.

Acquisition-specific Managerial Responsibilities

Acquisition-specific managerial responsibilities, such as, for example, an M&A team (Zollo and Winter, 2002), could have a positive effect on firms' acquisition performance (Helfat et al., 2007). Such dedicated tasks could be responsible for developing both the tacit and the codified knowledge associated with managing different stages of acquisitions (ibid.). These acquisition-specific managerial responsibilities convert experience into explicit learning mechanisms and ensure that it does not stay on a local level. Having certain acquisition responsibilities, therefore, could be vital for the management of acquisitions as has been shown in the context of alliances (ibid.; Heimeriks, 2008).

On a managerial level, the existence of acquisition-specific responsibilities enhances the creation of a common language, an understanding regarding the needed context, shared interpretations, and the creation of novel ideas to deal with post-acquisition reality. Acquisition-specific managerial responsibilities can do this through, for example, having cross-functional teams in which they discuss how knowledge best can be shared while also taking into account the needs of all the business functions that are involved. Thus, acquisition-specific managerial responsibilities help firms to move beyond their syntactic, semantic, and pragmatic knowledge boundaries on a managerial level in order to enhance post-acquisition knowledge sharing. These arguments lead to the following proposition:

Proposition 3: Acquisition-specific responsibilities at the managerial level will help firms to overcome their syntactic, semantic, and pragmatic knowledge boundaries and thus enhance post-acquisition knowledge sharing.

Learning Loop

Finally, our conceptual model as displayed in Figure 6.2 also recognizes the existence of an organizational learning loop. We have portrayed this loop with the arrow pointing from the managerial level of intervention to the operational level. This learning loop is kept in motion through firms' post-acquisition knowledge-sharing experience, along with the effort of acquisition-specific managerial responsibilities to accumulate this experience and adjust the use of engineered interventions and shared practices.

By reflecting on past acquisition performances, acquisition-specific managerial responsibilities can adjust the use of engineered interventions and shared practices and if needed create new ones. By doing this, in a perfect scenario, firms that have more acquisition experience would probably have more effective engineered interventions and shared practices in use since these firms can keep adjusting and creating new engineered interventions and shared practices until they are satisfied. The reflection on and adjustment of these interventions which results in reconfiguration of the way knowledge-based resources are used, will lead to the dynamic aspect of an acquisition-based dynamic reconfiguration capability. Thus, the organizational learning loop regarding the use of engineered interventions and shared practices is created and kept in motion through such acquisition-specific managerial responsibilities. Of course, also with regard to acquisition-specific managerial responsibilities, in a perfect scenario, firms that have more acquisition experience would probably have more effective managerial responsibilities in place. Thus, firms' experience regarding post-acquisition knowledge sharing affects the type and quality of engineered interventions, shared practices, and acquisition-specific managerial responsibilities in use. The effect on engineered interventions and shared practices, however, is mediated through acquisition-specific managerial responsibilities. These arguments lead to the following proposition:

Proposition 4:   The impact of engineered interventions, shared practices, and acquisition-specific managerial responsibilities on post-acquisition knowledge sharing would be positively greater when based on relatively more acquisition experience.

It could be, however, that acquisition experience does not affect the use of engineered interventions, shared practices, and acquisition-specific managerial responsibilities since organizations often do not learn from acquisitions (Zollo and Singh, 2004; Puranam and Srikanth, 2007). The assumption, however, is that, if carried out properly there is probably an organizational learning loop which enhances the use of such interventions. Thus, the conceptual model developed in this chapter is prescriptive, assuming an ideal situation.

Taking the above-mentioned into account, our conceptual model illustrates that engineered interventions, shared practices, and acquisition-specific managerial responsibilities along with an organizational learning loop, are the micro-foundations of an acquisition-based dynamic reconfiguration capability.

4   CONCLUDING REMARKS

The most important aspect affecting knowledge acquisitions' success is being able to combine knowledge-based resources through post-acquisition cross-boundary knowledge sharing, in order to innovate. Regardless of the increasing number of knowledge acquisitions, however, an understanding of how serial acquirers direct their post-acquisition cross-boundary knowledge-sharing activities remains absent. Clearly, there is a need for systematic research on cross-boundary knowledge sharing through knowledge acquisition. This chapter argues that an acquisition-based dynamic reconfiguration capability can be seen as a distinctive knowledge-sharing ability of serial acquirers. This capability could also be seen as their ability to move beyond their existing knowledge boundaries in order to share knowledge with the acquired firm. Trying to understand which underlying engineered interventions, shared practices, and acquisition-specific managerial responsibilities are the potential forces behind the creation of such capability, therefore, would be a step forward in understanding how to manage more successful knowledge acquisitions. This chapter has set a conceptual foundation for future empirical research.

Implications for Practice

Supporting knowledge sharing depends to a large extent on the uniqueness of the particular situation. What works well in one organization will not necessarily work in another. This has implications for the way organizations can intervene in the process of knowledge sharing. The expectation, however, would be that organizations can try to learn step by step from each acquisition in order to find out which engineered interventions and shared practices that enhance cross-boundary knowledge sharing work well according to their experience. With this in mind, when acquiring a knowledge-intensive firm a question that managers with acquisition-specific responsibilities could ask themselves is 'what type of knowledge boundary are we facing?'. If the knowledge boundary in question is a syntactic one on the operational level, then it is viable to bridge this boundary by using engineered interventions in order to enhance sharing of explicit knowledge. If the knowledge boundary in question is a semantic or pragmatic knowledge boundary on the operational level, then the most appropriate way to overcome this boundary is most likely by developing shared practices which contain frequent interactions among core knowledge workers in order to enhance sharing of tacit knowledge.

However, only using engineered interventions and developing shared practices is not enough. Firms involved in knowledge acquisitions need also to learn from their experiences. Therefore, after each acquisition is completed, an important task of acquisition-specific managerial responsibilities is to find out what they have learned from the acquisition in order to use this knowledge for subsequent acquisitions and thus keep the organizational learning loop in motion. It is expected that such managerial responsibilities can do this through adjusting the engineered interventions and shared practices in use and making different decisions when knowledge boundaries are faced in following acquisitions. Keeping this circle in motion will help create an acquisition-based dynamic reconfiguration capability which enables firms to move beyond their existing knowledge boundaries in order to have more successful knowledge acquisitions and thus probably sustain their competitive advantage.

Implications for Future Research

This chapter has introduced a conceptual model of micro-foundations of acquisition-based dynamic reconfiguration capability, which also contains knowledge boundaries that each of these micro-foundations helps to overcome. This conceptual model is prescriptive, assuming an ideal situation. Clearly, the value of the model introduced in this chapter needs to be validated by empirical research. To the best of our knowledge, up until now, no research has been conducted which has paired the cross-boundary knowledge-sharing activities of firms involved in knowledge acquisitions with the creation of an acquisition capability. This research, therefore, could make a significant contribution to the literature of the knowledge-based and dynamic capabilities views of the firm by linking these two fields. This has implications for future research. On the one hand, future research in search of dynamic reconfiguration capabilities of serial acquirers involved in knowledge acquisitions should take into account the knowledge-based view of the firm, considering that the foundation of these capabilities lies in the way firms conduct their cross-boundary knowledge-sharing activities. On the other, the same holds for future research in the field of the knowledge-based view of the firm. Researchers in search of cross-boundary knowledge-sharing activities within knowledge acquisitions should take into account that their findings could be the micro-foundations of a higher capability which enables firms to share knowledge across boundaries. Hence, researchers on a quest for revealing cross-boundary knowledge-sharing activities of serial-acquirers of knowledge-intensive firms must take into account that they are dealing with two different fields of research that are interrelated, and thus when conducting research both of these lenses must be used.

   It could be, however, that knowledge acquisitions are inherently too situation specific to provide a general causal explanation. Future research, therefore, will be conducted in an area that should be treated carefully with respect for organizational idiosyncrasies. Understanding the nature of knowledge-sharing processes only by conducting quantitative research is not enough since it is important to understand the micro-processes of knowledge sharing that are embedded in this process. Therefore, combining quantitative research and qualitative ethnographic research seems to be a good step forward, in order to understand the process of knowledge sharing within knowledge acquisitions and thus revealing the micro-foundations of an acquisition-based dynamic reconfiguration capability.

REFERENCES

Capron, L. and J. Anand (2007), 'Acquisition-based dynamic capability', in C.E. Helfat, S. Finkelstein, W. Mitchell, M.A. Peteraf, H. Singh and D.J. Teece (eds), *Dynamic Capabilities: Understanding Strategic Change in Organizations*, Oxford: Blackwell, pp. 80–99.

Carlile, P.R. (2002), 'A pragmatic view of knowledge and boundaries: boundary objects in new product development', *Organization Science*, **13** (4), 442–55.

Carlile, P.R. (2004), 'Transferring, translating, and transforming: an integrative framework for managing knowledge across boundaries', *Organization Science*, **15** (5), 555–68.

Collins, C.J. and K.G. Smith (2006), 'Knowledge exchange and combination: the role of human resource practices in the performance of high-technology firms', *Academy of Management Journal*, **49** (3), 544–60.

de Man, A.-P. and G. Duysters (2005), 'Collaboration and innovation: a review of the effects of mergers, acquisitions and alliances on innovation', *Technovation*, **25** (12), 1377–87.

Dyer, J.H. and K. Nobeoka (2000), 'Creating and managing a high-performance knowledge-sharing network: the Toyota case', *Strategic Management Journal*, **21** (3), 345–67.

Dyer, J.H. and H. Singh (1998), 'The relational view: cooperative strategy and sources of interorganizational competitive advantage', *Academy of Management Review*, **23** (4), 660–79.

Eisenhardt, K.M. and J.A. Martin (2000), 'Dynamic capabilities: what are they?', *Strategic Management Journal*, **21** (10/11), 1105–21.

Faems, D., M. Janssens and B. van Looy (2007), 'The initiation and evolution of interfirm knowledge transfer in R&D relationships', *Organization Studies*, **28** (11), 1699–728.

Felin, T. and N.J. Foss (2009), 'Organizational routines and capabilities: historical drift and a course-correction toward microfoundations', *Scandinavian Journal of Management*, **25** (2), 157–67.

Grant, R.M. (1996), 'Prospering in dynamically-competitive environments: organizational capability as knowledge integration', *Organization Science*, **7** (4), 375–87.

Heimeriks, K.H. (2008), *Developing Alliance Capabilities*, Basingstoke: Palgrave Macmillan.

Helfat, C., D. Finkelstein, W. Mitchell, M.A. Peteraf, H. Singh, D.J. Teece and S.G. Winter (2007), *Dynamic Capabilities: Understanding Strategic Change in Organizations*, Oxford: Blackwell.

Huber, G. (1991), 'Organizational learning: the contributing processes and literatures', *Organization Science*, **2** (1), 88–115.

Kogut, B. and U. Zander (1992), 'Knowledge of the firm, combinative capabilities, and the replication of technology', *Organization Science*, **3**, 383–97.

Kotlarsky, I., B. Van den Hooff and M. Huysman (2009), 'Bridging knowledge boundaries in cross-functional groups: the role of a transactive memory system', paper presented at the International Conference on Information Systems, Phoenix, AZ, December 14–18.

Laamanen, T. and T. Keil (2008), 'Performance of serial acquirers: toward an acquisition program perspective', *Strategic Management Journal*, **29** (6), 663–72.

Lam, A. (1997), 'Embedded firms, embedded knowledge: problems of collaboration and knowledge transfer in global cooperative ventures', *Organization Studies*, **18** (6), 973–96.

Levina, N. and E. Vaast (2005), 'The emergence of boundary spanning competence in practice: implications for implementation and use of information systems', *MIS Quarterly*, **29** (2), 335–63.

Nonaka, I. (1994), 'A dynamic theory of organizational knowledge creation', *Organization Science*, **5** (1), 14–37.

Puranam, P., H. Singh and M. Zollo (2003), 'A bird in the hand or two in the bush? Integration trade-offs in technology-grafting acquisitions', *European Management Journal*, **21** (2), 179–84.

Puranam, P. and K. Srikanth (2007), 'What they know versus what they do: how acquirers leverage technology acquisitions', *Strategic Management Journal*, **28** (8), 805–25.

Ranft, A. (1997), 'Preserving and transferring knowledge-based resources during post-acquisition implementation', PhD dissertation, University of North Carolina, Chapel Hill, NC.

Ranft, A.L. and M.D. Lord (2002), 'Acquiring new technologies and capabilities: a grounded model of acquisition implementation', *Organization Science*, **13** (4), 420–41.

Star, S.L. (1989), 'The structure of ill-structured solutions: boundary objects and heterogeneous distributed problem solving', in M. Huhns and L. Gasser (eds), *Distributed Artificial Intelligence*, Vol. 2, London: Morgan Kaufman, pp. 37–54.

Szulanski, G. (1996), 'Exploring internal stickiness: impediments to the transfer of best practice within the firm', *Strategic Management Journal*, **17**, 27–43.

Teece, D.J. (2007), 'Explicating dynamic capabilities: the nature and microfoundations of (sustainable) enterprise performance', *Strategic Management Journal*, **28** (13), 1319–50.

Teece, D.J., G. Pisano and A. Shuen (1997), 'Dynamic capabilities and strategic management', *Strategic Management Journal*, **18** (7), 509–33.

Van den Hooff, B. and M. Huysman (2009), 'Managing knowledge sharing: emergent and engineering approaches', *Information & Management*, **46** (1), 1–8.

Vermeulen, F. and H. Barkema (2001), 'Learning through acquisitions', *Academy of Management Journal*, **44** (3), 457–76.

Von Krogh, R.G.J. and K. Slocum (1994), 'An essay on corporate epistemology', *Strategic Management Journal*, **15**, 53–71.

Wenger, E. (1998), *Communities of Practice: Learning, Meaning, and Identity*, Cambridge: Cambridge University Press.

Zollo, M. and H. Singh (2004), 'Deliberate learning in corporate acquisitions: post-acquisition strategies and integration capability in U.S. bank mergers', *Strategic Management Journal*, **25**, 1233–56.

Zollo, M. and S.G. Winter (2002), 'Deliberate learning and the evolution of dynamic capabilities', *Organization Science*, **13** (3), 339–51.

7. When firms do not benefit from collaborative experience: differences in the intensity and nature of interorganizational relationships

Astrid A. ter Wiel and Paul W.L. Vlaar

1 INTRODUCTION

In order to cope with changing demands and to survive in turbulent environments, organizations are increasingly looking for solutions beyond their own boundaries and are joining forces with other firms. Entering into interorganizational relationships, such as research and development (R&D) alliances or buyer–supplier partnerships, creates new opportunities for firms, allowing them to share resources, to open up new markets or jointly develop new products. Firms can accordingly collaborate with suppliers, customers or competitors in different arrangements, such as informal collaborations and joint ventures. Conventional wisdom indicates that firms with more collaborative experience, gained while managing their relationship with those partners, become more successful in future collaborative initiatives, because they accumulate experience and learn how to manage their collaborative relationships.

In this chapter, we argue that experience with one type of collaborative relationships is different from experience with other types of collaborative relationships, depending on the intensity of cooperation (that is, transactional versus relational) and the type of interdependency of a relationship (that is, horizontal versus vertical). Lessons learned from repeated interactions with suppliers, for example, may not be applicable when the same firm enters a strategic alliance with its competitor. Worse, experience with certain types of collaborative relationships may even be detrimental to the performance of other types of relationships. The competitive attitude and short-term perspective that suits transactional relationships, for instance, may harm long-term cross-industrial alliance relationships, in which a focus on cooperation and long-term benefits is generally more appropriate. Based on extant theory and illustrating our arguments with quotes from managers of collaborative relationships, we contend that it is important to distinguish different forms of collaborative relationships and to recognize that relationship managers should adapt their management style to the type of interfirm relationship they are dealing with.

2 TYPES OF INTERORGANIZATIONAL RELATIONSHIPS

Interfirm relationships can take a variety of forms, including joint ventures, supplier relationships, joint marketing efforts, and collaborative R&D (Das and Teng, 1996). Scholars discussing such relationships usually specify the subjects they study based on the governance structure characterizing a relationship and the content of a relationship. Regarding governance structure, firms can collaborate informally, establish connections through contracts, or partially integrate through equity investments in, for example, joint ventures (Grandori and Soda, 1995). A commonly used distinction to group collaborative relations based on governance structure is the one between non-equity and equity agreements, the latter involving the creation of a new and independent jointly owned entity, or a minority equity position from an organization in their partner (Gulati, 1995). Other categorizations based on governance structure involve collaborative forms such as license agreements, cross-licensing, alliance contracts, joint ventures and several mixed modes (for example, Mowery et al., 1996).

Concerning relationship content, we observe that managers responsible for a collaborative relationship are often selected for the job because of their expertise in a certain area, which generally connotes the activities conducted in the relationship. Based on this content, various groups of relationships can be distinguished. Anand and Khanna (2000), for instance, distinguish marketing, production and R&D relationships. Other collaborations can entail joint purchasing agreements, or finance and logistics contracts, where partners combine forces to negotiate with their suppliers or outsource part of their operations.

Although each of the previously discussed dimensions has its merits, offering valuable means to characterize distinct types of collaborative initiatives, they do not directly concern the nature of the interaction process itself. Such a classification of collaborative relationships would be useful, since differences in the nature of this process may have different implications for managing collaborative activities. Moreover, presuming that different types of relationships and interaction processes require other kinds of management styles, collaborative experience with one type of

Table 7.1   Classification of interorganizational relationships

Linkage (interdependency)	Cooperation intensity (exchange relationship)	
	Low (transactional)	High (relational)
Horizontal (generally: pooled interdependency)	Cell A (Informal) joint agreements (pooling and exchanging information) with organizations from the same levels of the value-added chain	Cell B Formal and long-term partnerships with organizations from the same levels of the value-added chain
Vertical (generally: sequential interdependency)	Cell C Preferred connections (short list) – formal or informal – with organizations from different levels of the value-added chain	Cell D Formal and long-term partnerships with organizations from different levels of the value-added chain

relationship may be less valuable or even detrimental for firms managing a greater variety of collaborative relationships and a larger number of distinct relationship portfolios.

Extant literature has primarily referred to two dimensions to categorize the nature of collaborative relationships: (i) the intensity of cooperation, involving the exchange spectrum from transactional to relational exchanges; and (ii) the type of interdependency involved with cooperation, represented by the distinction between horizontal and vertical collaborative linkages. In Table 7.1, we have combined both dimensions to classify interorganizational relationships.

First, we consider cooperation intensity. Cooperation can range from simple exchanges of information or resources, to limited collaboration in accomplishing a specific functional purpose, to extensive cooperation involving the production of a product or service or collaboration across several domains and functions (Alter and Hage, 1993). Transactional exchanges on one side, and relational exchanges on the other, thus constitute the two extremes of the cooperation intensity spectrum (Macneil, 1978). Since true transactional exchanges are simple, discrete, one-time events (see Dwyer et al., 1987), we exclude such arm's-length market exchanges from our discussion. Similarly, extreme cases of relational exchanges generally connote new organizational forms, such as network organizations or virtual organizations, so we stop short of this extreme side of the aforementioned spectrum as well. Instead, we focus subsequent discussions on dyadic interorganizational relationships that emerge when two organizations go beyond the pure transactional type of exchange and move to ongoing (longer-term) connections involving repeated transactions.

Second, we consider different types of interdependency involved with interfirm relationships. In this respect, one can distinguish vertical and horizontal linkages. Vertical relationships occur when firms cooperate across different levels of the value-added chain, whereas horizontal linkages involve collaboration between actors at the same level (Kotabe and Swan, 1995). In these different linkages, the level of firms' interdependency varies. Kumar and Van Dissel (1996) have put Thompson's (1967) view, on how organizational units may depend on one another, in the interorganizational context. Where two firms share resources but are independent, they speak of 'pooled interdependency'. Pooled interdependency generally occurs in horizontal relations: firms may share products or knowledge but remain independent entities. When the output from one firm becomes input to the other we may speak of 'sequential dependency'. This is mainly the case in vertical relationships where one firm is dependent upon input from the other, vertically linked, firm. With 'reciprocal dependency', each firm receives input from and provides output to the other. This happens in vertical relationships; for example, an engineering team consisting of customers, suppliers and distributors that develops a new automobile (Kumar and Van Dissel, 1996), but also occurs in horizontal relationships, especially when firms collaborate across industries.

Before we indicate what it means for the management of a particular relationship to be classified in one cell rather than another, and which implications are involved when a relationship develops or degenerates from one cell to the next, we further explain each of the four cells presented in Table 7.1. We also illustrate each of these cells with quotes from a qualitative, explorative study conducted in 2009 and 2010 in the health care sector in the Netherlands.

The simplest form of horizontal cooperation – with low cooperation intensity and with a more transactional character – entails an exchange of information between firms in a dyadic relationship (cell A in Table 7.1). This kind of 'agreement' is often informal, witness the following example:

> With one other hospital, which we do not consider to be our competitor because of different geographical locations, we have 'friendly' relations so to say. We exchange, for example, information on prices of products or services that we both buy. (Relationship Manager 8)

An example of a relationship between two firms with a horizontal scope and a relational character (that is cell B in Table 7.1) consists of an R&D

alliance or a joint purchasing agreement between two competitors. In our empirical study several hospitals joined forces to approach suppliers for strategic purchases and share the resulting profits, as is illustrated by the following quote:

> We joined forces with four other hospitals in the Netherlands and a large foreign purchasing collaboration to negotiate better prices and conditions for our suppliers [. . .]. We share the generated savings pro rata: the bigger the organization, the bigger its share. (Relationship Manager 19)

Parties in vertical interfirm relationships of a more transactional character are often referred to as 'preferred' partners (cell C). If a firm, for instance, needs to purchase the same materials over and over again, and they tend to use the same supplier, we talk of a 'preferred' supplier:

> We have a list with a limited number of preferred suppliers. Some we use regularly and we have simple, standard contracts with them. Some we use incidentally, but they are – per event, let's say twice a year – selected without separate tenders simply because they are on our preferred supplier list. I do not actively monitor or manage the relationships with these suppliers, it is very operational. The guys in the back office stay in touch and order when necessary. (Relationship Manager 2)

Similarly, a firm may work with a preferred buyer or distributor. However, if a firm guarantees trade to a business partner – the supplier is assured that materials will be bought for a long period of time – and they work together more closely, interfirm linkages take on a more relational character. The same applies to firms working closely together with customers; partners may, for example, agree on a long-term contract and share the costs of investments in relation-specific assets. Firms could also develop a product jointly with a buyer or a supplier. All these connections with a relational character across different levels of the value-added chain fit in cell D in Table 7.1. An illustrative example is offered by a relationship manager:

> We just signed a contract with [one of our suppliers]. It is a three-year joint research project in which we improve part of an existing product and test it. The greater part of the development will be done by the supplier in which we take a more advisory role; the testing will take place in our hospital. We assigned a manager to this project and together with a director he coordinates. (Relationship Manager 11)

Now that we have illustrated the four different types of collaboration along both dimensions as presented in Table 7.1, we turn to explaining the differences between each type of relationship in terms of the appropriate management styles. Moreover, we pay attention to the managerial consequences associated with firms initiating and maintaining a wide variety of different types of relationships, or with relationships changing in terms of the nature of the interaction with partners along one or both dimensions. Finally, we combine these arguments to suggest that collaborative experience with one type of relationship is not necessarily beneficial, and can even be detrimental, to future collaborative initiatives of firms.

3 TYPES OF RELATIONSHIPS AND SKILLS

If the relational character of a horizontal relationship increases (moving from cell A to B or from C to D in Table 7.1), the properties of the relationship change. To explain the consequences for the management of the relationship, we summarized the most important properties of the two extremes of the interorganizational exchange spectrum, transactional versus relational exchanges, in Table 7.2. To explain the different approaches required for a transactional 'relationship' and those for a long-term relationship with high cooperation intensity, we label the manager responsible for the latter relationship 'MR' (manager relational), and the one responsible for the transactional connection 'MT' (manager transactional). We distinguish four main properties that define the different management approaches.

First, as is shown in Table 7.2, the MR needs to be able to focus on long-term results and invest in the relationship, even if the short term does not immediately pay off. Traditional purchasing managers, for example, are very much focused on monetary advantages and tend to overlook the long-term effects of their actions. If a manager negotiates prices and adopts a hostile approach in doing so, (s)he might damage the longer-term relationship with, in this example, the supplier. Second, the MR needs to realize that (s)he cannot just cross over to another partner should that desire arise, as could easily be done in a relationship of a more transactional nature. Related to a long-term management approach, this requires more tactical solutions in situations of stress or conflict. Third, the MT usually works with more straightforward content of limited scope and complexity. The MR, on the other hand, deals with more complicated matters, encounters all kinds of assumptions and needs to be able to develop, maintain and repair trust throughout the relationship. Fourth, the character of the interaction between partners differs for the MT and the MR. More is demanded from the MR because, for intense and long-term relationships, personal relationships are important and multiple

Table 7.2   Transactional versus relational exchanges

Properties	Transactional	Relational
1 Cooperation intensity and timing	Low cooperation intensity Short time perspective Distinct beginning, short duration, and sharp ending	High cooperation intensity Long time perspective Commencement traces to previous agreements; exchange is longer in duration; reflecting an ongoing process
2 Transferability	Complete transferability; it does not matter who fulfills contractual obligation	Limited transferability; exchange is heavily dependent on the identity of the parties
3 Scope	Discrete transactions are characterized by very limited communications and narrow content	The basis for future collaboration may be supported by implicit and explicit assumptions, trust, and planning
4 Communication, personal involvement and exchange	Minimal personal relationships; segmental, limited, non-unique, transferable, ritual-like communications predominate	Important personal relationships: whole person, unlimited, unique, non-transferable, non-economic satisfactions derived; both formal and informal communications are used
	Limited, linguistic, formal communication	Extensive, deep, not limited to linguistic, informal communication in addition to or in lieu of formal
	Simple, monetizable -economic exchange only	In addition to economic, complex personal non-economic satisfactions very important; social exchange
	The identity of parties to a transaction must be ignored or relationships creep in	Relational exchange participants can be expected to derive complex, personal, non-economic satisfactions and engage in social exchange

Source: Adapted from Macneil (1978), Dwyer et al. (1987) and Khanna et al. (1998).

Table 7.3   Horizontal versus vertical exchanges

	Properties	Horizontal	Vertical
1	Interdependence	Generally pooled Ambiguous	Generally sequential Clearer and more direct
2	Resources	Overlapping (scale)	Exclusive, more complementary (link)
3	Contracts	Open, tacit, output based	Closed, explicit, input and output based
4	Relationship strength	Stronger institutional and interpersonal connections	Weaker institutional and interpersonal connections
5	Expropriation	Higher potential	Lower potential

communication techniques are used. The social exchange component in relationships managed by the MR is much more prominent. The MT deals with relatively simple, often straightforward, economic exchanges while the MR takes care of complex, personal and non-economic satisfactions.

We now conduct a similar exercise for the dimension distinguishing horizontal and vertical relationships, as summarized in Table 7.3. Comparing horizontal to vertical relationships (cell A versus cell C, and cell B versus cell D in Table 7.1), we distinguish five main properties that can be used to explain what the distinction between horizontal and vertical relationships means for the management of collaborative relationships.

First, collaborations in vertical connections differ from those involving horizontal connections, primarily in terms of interdependence (Smith et al., 1995). The level of parties' interdependence will generally be clearer and more direct in vertical links than in horizontal links. With pooled interdependence the least amount of interdependence is involved: a firm can be plucked out, and as long as there is no significant corresponding withdrawal of resources, the others can continue to work uninterrupted. This shows that the level of interdependency between firms is key when assessing the potential for one firm to harm the operations of the other. A manager responsible for relationships with high interdependency, continuously has to be aware of the intentional or accidental harm the firm can inflict upon the other (Kumar and Van Dissel, 1996). With sequential interdependence the manager needs to realize that pulling out (or making the other pull out) is like breaking a chain whereby in extreme cases the whole subsequent set of activities may cease to function (in vertical relations). This implies that the relationship manager needs to thoroughly oversee the whole chain of activities. Changes or problems in a situation of reciprocal interdependence could affect downstream and also upstream parties, because the participants in the relationship feed work back and forth to each other (ibid.). Thus, different types of interdependence generate various degrees of risk and conflict to be managed by the responsible manager.

Second, related to the interdependence property, is the nature of the resources that are exchanged between partners. In horizontal connections in the same industry firms contribute similar resources pertaining to the same stage or stages in the value chain, while in vertical linkages firms aim at combining different and complementary skills and resources that each partner contributes (Dussauge et al., 2000). Hennart (1988) classified these as, respectively, scale and link alliances. Firms possessing complementary skills and resources have the incentive to reduce their interdependence by acquiring skills and other intangible capabilities that underlie their partner's contributions, as well as acquiring any new skills that arise as the result of combining their partner's complementary resources (Dussauge et al., 2000). Managers responsible for vertical partnerships have to find a balance between sharing enough knowledge and resources to make the collaboration work while not divulging their sources of competitive advantage.

Third, and again related to the interdependence being more direct in vertical relationships, 'vertical contracts' are often clearer and more quantitative than agreements between two horizontal partners. A buyer–supplier contract is more straightforward than the one in a joint-development project where the exact process is yet to be determined, only the outcomes might be roughly drafted, and a great deal more uncertainty is involved (Mayer and Teece, 2008). The contract content affects the restrictions concerning the management of the relationship, and some situations go beyond what is in the contract. More open contracts leave room for interpretation from both sides and the managers involved need the know-how and skills to deal with such contracts requiring communication that is most likely less explicit than in vertical relations.

Fourth, partners in horizontal interorganizational relationships display stronger institutional and interpersonal connections compared to participants in vertical interorganizational relationships (Rindfleisch, 2000). Managers may belong to a common social circle and are likely to share similar educational backgrounds or belong to the same associations. Prior to establishing a formal relationship, horizontally related firms often participate in informal information-sharing activities. To be able to establish the stronger interpersonal connection, it would help if the responsible manager has been involved in the linkages that occurred prior to the formal collaboration. While managing the formal relationship, the manager may draw from earlier experiences with the same partner.

Fifth, in horizontal alliances the potential for opportunism is high as partners may use the alliance only as a means to gain market position at the expense of a partner (Bucklin and Sengupta, 1993). The relationship manager needs to actively manage the partners' role, influence and actions in horizontal relationships to avoid expropriation.

The differences between horizontal and vertical relationships can affect both the organization's learning from collaborative experience and the management skills and styles that are necessary to effectively manage different interfirm linkages. Managers comfortable in personal and open relationships with their business partners, might encounter problems in dealing with relationships under strict and formal contracts. At the same time, those responsible for horizontal relationships have to guard over the expropriation potential when setting up and managing their inter-firm collaborations. Our explanation of the properties that define the dimensions along which we classified interorganizational relationships exemplifies the necessity of distinguishing different styles in managing collaborations. In the next sections, we explain how the classification of interfirm relationships as presented above is also relevant when trying to understand how collaborative experience may influence the perform-ance of future collaborative initiatives. In particular, we contend that the frequently promoted notion that this association tends to be positive has to be nuanced. In fact, we believe that experience with one type of relationship may not be applicable to other types of relationships, and that it could even have a negative effect on the performance of these relationships.

4   COLLABORATIVE EXPERIENCE

Organizations learn by direct experience; the more organizations engage in certain activities the better they are able to manage these types of activities (Harbison and Pekar, 1998; Sampson, 2005). Conventional wisdom suggests that firms repeatedly dealing with interfirm relationships gain collaborative experience (Simonin, 1997), which results in a host of positive outcomes, such as learning (Kale and Singh, 2007), collabora-tive capability development (Schilke and Goerzen, 2010), and eventually interorganizational performance (Sampson, 2005). The general assump-tion seems to be that the more organizations collaborate with other organizations, the better they are able to do so in the future. Authors have argued, for example, that systematically learning from alliance experience is extremely valuable as it influences firms' abilities to avoid pitfalls (Kale et al., 2002), and because it allows organizations to unleash the full potential of exchanging resources and managing joint activities (Sampson, 2005).

Previous studies, however, often deal with collaborative performance at the organizational level, not elaborating on the type of experience involved and thereby generalizing and tarring different interorganizational relationships with the same brush. As explained earlier, Anand and Khanna's article (2000) is an exception, but they do not look at the effects of collaborative experience within the organization itself – the intrafirm level of analysis. If firms do really well in managing buyer–supplier partnerships, for instance, this does not necessarily mean that they are able to successfully manage other interorganizational relationships, such as horizontal strategic alliances. We illustrate this point using several quotes from our qualitative study, suggesting that researchers should recognize the differences among collaborative relationships when ascertaining the influence of collaborative experience of interorganizational performance. In the study, 23 relationship managers were interviewed about the collaborative relationships in their organization. An alliance manager explains that the relationships his organization has with other organizations differ in nature, explaining why he is responsible for only a subset of these external relationships:

> The management of strategic supplier partnerships is very different from that of the management of other alliances. And the management of collaborations with other hospitals is again different from managing R&D alliances. It is a different setup with different goals, a different context and different interests. (Relationship Manager 3)

In this hospital, different managers are responsible for different types of collaborative relations. A procurement manager of another organization further clarifies that his organization also tends to change the person responsible for managing a relationship when relationships develop towards a different point on the transactional–relational dimension, for instance assuming a more strategic position in the relationship portfolio:

> When the relationship develops, the complexity of the relationship management increases. Often the person responsible for that relationship changes because we need someone with more competencies and capabilities to manage the relationship. (Relationship Manager 2)

The relationship manager herewith demonstrates that his organization distinguishes types of interorganizational relationships based on the intensity of cooperation. In this example, he talks of interorganizational relationships that can be plotted in cells C and D of Table 7.1; a buyer–supplier relationship with a relative low intensity of cooperation (cell C) develops into a relationship with high cooperation intensity (cell D). It is not surprising that one collaborative relationship is different from the other, but it remains unclear how experience with one type of relationship influences the performance of other types, now and in the future.

The four types of interorganizational relationships, as presented in Table 7.1, require different approaches regarding the management of the relationship itself. A manager of a Dutch teaching hospital explains:

> Managing a strategic supplier relationship is quite different from managing a collaborative relationship with another hospital. [. . .] I think that is the case because of the origin of the relationship. It requires adaptation from both sides if you have gone through some rough negotiations with a supplier before and eventually form a partnership. You have to be able to let go of your old habits and form new positions. That is similar to the difference between collaborating with a supplier or an associate hospital. Other things are involved. For example, the extent to which an alliance contract needs to be sound. (Relationship Manager 3)

Besides addressing differences between horizontal (collaboration with a competitor) and vertical relationships (collaboration with a supplier), this alliance manager elaborates on a situation where an interorganizational relationship that formerly fitted cell C in Table 7.1 shifts to cell D.

Several difficulties ensue from moving from a straightforward buyer–supplier connection (low cooperation intensity) to a vertical partnership (high cooperation intensity). In a straightforward buyer–supplier relationship, firms do not necessarily take a long-term perspective or consider transferability issues, for instance (see Table 7.2 for all differences in properties). The process of bargaining and negotiation is at least minimally adversarial and not always conducive to developing long-term relationships (Achrol, 1997), but inevitable in buyer–supplier relationships. The original (transactional) setup of the relationship described above required a different approach, not taking into account the effects of management decisions and tactics on a possible partnership with high cooperation intensity. Such a situation suggests that experience with one type of interfirm relationships can be detrimental to managing other types of collaborative relationships. As the manager states: 'You have to be able to let go of your old habits and form new positions'. Relationship management thus needs to be customized to the type of relationship that one is involved in, which may vary with the degree of interdependency between partners and the intensity of cooperation among them. The following quote from a manager of one of the leading hospitals in the Netherlands further clarifies this matter:

> Well, one type of relationship is different from the other. The experience that we have with our R&D alliances is not necessarily useful for other collaborative relationships. Collaborating with other hospitals, especially neighboring ones – our direct competitors – is much more pulling and pushing, than collaborating with, for example, research institutes. The way you work with competitive alliance partners, is different. We would be more careful with sharing certain information for instance. If you were to deal with all partners the same way, it might work out unfavorably. (Relationship Manager 1)

The position of this manager – that the management approach for horizontal relationships should be different from the approach in vertical relationships – is supported by literature suggesting that firms in horizontal alliances display lower levels of interorganizational trust compared to firms in vertical alliances. This differential role of trust results, among others, from the opportunity that firms in such relationships have to behave opportunistically, from lower interdependency, and from stronger institutional and interpersonal linkages among horizontal collaborators (Rindfleisch, 2000). Imagine a situation where a manager, responsible for collaborative relationships with competitors in the same market as the focal firm, is made responsible for an interorganizational relationship with a research institute. He or she might be reluctant to share information, remain hesitant to share insights, knowledge, or experience with the staff from the partnering organization, simply because the person is used to working with business partners that simultaneously have to be regarded as competitors. Sticking to the management style appropriate for such relations, however, might jeopardize an effective collaborative relationship with the research institute.

Not only are there differences between horizontal and vertical collaborations, but within these portfolios interorganizational relationships may also vary in terms of the intensity with which they cooperate with various partners (see Table 7.2). This is illustrated by the following quote:

> Our hospital has had an alliance with [a big neighboring hospital] for a long time. There are a lot of dyadic relationships between physicians here and there, but it is a relatively low key alliance. We leave the intensity of the collaboration up to the separate divisions. [. . .] In our alliance with a smaller hospital the board of directors is much more involved in the collaboration and has a leading role; in contrast to the bigger hospital where the principal part of the collaboration lies in the lower regions of our organization and the alliance agreement covers it all. These physicians would not accept us being too much on top of the collaborative activities. (Relationship Manager 8)

This manager adapts his management style to the type of alliance he is dealing with. In the case of the low-key alliance with the bigger hospital, he adopts a more *laissez-faire* approach and takes a peripheral role. Besides highlighting the differences between managing various types of interfirm relationships, the last two quotes illustrate that collaborative experience with one type of interorganizational relationships might have detrimental effects on other types of future collaborative relationships.

5   CONCLUSIONS AND IMPLICATIONS

Our primary aim in this chapter was to explain the importance of recognizing the differences between distinct types of collaborative relationships and some peculiarities that enter into the management of those relationships. We distinguished four (extreme) categories of interorganizational relationships based on horizontal versus vertical linkages, and low versus high cooperation intensity. Our quotes from relationship managers illustrate the nuances in managing different types of interfirm relationships, for example a procurement manager who is responsible for strategic buyer–supplier relationships would not necessarily be the right person to manage an interfirm joint development project. We further suggest that applying experience from managing one type of collaborative relationship to other types of interorganizational relationships may not necessarily be beneficial and can even be detrimental to their performance. In fact, relationship management needs to be customized to the nature of the collaboration, which may vary with the degree of interdependency and the cooperation intensity between partners. We have nuanced the presumed positive effect of more experience with interfirm collaboration on future relationships by distinguishing different types of experience. Additionally, if one type of collaborative experience is not complementary to the other, it depends on the relationship whether firms and relationship managers can apply their experience from the past. We suggest organizations looking for collaborative opportunities beyond their own boundaries take into account that different skills are required for the effective management of various types of interfirm relationships.

REFERENCES

Achrol, R. (1997), 'Changes in the theory of interorganizational relations in marketing: toward a network paradigm', *Journal of the Academy of Marketing Science*, **25** (1): 56–71.

Alter, C. and J. Hage (1993), *Organizations Working Together*, Newbury Park, CA: Sage.

Anand, B.N. and T. Khanna (2000), 'Do firms learn to create value? The case of alliances', *Strategic Management Journal*, **21** (3): 295–315.

Bucklin, L.P. and S. Sengupta (1993), 'Organizing successful co-marketing alliances', *Journal of Marketing*, **57** (April): 32–46.

Das, T.K. and B.S. Teng (1996), 'Risk types and interfirm alliance structures', *Journal of Management Studies*, **33**: 827–43.

Dussauge, P., B. Garrette and W. Mitchell (2000), 'Learning from competing partners: outcomes and durations of scale and link alliances in Europe, North America and Asia', *Strategic Management Journal*, **21** (2): 99–126.

Dwyer, F.R., P.H. Schurr and S. Oh (1987), 'Developing buyer–seller relationships', *Journal of Marketing*, **51** (2): 11–27.

Grandori, A. and G. Soda (1995), 'Interfirm networks: antecedents, mechanisms and forms', *Organization Studies*, **16** (2): 183–214.

Gulati, R. (1995), 'Does familiarity breed trust? The implications of repeated ties for contractual choice in alliances', *Academy of Management Journal*, **38** (1): 85–112.

Harbison, J.R. and P. Pekar (1998), *Smart Alliances: A Guide to Repeatable Success*, San Francisco, CA: Jossey-Bass.

Hennart, J.F. (1988), 'A transaction costs theory of equity joint ventures', *Strategic Management Journal*, **9** (4): 361–74.

Kale, P., J.H. Dyer and H. Singh (2002), 'Alliance capability, stock market response, and long-term alliance success: the role of the alliance function', *Strategic Management Journal*, **23** (8): 747–67.

Kale, P. and H. Singh (2007), 'Building firm capabilities through learning: the role of the alliance learning process in alliance capability and firm-level alliance success', *Strategic Management Journal*, **28** (10): 981–1000.

Khanna, T., R. Gulati and N. Nohria (1998), 'The dynamics of learning alliances: competition, cooperation, and relative scope', *Strategic Management Journal*, **19** (3): 193–210.

Kotabe, M. and K.S. Swan (1995), 'The role of strategic alliances in high-technology new product development', *Strategic Management Journal*, **16** (8): 621–36.

Kumar, K. and H.G. Van Dissel (1996), 'Sustainable collaboration: managing conflict and cooperation in interorganizational systems', *MIS Quarterly*, **20** (3): 279–300.

Macneil, I.R. (1978), 'Contracts: adjustment of long-term economic relations under classical, neoclassical, and relational contract law', *Northwestern University Law Review*, **72** (6): 854–905.

Mayer, K.J. and D.J. Teece (2008), 'Unpacking strategic alliances: the structure and purpose of alliance versus supplier relationships', *Journal of Economic Behavior and Organization*, **66** (1): 106–27.

Mowery, D.C., J.E. Oxley and B.S. Silverman (1996), 'Strategic alliances and interfirm knowledge transfer', *Strategic Management Journal*, **17**: 77–91.

Rindfleisch, A. (2000), 'Organizational trust and interfirm cooperation: an examination of horizontal versus vertical alliances', *Marketing Letters*, **11** (1): 81–95.

Sampson, R. (2005), 'Experience effects and collaborative returns in R&D alliances', *Strategic Management Journal*, **26** (11): 1009–31.

Schilke, O. and A. Goerzen (2010), 'Alliance management capability: an investigation of the construct and its measurement', *Journal of Management*, **36** (5): 1192–219.

Simonin, B.L. (1997), 'The importance of collaborative know-how: an empirical test of the learning organization', *Academy of Management Journal*, **40** (5): 1150–74.

Smith, K.G., S.J. Carroll and S.J. Ashford (1995), 'Intra- and interorganizational cooperation: toward a research agenda', *Academy of Management Journal*, **38** (1): 7–23.

Thompson, J.D. (1967), *Organizations in Action; Social Science Bases of Administrative Theory*, New York: McGraw-Hill.

PART III

Between firms and society

Introduction to Part III: Exploring the logic of organizational boundaries

Peter Groenewegen

The chapters in this section deal with the issues of trust, and of boundaries between workers and management, between the clients of the organization, and the building of relations in the market.

One of the by now classic discussions on organizational boundaries is on the three forms of organizing: markets, networks and hierarchies. Powell (1990) introduced the network form, in an attempt to order the ongoing discussion of changes in organizing. Networks, it is suggested, are considered different from the two archetypes hierarchy (according to rules and positions) and market (transactions according to price), insofar as networks allow for more flexible arrangements. Furthermore, a network organization is defined as a 'a unique set of internal and external linkages for each unique project' (Baker, 1992 p. 398). The discussion of the changing function of organizations in society has, however, also touched upon other distinctions, such as those between public and market-based organizational forms, profit and nonprofit organizations, as well as entrepreneurial action as compared to internal innovation. Thus Powell's threefold characterization of organizing principles – which has been applied rather broadly to many phenomena such as efficient government organization, connecting firms with compatible qualities, designing efficient and flexible organizations – can be seen to be rather open with regard to the actual configurations to be expected in and around organizations.

The manner in which connections between workers and management function is nicely illustrated in this volume, in the different stances on reorganizations by work councils, in the contribution by Sapulete et al. (Chapter 8). The authors argue that trust in the relationship between management and workers is crucial to understanding the effect of works councils on productivity during reorganizations. When trust is present, they suggest, works councils and management can be considered as part of a closely-knit network, which enhances the functioning of organizations. Thus reorganizations that avoid layoffs leave the relationship between workers and management intact, and the authors show that maintaining productive networks requires trust and understanding. However, during reorganizations where management attempts to separate the workers' networks into workers to be laid off and workers to be retained, the relationship between the two parties can lead to conflict, and a disjointed network. Then, almost by definition, Sapulete et al. suggest that distrust in networks leads to lowered productivity, and must therefore be managed.

Organizations also struggle internally with the control issues related to networked organizing when hierarchical lines are blurred. This has frequently been shown to be the case when a network-like perspective is applied to the core of organizing. The flattening of hierarchical lines within organizations is frequently demonstrated in the cases of intrapreneurship, temporary teams, project organizations and so on (Dahlander and O'Mahony, 2010). The discussion by Fiolet (Chapter 9) on the changing patterns of activity in organizations reflects this need for exploration into new forms of organizing. Due to external changes in mission, Fiolet suggests that there is an increased need to really change from internal logics to demand-driven care. This new logic crosses the boundary between two forms of control: one derived from care demands, and the other from cost control. The process requires the development of trust relations, it is suggested, between different departments and disciplines in health-care organizations. Fiolet's research indicates that new organizational forms increasingly emerge as a consequence of a patchwork of solutions to the problems of organizations. Echoing prior contributions to this volume, Fiolet thus suggests that managerial responsibility requires some degree of control, but that the new services also require management control.

In both the research and management domain, networks are a key concept, enabling proper external positioning of the organization. Therefore external relations and positioning also become increasingly important to all organizations. Marketing tools are of increasing importance in finding audiences for both social and nonprofit organizations, as argued by Weinberg and Lee, in the last contribution to this volume (Chapter 10). Marketing, they suggest, can be described as establishing relations with new publics. And in order to succeed in marketing, trust is subsequently seen to be an essential ingredient. Thus for marketing to work effectively, the authors suggest that the organization needs to pay attention to building relationships with publics, and make clear the fact that networks are of broader importance. The growth in the number of nonprofit providers catering for the same social needs, they suggest, shows that networking with 'competitors' is essential for success.

REFERENCES

Baker, W.E. (1992), 'The network organization in theory and practice', in N. Nohria and R.G. Eccles (eds), *Networks and Organizations*, Boston, MA: Harvard Business School Press, pp. 397–429.

Dahlander, L. and S. O'Mahony (2010), 'Progressing to the center: coordinating project work', *Organization Science*, doi: 10.1287/orsc.1100.0571.

Powell, W.W. (1990), 'Neither market nor hierarchy – network forms of organization', *Research in Organizational Behavior*, **12**: 295–336.

8. The impact of works councils on productivity in times of reorganization

Saraï Sapulete, Arjen van Witteloostuijn, Annette van den Berg and Yolanda Grift[1]

1 INTRODUCTION

The traditional gap between management and workforce is considered by many to be a major internal boundary within organizations. One possible way to bridge this gap is through codetermination, although its effectiveness depends on several institutional and economic conditions (Engelen, 2000; Wigboldus et al., 2008). A good relationship between management and workforce is believed to enhance performance by means of boosting morale and motivation, which, in turn, stimulates higher productivity (Lazear, 1998). Indeed, there is some evidence, particularly for Germany, that a good relationship between management and works council is beneficial for organizational performance (van den Berg et al., 2011a, b). In the Dutch context, a good relationship between management and workforce can be established through a works council, as embedded in Dutch corporate law.

Codetermination is defined as the right of employees to participate in the decision-making processes of an organization. It can take different forms in organizations, mostly depending on the culture and law of the country at hand. We study the effect of codetermination by analyzing data on Dutch works councils. Works councils in the Netherlands, similar to in Germany, have a large number of far-reaching legal rights, compared to other countries (van den Berg et al., 2011a). Dutch works councils have the right to be informed on all relevant matters in order to carry out their legal tasks optimally. Furthermore, they have the right to give advice on a large number of strategic decisions, irrespective of whether or not the direct interests of the employees are at stake (van het Kaar, 2008). In addition, they have the right of initiative – that is, to come up with ideas on how to improve organizational matters.

The most far-reaching power is the right of consent, which is the right to agree or disagree, on social matters (van den Berg, 2004). Typical for the Dutch case is the dualistic task of the works council, who have to operate not only in the interests of the employees, but also in the interest of the organization as a whole. The task of negotiating on terms of employment is usually performed by the trade unions, and *not* by works councils, through collective labor agreements at the sector and/or national level (ibid.). In this way, the likelihood that conflicts of interest for works councils arise is substantially reduced, increasing the chance that the works council is able to fulfill its dualistic task properly.

In the present study, we are interested in the way in which works councils can reduce the gap between management and employees, thereby blurring a critical boundary *within* the organization, rather than boundaries across organizations. It is in this sense that this chapter fits with this book's theme. We argue that this is especially important in times of reorganization, because such times typically provide the conditions in which the works council can exercise its rights to the fullest, potentially, by seeking to represent the interests of both the employees and the organization as a whole. However, van den Berg et al. (2011b) argue that works councils may work well in good times, but are put to the test in bad times. Our aim is to gain insights into the role of codetermination in times of reorganization to see whether or not works councils are able in such circumstances to serve the interests of both employees *and* the organization as a whole. Specifically, the central question in this study is: can codetermination help to enhance the effectiveness of reorganizations and, in doing so, contribute to increasing organizational productivity?

It is important to look into this question because the evidence as to the effect of codetermination on organizational performance is still mixed. Hence, further work in this area is badly needed, as this is instrumental in pinning down the conditions under which works councils can function optimally. Here, reorganizations offer a particularly demanding context. On the one hand, they might be necessary to safeguard the successful continuation of organizations. On the other hand, reorganizations tend to threaten the position of (a subset of) the employees. If we are able to gain more insights into the role of codetermination in reorganizations, beneficial or harmful for employees and/or the organization as a whole, we can formulate practical implications for organizations undergoing or planning reorganizations.

Of course, research on the effect of reorganization on organizational performance has been done before, extensively (Janod and Saint-Martin, 2004), as has research on the direct relationship between codetermination and organizational performance (Addison et al., 2001). However, the role of codetermination in reorganizations has barely been studied, apart from in a few case studies such as Haipeter (2006). With the current study, we aim to contribute to the literature on codetermination by analyzing a large Dutch dataset that includes information that can help to provide insights into the role of works councils in times of reorganizations.

This chapter is organized as follows. Section 2 presents the conceptual model and develops three hypotheses, based on prior work. In Section 3, the data and method used to test the hypotheses are discussed, followed by a report of the empirical results in Section 4. The final section is a discussion.

2   PRIOR WORK AND CONCEPTUAL MODEL

Since the 1990s, economists have conducted research into the (likely) effects of codetermination. Because worker participation is predominantly a European phenomenon, most studies focus on the impact of works councils. Virtually all theoretical studies are influenced by the seminal work by Freeman and Lazear (1995), who demonstrate in an abstract way that the legal rights of works councils can improve communication and enhance trust, thereby contributing to organizational performance. In the corporate governance literature, which is still dominated by the Anglo-Saxon perspective, hardly any attention is given to the potentially beneficial role of worker codetermination. A notable exception is the edited work by Blair and Roe (1999: 1–2), who argue that 'human capital is often as important as physical capital in creating value', followed by a range of arguments as to why employee involvement can improve corporate decision making. In the same tradition, Goodijk (2000) is a strong supporter of a stakeholder model, in which there is ample room for worker codetermination.

Previous empirical research relating codetermination to organizational performance generated mixed evidence. Addison et al. (2001) find positive effects on productivity, but negative effects on profitability. Wever (1994) compares five cases and reports that, overall, works councils can make effective strategic choices and can serve management interests. Van den Berg et al. (2011a) reveal that a positive attitude of management toward the works council is associated with higher organizational performance. Hence, even though the results are mixed, implying lack of general consensus regarding the positive or negative effects of works councils in practice, quite a few studies provide evidence as to the importance of works councils for organizational performance in several areas, indicating a possible role for works councils in blurring employee–employer boundaries within organizations.

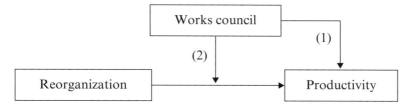

Figure 8.1   Conceptual model of the effect of codetermination on productivity

We focus on two effects of works councils in bridging the gap between employees and management: a direct and a moderating effect on the relation between reorganization and productivity. The conceptual model in Figure 8.1 visualizes these effects, where the direct effect is represented by Path 1 and the indirect effect by Path 2.

The Direct Effect of Codetermination (Path 1)

The role of codetermination can be studied in the light of institutional theory. Institutions are 'systems of hierarchical, man-made rules that structure behavior and social interaction' (Groenewegen et al., 2010: 25). A works council can be perceived as an institution, being a formal body that has legal rights to structure behavior and social interaction within organizations. Van den Berg (2004) argues that codetermination can lead to an efficient governance structure by diminishing the agency cost caused by information asymmetry and transaction-specific investment. She states that managers and employees are involved in an agency relationship, with the danger that employees might not perform entirely in the interest of the organization. Due to information asymmetry, workers can choose to shirk. Furthermore, transaction-specific investments arise, for example, when an employee has knowledge that can only be used in the organization s/he works for, limiting job-switching opportunities. This is also known as 'hold-up' (Groenewegen et al., 2010).

On the one hand, giving employees a say in decision-making processes may encourage them to behave more cooperatively, and consequently not act opportunistically, but rather in the interest of the organization as a whole. Moreover, such codetermination may give employees the feeling that they have control over their jobs, leading to less reluctance to engage in transaction-specific investments. Granting employees codetermination rights creates mutual trust (van den Berg et al., 2011b), which brings employees and management closer to each other, diminishing the boundaries between them. This is confirmed by the study of Kato and Morishima

(2002), who find that by goal alignment of employees and management via information provision, such that asymmetry is reduced and loyalty is enhanced, organizational productivity is improved.

On the other hand, codetermination can be perceived as costly. For example, when managers regard codetermination as slowing down the decision-making process, the institution of a works council might not add to the organization's productivity. However, managers may be wrong here, as faster and one-sided decision making does not necessarily lead to higher productivity than a somewhat slower but more balanced decision-making process. For example, van den Berg et al. (2011b) find that, in good times, delaying the decision-making process might even be beneficial for organizational performance, because the works council can then take time to follow a more careful procedure that leads to a more balanced decision. Similarly, Engelen (2000) argues that works councils, due to their contribution to more careful decision making, can have a positive effect on the efficiency of their organizations.

In all, these arguments indicate that a works council may well generate a positive effect on organizational productivity. This gives:

Hypothesis 1:   Organizations with a works council are more productive than organizations without a works council.

The Moderating Effect of Codetermination (Path 2)

The direct effect of codetermination on organizational productivity is not unconditional, as implied by Hypothesis 1. For instance, in times of reorganization, conflicting interests may arise. On the one hand, management may want to reorganize to achieve higher performance, even though this might be at the cost of jobs or come with wage cuts. On the other hand, employees will most likely want to maintain the organization's workforce with reasonable terms of employment. Given this conflict of interests, the question is whether works councils are able to bring both parties nearer to each other to support the reorganization on the basis of good communication and mutual trust. For both parties, in the end, emerging out of the reorganization process as advantageously as possible is critical. In order to do that, works councils may decide to support the reorganization optimally so as to generate the best result for management as well as for employees. If negative effects of the reorganization for employees are inevitable, and also seen as such in the eyes of the works council, then the role of the works council may become one of creating acceptance among employees (Lazear, 1998).

The right implementation of reorganizations is one of the most important elements needed to make reorganizations work. As Sorge and van

Witteloostuijn (2004: 1221) argue: 'An effective implementation of a second-best strategy produces higher performance than the inferior execution of a brilliant first-best strategy'. We believe that successful implementation can be enhanced by involving employees in the reorganization process. We expect a works council to support organizational changes in an efficient way, because the works council knows what happens on the shop floor and accordingly might provide useful ideas for improvement. In addition to the important role that works councils may play in the implementation process of reorganizations, they can also generate an understanding among employees as to the possible negative consequences, which is instrumental in adequately dealing with such downsides (for example, Wigboldus et al., 2008). This argument is supported by the findings of DiFonzo and Bordia (1999), who show that communication is extremely important in processes of organizational change, because poor communication can lead to rumors and a negative atmosphere, which are, in turn, bad for organizational productivity. If employees are being kept informed and if the reorganization's rationale is communicated convincingly, their willingness to give up some of their interests for the greater interest of the organization as a whole might well increase (Lazear, 1998; van den Berg, 2004).

Not surprisingly, reorganization is often interpreted as a negative and threatening event, being associated with layoffs of and changes for employees. However, reorganization can be positive as well as negative, since organizational change destroys and creates at the same time (Biggart, 1977). Negative associations with reorganizations can lead to ineffectiveness and instability. For example, Sorge and van Witteloostuijn (2004) argue that downsizing often generates ineffective – if not downright counterproductive – results. They suggest that this might be due to ill-directed or improperly implemented reorganizing processes. Their paper mainly emphasizes why reorganizations often tend not to be effective. Positive associations with reorganizations are mostly related to labor productivity: work reorganization is argued to generate improved performance due to more efficient use of labor and capital (Bertschek and Kaiser, 2004; Janod and Saint-Martin, 2004). Codetermination is an important aspect in this process, because a works council can fulfill the mediating role between management and employees. Ultimately, after all, the (remaining) employees are the people who must enhance higher productivity.

Of course, there is no clear black-or-white distinction between negative and positive reorganizations, even more so because such associations depend on whose point of view is considered. We distinguish two types of reorganizations: those with layoffs and those without layoffs. Because employees' constructive involvement is believed to improve the chances of success of reorganization processes, we expect organizations that reorganize without layoffs to have a higher likelihood of leading to effective reorganization. As a consequence of this effectiveness, we expect these reorganizations to be beneficial for organizational productivity. This is also implied by the study of Janod and Saint-Martin (2004), who find a positive effect of reorganization on organizational performance because labor and capital are employed more efficiently. Furthermore, the case study by Wigboldus et al. (2008) shows that the increased acceptance the works council generates for necessary relocations, contributes to higher productivity. However, this may work out very differently in the context of reorganizations that involve layoffs. Cascio and Wynn (2004) find that the organizational performance impact of employment downsizing is negative. Zwick (2002) reports that when reorganizations endanger employees' jobs, employees are more resistant. We add to this argument the expectation that a works council can hamper this effect by creating acceptance and trust (Lazear, 1998). This gives:

Hypothesis 2:　The positive effect of reorganization without *layoffs on productivity is reinforced when a works council is present.*

Hypothesis 3:　The negative effect of reorganization with *layoffs on productivity is hampered when a works council is present.*

3　METHODS

Data and Measures

We use data from the Labour Demand Panel of the SCP (Sociaal Cultureel Planbureau, The Netherlands Institute for Social Research). These data have formerly been gathered by OSA (Organisatie voor Strategisch Arbeidsmarktonderzoek, or Institute for Labour Studies) from 1991 onwards, interviewing samples of organizations every two years by means of a face-to-face interview and a written questionnaire. In the current study, we use two of the available waves with relevant information on works councils, namely those of 1999 and 2001. In other waves, regrettably, the organizations have not been asked whether they had a works council or not (before 1999, with the exception of 1993, and after 2001). We focus on the private sector, thus leaving out organizations from the nonprofit sector, given the nature of our dependent variable: organizational performance in terms of productivity.

Table 8.1 reports the descriptive statistics for the variables used in the analyses, and Tables 8.2 and 8.3 show the correlations between these variables. Our dependent variable is organizational performance in terms of *Productivity*. We construct this variable by dividing annual revenues by the total office hours in the same year, subsequently taking the log of this ratio to generate a less skewed distribution. We divide annual revenues by total office hours, because this gives a better productivity indicator than dividing annual revenues by number of employees. The latter would not control for part-time versus full-time employees, so we cannot be sure about productivity per employee. With respect to the current measure, total annual office hours are aggregated over all employees, implying that their full-time or part-time status is accounted for. Our productivity variable ranges from 7.39 to 19.01 in 1999, and from 7.47 to 18.52 in 2001.

Our first independent variable is codetermination as measured by the presence of a *Works council*. In Dutch organizations, codetermination is mostly arranged by establishing a works council. By law, organizations should have a works council when they employ 50 or more people. Organizations with fewer than 50 employees can decide to voluntarily install a works council. Our second and third hypotheses relate to reorganization, which is measured by two dummies reflecting reorganization with and without layoffs. The OSA data include downsizing (with and without layoffs), reassigning employees, schooling employees, and hiring more personnel as indicators of reorganization. We sum up the four variables that refer to *Reorganization without layoffs* and code them as a no (0)–yes (1) dummy. We compare that to *Reorganization with layoffs*, which is a similar 0–1 dummy variable. Reorganizations with layoffs are not very frequent, either in 1999 or in 2001: only 4 percent of the organizations indicate that they engaged in these kinds of reorganization. The percentage of reorganizations without layoffs is much higher, with 20 percent in 1999 and 26 percent in 2001. These measures refer to reorganizations in the two years before the interview/questionnaire took place. So, by construction of the measures, our reorganization variables are lagged, implying that reciprocal causality – from productivity to reorganization – is not an issue in our dataset. To estimate the hypothesized *interaction* effects, we create two interaction dummies of the works council dummy with the different types of reorganization: *Layoffs*Works council* and *Without layoffs*Works council*.

With our set of control variables, we aim to filter out the impact of other factors that may be important alternative determinants of organizational productivity. The first *market* indicator is the *Change in price* in the previous two years, with four categories: no difference, increase, decrease and fluctuation. Most organizations have benefited from increasing prices in the

Table 8.1 Descriptive statistics for the 1999 and 2001 waves

Variables	1999					2001				
	N	Mean	SD	Min	Max	N	Mean	SD	Min	Max
Dependent variable										
Productivity	858	12.16	1.88	7.39	19.01	789	12.16	1.79	7.47	18.52
Independent variables										
Works council	858	0.34	0.48	0	1	789	0.40	0.49	0	1
Reorganization with layoffs	858	0.04	0.19	0	1	789	0.04	0.20	0	1
Reorganization without layoffs	858	0.20	0.40	0	1	789	0.26	0.44	0	1
Interaction terms										
Layoffs*Works council	858	0.02	0.15	0	1	789	0.02	0.15	0	1
Without layoffs*Works council	858	0.12	0.33	0	1	789	0.16	0.37	0	1
Market control variables										
Change in price	858					789				
0 – No difference	212	24.71				128	16.22			
1 – Increase	396	46.15				488	61.85			
2 – Decrease	60	6.99				25	3.17			
3 – Fluctuating	190	22.14				148	18.76			
Business cycle	858					789				
0 – No/hardly	158	18.41				214	27.12			
1 – Slightly	354	41.26				369	46.77			
2 – Yes/very	346	40.33				206	26.11			
Process control variables										
R&D	858	0.40	0.49	0	1	789	0.49	0.50	0	1
Outsourcing	858	0.25	0.43	0	1	789	0.29	0.45	0	1

Organizational control variables

	N	Mean	SD	Min	Max	N	Mean	SD	Min	Max
Size	858	139.91	393.84	5	5,500	789	176.19	515.72	5	5,600
Age	858	27.99	25.51	3	102	789	27.40	26.79	0	102
Subsidiary	858	0.41	0.49	0	1	789	0.47	0.50	0	1
Hierarchical levels	858	2.38	0.86	1	7	789	2.46	0.79	1	7
Percentage of managers	858	16.30	10.65	0	83.30	789	15.46	10.49	0.24	83.33
Industry	858					789				
1 – Industry and agriculture	330	38.46				308	39.04			
2 – Construction	130	15.15				125	15.84			
3 – Commercial, catering, repair	162	18.88				161	20.41			
4 – Transport	78	9.09				69	8.75			
5 – Business services	158	18.41				126	15.97			
Personnel control variables										
Staffing	858					789				
0 – Fitting staff	468	54.55				447	56.65			
1 – Understaffing	334	38.93				297	37.64			
2 – Overstaffing	56	6.53				45	5.70			
Performance pay	858	0.44	0.50	0	1	789	0.49	0.50	0	1
Works council missing	858	0.57	0.50	0	1	–	–	–	–	–
Dummies										
D-age = 102	858	0.03	0.17	0	1	789	0.03	0.18	0	1
D-size > 4,000	858	0.00	0.05	0	1	789	0.01	0.08	0	1
D-man > 65	858	0.00	0.07	0	1	789	0.00	0.05	0	1
Inverse Mills ratio										
Inverse Mills ratio	858	0.42	0.10	0.16	0.83	789	0.49	0.17	0.17	1.49

Table 8.2   Pearson correlations for the 1999 wave

	1	2	3	4	5	6	7	8
1. Productivity	1.00							
2. R&D	0.23***	1.00						
3. Outsourcing	0.13***	0.13***	1.00					
4. Layoffs	0.11***	0.06*	0.12***	1.00				
5. Without layoffs	0.22***	0.18***	0.10***	0.31***	1.00			
6. Size	0.47***	0.22***	0.06*	0.02	0.22***	1.00		
7. Age	0.16***	−0.04	−0.00	−0.04	−0.05	0.11***	1.00	
8. Subsidiary	0.35***	0.12***	0.08***	0.07**	0.12***	0.12***	−0.05	1.00
9. Hierarchical levels	0.56***	0.23***	0.10***	0.04	0.21***	0.47***	0.10***	0.31***
10. Percentage managers	−0.28***	−0.14***	−0.05	−0.03	−0.06*	−0.18***	−0.06*	−0.22***
11. Performance pay	0.18***	0.06*	0.12***	0.00	0.08**	0.12***	−0.00	0.14***
12. Works council (WC)	0.63***	0.27***	0.11***	0.14***	0.29***	0.40***	0.13***	0.34***
13. WC missing	−0.65***	−0.23***	−0.10***	−0.12***	−0.26***	−0.37***	−0.14***	−0.35***
14. D-age	0.05	−0.03	−0.02	0.00	0.00	0.17***	0.50***	−0.02
15. D-size	0.09***	0.06*	−0.03	−0.10	0.04	0.63***	0.07**	0.01
16. D-man	−0.05	−0.02	−0.00	−0.01	0.10	−0.02	0.00	−0.06*
17. Layoff*WC	0.14***	0.09***	0.13***	0.81***	0.30***	0.05	−0.03	0.07**
18. Without layoff*WC	0.35***	0.21***	0.13***	0.31***	0.76***	0.33***	0.02	0.12***
19. Inverse Mills ratio	0.21***	0.19***	0.03	0.07**	0.14***	0.13***	0.02	0.39***

Note: ***$p < 0.01$, **$p < 0.05$ and *$p < 0.1$.

preceding two years (46 percent in 1999 and 62 percent in 2001). A fluctuating price signals a combination of two of the three the categories 'no differences', 'increase' and 'decrease' over the last two years: for example, a price decrease in 1997, but an increase in 1998. We expect an increase in price to

9	10	11	12	13	14	15	16	17	18
1.00									
−0.14***	1.00								
0.13***	−0.05	1.00							
0.56***	−0.34	0.10***	1.00						
−0.57***	0.42***	−0.13***	−0.83***	1.00					
0.05	−0.07**	−0.00	0.03	−0.04	1.00				
0.15***	−0.03	0.05	0.07**	−0.06	0.14***	1.00			
−0.03	0.40***	0.01	−0.05	0.06*	−0.01	−0.00	1.00		
0.08**	−0.06*	0.03	0.22***	−0.18***	−0.03	−0.01	−0.01	1.00	
0.31***	−0.18***	0.08**	0.51***	−0.43***	0.02	0.06	−0.03	0.40***	1.00
0.30***	−0.16***	0.00	0.40***	−0.34***	0.01	−0.05	−0.05	0.09***	0.21***

be positively related to productivity and price decrease or fluctuation to be negatively related to productivity. The second market indicator is sensitivity to *Business cycles*, for which three categories are distinguished: no/hardly, slightly, yes/very. In 1999, most organizations are slightly or very sensitive

Table 8.3   Pearson correlations for the 2001 wave

	1	2	3	4	5	6	7	8
1. Productivity	1.00							
2. R&D	0.32***	1.00						
3. Outsourcing	0.07*	0.10***	1.00					
4. Lay-offs	0.10**	0.04	0.08**	1.00				
5. Without layoffs	0.29***	0.22***	0.12***	0.26***	1.00			
6. Size	0.40***	0.19***	0.07*	0.01	0.30***	1.00		
7. Age	0.15***	0.06*	0.08**	0.08**	−0.07**	−0.02	1.00	
8. Subsidiary	0.34***	0.15***	−0.06*	0.04	0.10***	0.13***	0.01	1.00
9. Hierarchical levels	0.44***	0.23***	0.06*	0.06*	0.18***	0.35***	0.06*	0.25***
10. Percentage managers	−0.30***	−0.12***	−0.04	−0.02	−0.19***	−0.23***	−0.08**	−0.20***
11. Performance pay	0.17***	0.10***	0.09***	0.01	0.12***	0.13***	−0.03	0.11***
12. Works council (WC)	0.57***	0.19***	−0.02	0.08**	0.29***	0.35***	0.08**	0.41***
13. D-age	0.12***	0.02	0.01	0.11***	−0.02	−0.00	0.50***	0.08**
14. D-size	0.18***	0.08**	0.02	−0.02	0.14***	0.74***	−0.05	0.02
15. D-man	−0.04	0.00	−0.03	−0.01	−0.03	−0.02	−0.03	−0.05
16. Lay-off*WC	0.16***	0.09***	0.06*	0.76***	0.23***	0.04	0.08**	0.10***
17. Without lay-off*WC	0.42***	0.21***	0.06*	0.20***	0.75***	0.43***	−0.03	0.22***
18. Inverse Mills ratio	0.19***	0.09***	−0.06*	0.03	0.07**	0.31***	0.01	0.51***

Note: ***$p < 0.01$, **$p < 0.05$ and *$p < 0.1$.

to the business cycle (41 and 40 percent, respectively). In 2001, most organizations are slightly business cycle sensitive (47 percent). We expect that organizations that are sensitive to business cycles are associated with higher productivity than organizations that are not so sensitive, because the former need to be more flexible to quickly adjust to business cycle movements.

Two *process* indicators relate to research and development (R&D) and

9	10	11	12	13	14	15	16	17
1.00								
−0.15***	1.00							
0.10***	−0.00	1.00						
0.47***	−0.36***	0.06*	1.00					
0.04	−0.06*	0.01	0.04	1.00				
0.13***	−0.06*	0.08**	0.10***	−0.01	1.00			
−0.02	0.32***	0.00	−0.04	−0.01	−0.00	1.00		
0.08**	−0.06*	0.00	0.19***	0.11***	−0.01	−0.01	1.00	
0.28***	−0.27***	0.15***	0.54***	−0.00	0.18***	−0.02	0.31***	1.00
0.21***	−0.24***	0.05	0.34***	0.00	0.21***	−0.02	0.05	0.19***

outsourcing. *R&D* is measured by the question whether the organization had R&D activities in the previous year, and is included as a no (0)–yes (1) dummy variable. Of the organizations in 1999, 40 percent have R&D activities; in 2001, 49 percent. We expect R&D to have a positive effect on productivity. *Outsourcing* is measured by a dummy, indicating whether the organization currently outsources tasks that it performed internally two years earlier (1) or not (0). In 1999, 25 percent of the organizations engaged in outsourcing tasks; in 2001, 29 percent. We expect this variable to be positively related to organizational productivity.

We also control for a number of *organizational* characteristics. We control for the employment *Size* of the organization, because larger organizations tend to have higher revenues and, due to scale economies, may have higher productivity. The mean size in 1999 is 140 and in 2001, 176. We include organizational *Age*. This variable ranges from 3 to 102 in 1999, and from 0 to 102 in 2001. The maximum value is 102, as all organizations established in 1900 and before receive the value of 102. Organizational age is believed to have a positive effect on performance, because organizations become more reliable and accountable as they grow older (Hannan and Freeman, 1984). We add a variable *Subsidiary* to indicate whether the organization is part of a larger organization (1) or not (0). Following van den Berg et al. (2011b), we expect subsidiaries to have lower performance than non-subsidiaries: 41 percent of the organizations are part of a larger organization in 1999, and 47 percent in 2001.

We include two variables to measure the degree of hierarchy in an organization: the number of *Hierarchical levels* and the *Percentage of managers* present in the organization. More hierarchical levels in organizations are associated with loss of control, and are therefore considered to be harmful for performance (Williamson, 1967). Hazeu (2007) argues that the more hierarchical layers, the harder it is to judge employee activities, and the higher is the chance of shirking behavior, implying lower productivity. Zwick (2004) finds that productivity might be enhanced by flattening the hierarchy, because in so doing labor costs of redundant middle managers can be avoided. Moreover, for the functioning of works councils, hierarchy might not be beneficial. For example, the manager interviewed in the case study by Romme and van Witteloostuijn (1999) believes that a hierarchical structure, where power and authority only flow in one direction, is not the right one to make employee participation work. Therefore, in testing the effects of codetermination and reorganization, we control for the hierarchical structure of the organization. In 1999, the average number of hierarchical levels is 2.4 with 16 percent managers. In 2001, these averages are 2.5 and 15, respectively.

The fifth organizational characteristic we control for is *Industry*. Industries differ in characteristics and, accordingly, in their performance. It is likely that cross-industry variation in terms of codetermination and reorganization activities is substantial as well. This variable is related to five industries in the private sector, based on standard codes of the CBS (the Dutch Central Bureau of Statistics), and is added to the analysis in the form of dummy variables. Our sample is quite representative for the

Dutch private sector population, although 'transport' is slightly over-represented while 'commercial, catering and repair' is slightly underrepresented in our sample.

To control for *personnel* characteristics, we include staffing, performance pay and works council information. *Staffing* is measured by three categories: fitting, understaffing and overstaffing. In 1999 and 2001, most organizations have a fitting staff, but 39 percent report understaffing in 1999. In 2001, this is marginally reduced to 38 percent. Indeed, in this time period, the Dutch labor market was very tight. We expect that overstaffing is negatively related to productivity. *Performance pay* indicates whether (1) or not (0) the organization adopts performance-related wages. We expect that performance pay will increase organizational productivity. In 1999, 44 percent of the sampled organizations used a form of performance pay; in 2001, 49 percent did so.

For 1999, Table 8.1 shows that 34 percent of the organizations in the sample operated a works council; in 2001, 40 percent did so. These seem to be quite low percentages in view of the fact that about 78 percent of all organizations in the Netherlands had a works council at the beginning of the twentieth century (Van der Veen et al., 2002). This high percentage, however, refers to organizations that employ 50 or more employees, and thus are obliged by law to have installed a works council. Moreover, the compliance to the works council act increases with organizational size: larger organizations tend to have a higher compliance rate (up to 95 percent for organizations with more than 200 employees), while the smaller ones only score around 18 percent, on average (ibid.). This is confirmed by the percentages in our sample: the 40 percent of larger organizations have an average compliance rate of 85 percent, which for the smaller organizations is 60 percent.

Note that this difference may well be biased, though, because for a relatively high percentage of the smaller organizations the answer to the question about having a works council or not is not recorded in the 1999 wave. This is due to the fact that the OSA did not ask organizations with less than 35 employees whether they operated a works council or not. The total number of organizations in our sample that answered the works council question is 372, of which 80 percent report having a works council. This number is higher than the 34 percent in the variable we use. In order not to miss a large number of observations, we therefore decided to include the observations with missing values. They receive the 0 code of the no works council option. In the analyses, we control for this by including a dummy indicating whether this variable is missing or not. This is referred to as *Works council missing*. As can be seen in Table 8.1, about 57 percent of the participating organizations in 1999 did not have a record of whether or not they have a works council in place. In 2001, this record was always filled in, implying that this control variable is not included in the analyses for the 2001 wave.

We include three dummies to control for possible *outliers*. We do this for organizational size, creating *D-size* for organizations with 4,000 or more employees (two in 1999 and five in 2001). Similarly, we include *D-man* to control for extremely high percentages of managers. These are mostly found in organizations with very few employees. We include this dummy for organizations with more than 65 percent of managers (four in 1999 and two in 2001). Moreover, there are 25 organizations with a value of 102 for age. Because these organizations can be 102 or older, we include a dummy *D-age* to control for the possibly biased effect of the organizational age variable as a result of left censoring.

The data suffer from selectivity on the revenues measure, which we use to construct our dependent variable: *Productivity*. In 1999, 26 percent in our sample of organizations did not answer the question regarding revenues, and 32 percent did not do so in 2001. To control for selectivity, we perform a Heckman two-step analysis (Heckman, 1979). In the first step, we estimate a probit model, with a number of non-zero exclusion restrictions. The dependent variable is whether or not the question of revenues was answered. Subsequently, an *Inverse Mills ratio* is calculated and inserted into the regression of interest in the second step. If this term is significant, this indicates that we cannot reject the hypotheses of a selectivity effect in the dependent variable. Including this term controls for the selectivity bias that would otherwise have occurred. If the term is negatively significant, the coefficients would have been underestimated, and vice versa. Results of the probit analysis are available upon request.

We exclude a total of 20 outliers from the analyses: four for 1999, and 16 for 2001. The reason for this is that the associated data entries are suspicious. An example of this is organizations that indicate having no hierarchical levels at all in combination with a large percentage of managers. Another example relates to an organization that reports having 17 employees and 12 hierarchical levels. In 2001, in addition to cases with these kinds of suspicious data entries, we also exclude organizations that report implausibly low yearly revenues (ranging from 1 to 460 euros).

Data Analysis

We perform two hierarchical ordinary least squares (OLS) regression analyses (for the 1999 and the 2001 waves separately). In the first model, the direct effect of works councils on organizational performance (Path 1 in Figure 8.1) is analyzed. In the second model, the different types of reorganization are added. In the third model, the interactions between works council and the types of reorganization are added (Path 2 in Figure 8.1). We first analyze the model for the whole sample, and subsequently for two subsamples after splitting the sample into two subgroups – with organizations less than and more than 50 employees. We do this so as to see what the effects are in the group of organizations (less than 50 employees) that are not obliged by law to have a works council, implying that here operating a works council is done on a voluntary basis. In such cases, the effect of codetermination may be more pronounced. Note that the interaction terms have to be interpreted in combination with their constituent elements. If the separate coefficients (X and Z) and the interaction coefficient (XZ) are jointly significant, an interaction effect is indicated. Then, a positive coefficient would mean that the impact of reorganization on productivity is positive when a works council is present, and vice versa if the coefficient is negative.

The data suffer from attrition and selectivity over the years. OSA compensates for attrition by including new organizations in every new sample. However, taking the balanced panel over the years of organizations that stay in the sample is likely to be biased, since organizations that have poor organizational performance or do not survive over time are (likely to) have dropped out from the second data wave. OSA notes differences across industries in their participation rate over time: organizations in 'transport' have a lower chance of dropping out *vis-à-vis* all other industries. This is not the case for organizational size: large and small organizations have the same chance of dropping out of the sample over time (Bekker et al., 2003). The balanced panel that remains after attrition gives only 247 observations. Furthermore, the Hausman specification test indicates that we cannot perform a random effects panel analysis. Over time, only six of these 247 organizations change on the works council variable, which is not very surprising in the Dutch context. Thus, a fixed effects panel analysis, in our opinion, would not be appropriate. We performed a Chow test to find out whether we can pool the two data waves. The Chow test indicates that the data cannot be pooled, because the year waves differ too much from each other. Heteroskedasticity is an issue. We therefore include robust standard errors. Furthermore, to check for multicollinearity, we calculate variance inflation factors (VIFs). As none of the bivariate correlation coefficients is above 0.7 and since none of the VIF scores is above 10, the data do not suffer from multicollinearity.

4   RESULTS

Tables 8.4 and 8.5 report the results for both regressions, for the 1999 and 2001 waves separately. In both tables, Models 1 to 3 relate to the whole sample, Models 4 to 6 to the group of organizations with fewer than 50 employees, and Models 7 to 9 to the group of organizations with more than 50 employees. To start with, we are interested in the direct effect of works councils on organizational productivity. In Table 8.4, we can see that there is a positive effect of works councils on organizational productivity: the productivity of organizations with a works council is, on average, 66 percent higher than that of organizations without a works council. In 2001, this effect is even larger, with an average 135 percent higher productivity for organizations with *vis-à-vis* those without works councils. Looking at the group of organizations with fewer than 50 employees, we see that there is no effect of works councils in 1999, but the 2001 coefficients are significant. In 2001, organizations with a works council are associated with, on average, 40 percent higher productivity than their counterparts without a works council. In Model 7, for both years, we can observe that works council presence has a positive direct effect of 63 percent in 1999 and 80 percent in 2001. These results are perfectly in line with our first hypothesis.

The main effect of reorganization shows that reorganizations with layoffs have a positive effect in 1999, even though the effect is only marginally significant. In 2001, reorganizations without layoffs reveal a positive effect. The effect in 1999 is against our expectations, because we argued that reorganizations with layoffs would harm organizational productivity. In addition to the direct effect, we are interested in the moderating effect of works councils on the relationship between reorganization and organizational productivity. We find no significant interaction effects in the analyses for the whole sample. However, if we look at the effects in the group with organizations that employ fewer than 50 employees, we see that in both 1999 and 2001 there are significant interaction effects. In 2001, we find a significant interaction effect between reorganization without layoffs and works council involvement. This effect is represented in Figure 8.2. In reorganizations without layoffs, the works councils' role tends to be positive. In these kinds of reorganization, works councils can positively add to organizational productivity, as hypothesized. Contrary to our expectation, the impact of involvement of the works council in reorganizations with layoffs is significantly negative in 1999 and in 2001. When this type of reorganization occurs and the works council is involved, this tends to negatively affect organizational productivity. Figures 8.3 and 8.4 show these interaction effects. Our second hypothesis is partly confirmed

Table 8.4   Explaining productivity for the 1999 wave

Variables	Model 1	Model 2	Model 3	Model 4	Model 5	Model 6	Model 7	Model 8	Model 9
Independent variables									
Works council	0.657***	0.648***	0.696***	0.002	−0.002	0.135	0.626***	0.623***	0.585**
	(0.166)	(0.166)	(0.177)	(0.343)	(0.345)	(0.384)	(0.197)	(0.198)	(0.234)
Layoffs		0.437*	0.681		0.208	0.514		0.494*	1.020*
		(0.254)	(0.437)		(0.362)	(0.345)		(0.291)	(0.519)
Without layoffs		−0.096	−0.014		−0.078	−0.072		−0.171	−0.466
		(0.114)	(0.148)		(0.141)	(0.144)		(0.171)	(0.449)
Interactions									
Layoffs*WC			−0.341			−1.925**			−0.550
			(0.530)			(0.935)			(0.570)
Without layoffs*WC			−0.154			0.170			0.324
			(0.222)			(0.602)			(0.479)
Market									
Change in price									
1 – Increase	0.074	0.064	0.059	−0.040	−0.044	−0.061	0.360*	0.348*	0.350*
	(0.119)	(0.119)	(0.119)	(0.145)	(0.145)	(0.146)	(0.194)	(0.193)	(0.194)
2 – Decrease	0.340**	0.322*	0.338*	0.561***	0.568***	0.571***	0.190	0.160	0.159
	(0.172)	(0.175)	(0.177)	(0.194)	(0.194)	(0.194)	(0.271)	(0.284)	(0.284)
3 – Fluctuating	−0.401***	−0.389***	−0.389***	−0.643***	−0.638***	−0.637***	−0.313	−0.281	−0.277
	(0.146)	(0.147)	(0.147)	(0.170)	(0.172)	(0.172)	(0.234)	(0.237)	(0.239)

179

Table 8.4 (continued)

Variables	Model 1	Model 2	Model 3	Model 4	Model 5	Model 6	Model 7	Model 8	Model 9
Business cycle									
1 – Slightly	0.145	0.151	0.148	0.227*	0.227*	0.232*	−0.127	−0.102	−0.095
	(0.118)	(0.117)	(0.118)	(0.127)	(0.128)	(0.128)	(0.234)	(0.229)	(0.228)
2 – Yes/very	0.199*	0.202*	0.198*	0.251*	0.250*	0.260**	−0.048	−0.025	−0.015
	(0.117)	(0.117)	(0.117)	(0.128)	(0.129)	(0.130)	(0.217)	(0.216)	(0.213)
Process									
R&D	0.062	0.066	0.065	−0.035	−0.027	−0.027	−0.075	−0.081	−0.091
	(0.097)	(0.097)	(0.097)	(0.121)	(0.123)	(0.123)	(0.161)	(0.162)	(0.165)
Outsourcing	0.141	0.127	0.134	−0.020	−0.020	−0.021	0.154	0.128	0.121
	(0.106)	(0.107)	(0.107)	(0.140)	(0.140)	(0.141)	(0.139)	(0.141)	(0.143)
Organization									
Size	0.001***	0.002***	0.002***	0.080***	0.080***	0.079***	0.002***	0.002***	0.002***
	(0.000)	(0.000)	(0.000)	(0.009)	(0.009)	(0.009)	(0.000)	(0.000)	(0.000)
Age	0.008***	0.008***	0.008***	0.005*	0.005*	0.006*	0.006**	0.006**	0.006**
	(0.002)	(0.002)	(0.002)	(0.003)	(0.003)	(0.003)	(0.003)	(0.003)	(0.003)
Subsidiary	0.730***	0.725***	0.715***	0.627***	0.631***	0.633***	0.672***	0.649***	0.649***
	(0.109)	(0.109)	(0.108)	(0.140)	(0.139)	(0.139)	(0.164)	(0.163)	(0.164)
Hierarchical levels	0.331***	0.337***	0.335***	0.110	0.108	0.109	0.233**	0.248**	0.254**
	(0.066)	(0.066)	(0.066)	(0.091)	(0.091)	(0.091)	(0.099)	(0.098)	(0.101)
Percentage managers	−0.003	−0.003	−0.003	0.014***	0.014***	0.014***	0.008	0.007	0.008
	(0.005)	(0.005)	(0.005)	(0.005)	(0.005)	(0.005)	(0.010)	(0.010)	(0.011)
Industry (included)									

Personnel									
Staffing								
1 – Understaffing	0.091	0.102	0.100	0.037	0.038	0.039	0.062	0.094	0.103
	(0.095)	(0.096)	(0.096)	(0.116)	(0.117)	(0.117)	(0.153)	(0.156)	(0.154)
2 – Overstaffing	−0.278**	−0.296**	−0.302**	−0.352***	−0.365***	−0.357***	−0.258	−0.234	−0.235
	(0.126)	(0.128)	(0.129)	(0.131)	(0.137)	(0.137)	(0.222)	(0.221)	(0.222)
Performance pay	0.184**	0.190**	0.191**	0.097	0.099	0.100	0.390***	0.396***	0.402***
	(0.092)	(0.092)	(0.092)	(0.116)	(0.116)	(0.116)	(0.145)	(0.147)	(0.151)
Dummies								
D-age > 102	−0.720***	−0.735***	−0.751***	−0.654**	−0.664**	−0.705**	−0.659*	−0.667*	−0.673*
	(0.254)	(0.254)	(0.256)	(0.313)	(0.317)	(0.324)	(0.364)	(0.367)	(0.369)
D-size > 4000	−7.038***	−7.122***	−7.180***				−6.921***	−7.051***	−7.005***
	(0.888)	(0.903)	(0.918)				(0.908)	(0.937)	(0.941)
D-man > 65	−0.058	−0.035	−0.029	−0.706	−0.700	−0.692			
	(0.478)	(0.487)	(0.479)	(0.624)	(0.631)	(0.636)			
Inverse Mills ratio								
Inverse Mills ratio	−4.968***	−4.914***	−4.930***	−7.295***	−7.273***	−7.356***	−3.625***	−3.503***	−3.517***
	(0.717)	(0.717)	(0.717)	(0.960)	(0.966)	(0.968)	(0.939)	(0.934)	(0.940)
Constant	13.14***	13.10***	13.10***	11.47***	11.46***	11.52***	12.89***	12.78***	12.79***
	(0.411)	(0.411)	(0.411)	(0.539)	(0.544)	(0.541)	(0.569)	(0.566)	(0.568)
Observations	858	858	858	532	532	532	326	326	326
R-squared	0.585	0.586	0.587	0.347	0.347	0.352	0.423	0.429	0.430

Note: Robust standard errors in parentheses; ***$p < 0.01$, **$p < 0.05$ and *$p < 0.1$.

Table 8.5 Explaining productivity for the 2001 wave

Variables	Model 1	Model 2	Model 3	Model 4	Model 5	Model 6	Model 7	Model 8	Model 9
Independent variables									
Works council	1.345***	1.296***	1.295***	0.397**	0.400**	0.305	0.803***	0.781***	0.853***
	(0.147)	(0.145)	(0.152)	(0.168)	(0.168)	(0.187)	(0.250)	(0.249)	(0.262)
Layoffs		0.270	0.237		-0.222	-0.128		0.430	1.304
		(0.253)	(0.365)		(0.209)	(0.223)		(0.321)	(1.335)
Without layoffs		0.278**	0.280**		0.090	0.010		0.095	0.214
		(0.110)	(0.142)		(0.135)	(0.143)		(0.157)	(0.540)
Interactions									
Layoffs*WC			0.057			-0.976**			-0.981
			(0.473)			(0.488)			(1.380)
Without layoffs*WC			-0.004			0.688*			-0.147
			(0.219)			(0.397)			(0.563)
Market									
Change in price									
1 – Increase	0.079	0.091	0.092	0.056	0.064	0.056	0.113	0.133	0.125
	(0.148)	(0.147)	(0.147)	(0.172)	(0.173)	(0.174)	(0.207)	(0.207)	(0.208)
2 – Decrease	-0.466	-0.468	-0.467	-1.022**	-1.018**	-1.071**	-0.192	-0.171	-0.156
	(0.391)	(0.388)	(0.390)	(0.473)	(0.472)	(0.476)	(0.498)	(0.505)	(0.504)
3 – Fluctuating	-0.034	-0.022	-0.021	-0.090	-0.078	-0.091	-0.097	-0.058	-0.060
	(0.184)	(0.183)	(0.182)	(0.218)	(0.220)	(0.219)	(0.273)	(0.273)	(0.272)

	(1)	(2)	(3)	(4)	(5)	(6)	(7)	(8)	(9)
Business cycle									
1 – Slightly	−0.055	−0.067	−0.066	−0.035	−0.038	−0.044	−0.039	−0.044	−0.057
	(0.106)	(0.106)	(0.106)	(0.118)	(0.120)	(0.121)	(0.181)	(0.181)	(0.180)
2 – Yes/very	0.038	0.013	0.012	−0.056	−0.056	−0.063	−0.033	−0.065	−0.063
	(0.126)	(0.126)	(0.126)	(0.127)	(0.127)	(0.127)	(0.219)	(0.221)	(0.220)
Process									
R&D	0.588***	0.559***	0.558***	0.318***	0.309***	0.326***	0.703***	0.691***	0.709***
	(0.105)	(0.105)	(0.105)	(0.114)	(0.114)	(0.114)	(0.166)	(0.164)	(0.165)
Outsourcing	0.087	0.054	0.054	0.075	0.071	0.078	0.089	0.067	0.068
	(0.107)	(0.108)	(0.109)	(0.122)	(0.123)	(0.124)	(0.159)	(0.162)	(0.162)
Organization									
Size	0.001***	0.001**	0.001**	0.046***	0.046***	0.047***	0.001**	0.001**	0.001**
	(0.000)	(0.000)	(0.000)	(0.005)	(0.005)	(0.005)	(0.000)	(0.000)	(0.000)
Age	0.005***	0.006***	0.006***	0.004*	0.004*	0.005*	0.004	0.004	0.004
	(0.002)	(0.002)	(0.002)	(0.002)	(0.002)	(0.002)	(0.003)	(0.003)	(0.003)
Subsidiary	0.595***	0.601***	0.601***	0.863***	0.855***	0.851***	0.363*	0.353*	0.337*
	(0.125)	(0.124)	(0.125)	(0.147)	(0.149)	(0.149)	(0.188)	(0.187)	(0.189)
Hierarchical levels	0.242***	0.244***	0.244***	−0.011	−0.006	−0.006	−0.088	−0.076	−0.073
	(0.070)	(0.069)	(0.069)	(0.088)	(0.089)	(0.090)	(0.100)	(0.099)	(0.100)
Percentage managers	−0.018***	−0.018***	−0.018***	0.004	0.004	0.004	0.059***	0.058***	0.057***
	(0.006)	(0.006)	(0.006)	(0.006)	(0.006)	(0.006)	(0.015)	(0.015)	(0.015)
Industry (included)									

Table 8.5 (continued)

Variables	Model 1	Model 2	Model 3	Model 4	Model 5	Model 6	Model 7	Model 8	Model 9
Personnel Staffing									
1 – Understaffing	-0.102	-0.103	-0.103	0.083	0.083	0.076	-0.233	-0.227	-0.233
	(0.103)	(0.103)	(0.103)	(0.111)	(0.112)	(0.111)	(0.162)	(0.164)	(0.165)
2 – Overstaffing	-0.328*	-0.427**	-0.428**	-0.306**	-0.305*	-0.274*	-0.449*	-0.520*	-0.502*
	(0.169)	(0.173)	(0.174)	(0.151)	(0.160)	(0.162)	(0.261)	(0.268)	(0.271)
Performance pay	0.261***	0.247***	0.247***	0.081	0.080	0.065	0.434***	0.433***	0.423***
	(0.095)	(0.094)	(0.095)	(0.102)	(0.102)	(0.103)	(0.158)	(0.159)	(0.160)
Dummies									
D-age > 102	0.376	0.354	0.353	0.327	0.336	0.314	0.424	0.369	0.377
	(0.365)	(0.370)	(0.370)	(0.499)	(0.501)	(0.504)	(0.480)	(0.485)	(0.485)
D-size > 4000	-0.581	-0.403	-0.403				-0.104	-0.007	-0.012
	(1.443)	(1.451)	(1.459)				(1.449)	(1.456)	(1.458)
D-man > 65	0.769	0.786	0.786	0.109	0.122	0.057			
	(0.825)	(0.812)	(0.813)	(0.574)	(0.573)	(0.589)			
Inverse Mills ratio									
Inverse Mills ratio	-1.733***	-1.720***	-1.718***	-3.018***	-2.983***	-2.971***	-1.731***	-1.743***	-1.747***
	(0.427)	(0.426)	(0.425)	(0.543)	(0.548)	(0.550)	(0.575)	(0.571)	(0.567)
Constant	11.08***	11.04***	11.03***	11.01***	10.98***	10.97***	12.22***	12.18***	12.14***
	(0.307)	(0.308)	(0.309)	(0.354)	(0.362)	(0.362)	(0.511)	(0.517)	(0.524)
Observations	789	789	789	470	470	470	319	319	319
R-squared	0.481	0.487	0.487	0.327	0.328	0.332	0.372	0.378	0.380

Note: Robust standard errors in parentheses; ***$p < 0.01$, **$p < 0.05$ and *$p < 0.1$.

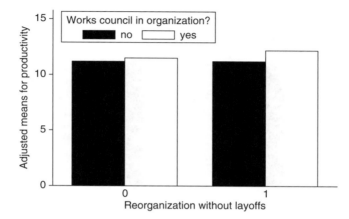

Figure 8.2   *Interaction effect* Without layoffs*Works council *for the 2001 wave*

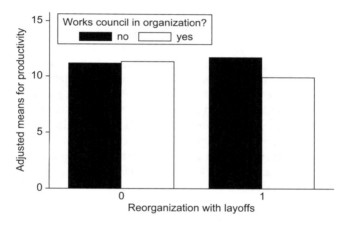

Figure 8.3   *Interaction effect* Layoffs*Works council *for the 1999 wave*

by these results, namely for small organizations in 2001, and our third hypothesis does not receive any support.

We control for a number of alternative explanations. In 1999, the market indicators prove significant: decreasing prices are good and fluctuating prices are bad for organizational productivity. Being sensitive to business cycles is positively related to organizational productivity. The process indicators are not significant with one exception: reorganization with layoffs, which positively impacts on organizational productivity. The organizational characteristics are almost all significant: organizational size

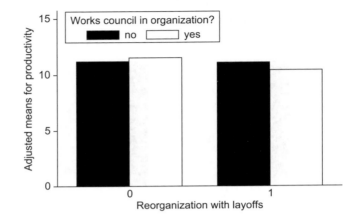

Figure 8.4   Interaction effect Layoffs*Works council *for the 2001 wave*

is positively related to organizational productivity, as is organizational age. Furthermore, there are differences between industries: 'construction' and 'transport' are less productive compared to 'industry and agriculture'. Being part of a larger organization has a positive effect on the organization's productivity, as has the number of hierarchical levels. The latter effects are contrary to what we expected. It might be that being part of a larger enterprise gives organizations more security: because they experience less risk as a result, they can enhance their productivity. Further, the positive effect of the number of hierarchical levels might indicate that organizational productivity increases because of more direct monitoring and supervision on the shop floor.

The personnel characteristics reveal that overstaffing tends to be bad for organizational productivity, whereas performance pay is positively related to the organization's productivity. Furthermore, a few of the control dummies are significant, namely those for extreme values of organizational age and size. These extreme values appear to be negatively related to organizational productivity. The inverse Mills ratio is significant and negative.

For 2001, the control variables show, in part, different patterns. The Chow test already indicated that both wave models differ too much to pool the data. This is confirmed by the different results for the two sets of model outcomes. In 2001, the market indicators are not significant. The process variables reveal that R&D improves organizational productivity. Furthermore, all organizational characteristics are significant, all in the same direction as in 1999. In 2001, contrary to in 1999, the percentage of managers is negatively significant. This is what we expected. However, again, the number of hierarchical levels is significant and positive. This indicates that more hierarchical levels tend to be good for organizational productivity, albeit in combination with a low number of managers. Moreover, the 'commercial' industry is more productive compared to the 'industry and agriculture' sector. The personnel indicators show that over-staffing tends to be bad and performance pay good for the organization's productivity. The dummies to control for extreme values are not significant. Again, the inverse Mills ratio is negatively significant.

5 DISCUSSION

The current study investigates the way in which works councils can narrow down the gap between management and employees and, in doing so, blur boundaries between different groups of actors *within* the organization. The question we aimed to answer is: can codetermination help to enhance effective reorganizations and, accordingly, help to boost organizational productivity? This study argues that codetermination is an important institution within organizations, which can help organizations to improve their productivity, even in times of reorganization. The process of reor-ganizational change can, in this way, be perceived as a process in which an organization can benefit from the involvement of a codetermination institution. Codetermination can either hamper the negative effects of reorganizations (particularly those involving layoffs), or even reinforce positive effects of reorganizations (particularly those without layoffs).

Our first hypothesis is supported: having a works council is associ-ated with direct positive effects on organizational productivity. That is, organizations with a works council have significantly higher productivity than organizations without one. This finding indicates that works councils are able to play a role in blurring boundaries between management and employees, by representing the interests of both parties. This confirms earlier findings of Addison et al. (2001) and Zwick (2004), who also found positive effects of works council presence on organizational productivity. Regarding reorganizations with *vis-à-vis* without layoffs, reorganizations appear to have a positive effect on organizational productivity. In 1999, this holds for reorganizations with layoffs; and in 2001, this is true for reorganizations without layoffs. We did not expect reorganizations with layoffs to show positive effects, as most research on reorganizations indi-cated negative effects on performance (Cascio and Wynn, 2004; Sorge and van Witteloostuijn, 2004). However, in the current study's sample, laying off people apparently gives a boost to efficiency, and hence to productiv-ity. What might explain this is the short-run nature of our performance measure. It may well be that the long-run impact of reorganizations, particularly in the case of organizations that engage in a string of these, will harm organizational performance. This is an interesting avenue for further work.

Interestingly, the results suggest that works councils play a significant role in reorganizations in smaller organizations, with fewer than 50 employees. In contrast, no interaction effects were found for organizations with more than 50 employees. This difference is noteworthy, because organizations employing fewer than 50 employees are legally free to choose whether or not to install a works council, while larger organizations are obliged by law to do so. Our findings indicate that in organizations in which works councils are voluntarily installed, they have a larger chance of making a difference, perhaps because both management and employees in these organizations believe that a works council adds value to the organization, making them more willing to invest in the council's effectiveness.

However, even though works councils potentially have an influential role to play in reorganizations, this influence is not always positive, contrary to what we expected. Specifically, the works council effect on productivity turns out to be positive in the context of reorganizations without layoffs. These results might be due to the fact that works councils facilitate the creation of a basis for understanding among the employees, so that reorganization can take place relatively smoothly. These results are in line with earlier case study work, showing that reorganizations can be beneficial for performance (Janod and Saint-Martin, 2004). In reorganizations with layoffs, however, involvement of the works council is associated with lower productivity. This might be due to a lack of adequate information provision, leading to a disrupted trust relation of management with employees. This process and the importance of communication have been revealed before in prior work (for example, Bastien, 1987; DiFonzo and Bordia, 1999). These case studies show that communication is one of the most important factors to facilitate the successful implementation of a reorganization such that it will not hamper productivity. One of the reasons why works council involvement can lead to negative results of a layoff-involving reorganization on productivity might be the works councils' legal obligation of secrecy. This can imply that the works council is informed in an early stage without being able to inform employees. This is a source of conflict and distrust later in the process.

Rumors in an organization might already spread the word of forthcoming layoffs, which may trigger a drop in morale and motivation to work (ibid.; Zwick, 2002). When employees suspect works council members of having the information without taking any counteraction, this might generate a lack of trust in the works council as well as in management. Employees might feel betrayed by both management and works council, both representing only organizational interests. Low morale and low motivation negatively affect productivity. Therefore, we believe that to let works councils play a constructive role in the process of reorganizing, they (and also management) should be able to communicate openly to employees at an early stage (for example, Bastien, 1987; DiFonzo and Bordia, 1999). To look into these processes and the important role of communication, we suggest future research that focuses on the study of the relations between management, employees and works council. This can be done, for example, by means of social network analysis.

A study such as ours is not without limitations. The first limitation relates to the fact that the current study's data indicated only whether a works council was present or not. This is a rather coarse-grained measure of codetermination. Moreover, this dummy measure may introduce a bias, because large organizations tend to have higher revenues *and* tend to have works councils more often than smaller organizations. Hence, the results have to be interpreted with caution. Therefore, it would be interesting to study the influence of different processual and structural characteristics of works councils, not only their presence. For example, the amount of influence a works council has in combination with the actual role this council plays in reorganizations are relevant.

A second limitation of this study is that data on smaller organizations concerning works councils were not gathered in 1999. These organizations would have been interesting to study, because they might have chosen to install a works council voluntarily. With this information, we would also have been able to perform analyses on the subgroup level. This offers another opportunity for future research, using a different (but to-be-collected) dataset. Furthermore, the number of organizations that had experienced a reorganization with layoffs in our sample is quite low. The interaction effects are thus based on only a small number of organizations. Data on later years, for example relating to the years of the global credit crisis (from 2007 onwards), could provide additional insights into the role of works councils in reorganizations with layoffs.

Furthermore, a third limitation is that the data suffer from attrition. Indeed, the Chow test reveals that pooling both waves of data is not allowed. This implies that we were not able to conduct panel analyses, but had to stick to separate sets of year-specific cross-section regressions (albeit including lagged reorganization variables). Future research could study longitudinal effects of works councils in the context of reorganization processes, to be able to unravel causal relationships, including measures of short *vis-à-vis* long-run organizational performance. Such an analysis could reveal whether the positive effect of codetermination on the relationship between reorganization and organizational performance persists over time.

NOTE

1. Annette van den Berg and Arjen van Witteloostuijn gratefully acknowledge the financial support of the Flemish government through the SBO program. We would like to thank the SCP (Sociaal Cultureel Planbureau, The Netherlands Institute for Social Research) for providing us with the data from their Labour Demand Panel. Furthermore, we would like to thank the participants of the PREBEM conference for their valuable comments.

REFERENCES

Addison, J.T., C. Schnabel and J. Wagner (2001), 'Works councils in Germany: their effects on establishment performance', *Oxford Economic Papers*, **53**, 659–64.

Bastien, D.T. (1987), 'Common patterns of behavior and communication in corporate mergers and acquisitions', *Human Resource Management*, **26** (1), 17–33.

Bekker, S., D. Fouarge, M. Kerkhofs, A. Román, M. De Voogd-Hamelink, T. Wilthagen and C. De Wolff (2003), *Trendrapport Vraag naar Arbeid 2002*, OSA (Organisatie voor Strategisch Arbeidsmarktonderzoek) (OSA) (Institute for Labour Studies), Tilburg University.

Bertschek, I. and U. Kaiser (2004), 'Productivity effects of organizational change: microeconometric evidence', *Management Science*, **50** (3), 394–404.

Biggart, N.W. (1977), 'The creative-destructive process of organizational change: the case of the post office', *Administrative Science Quarterly*, **22** (3), 410–26.

Blair, M.M. and M.J. Roe (eds) (1999), *Employees and Corporate Governance*, Washington, DC: Brookings Institution Press.

Cascio, W.F. and P. Wynn (2004), 'Managing a downsizing process', *Human Resource Management*, **43** (4), 425–36.

DiFonzo, N. and P. Bordia (1999), 'A tale of two corporations: managing uncertainty during organizational change', *Human Resource Management*, **37** (3–4), 295–303.

Engelen, E.R. (2000), 'Economisch burgerschap in de onderneming. Een oefening in concreet utopisme', Doctoral dissertation, Universiteit van Amsterdam.

Freeman, R.B. and E.P. Lazear (1995), 'An econometric analysis of works councils', in J. Rogers and W. Streeck (eds), *Works Councils: Consultation, Representation and Cooperation in Industrial Relations*, Chicago, IL: Chicago University Press, pp. 27–52.

Goodijk, R. (2000), 'Corporate governance and workers' participation', *Corporate Governance. An International Review*, **8** (4), 303–10.

Groenewegen, J., A. Spithoven and A. van den Berg (2010), *Institutional Economics: An Introduction*, Basingstoke: Palgrave Macmillan.

Haipeter, T. (2006), 'Recent developments in co-determination at Volkswagen: challenges and changes', *Journal of Industrial Relations*, **48** (4), 541–47.

Hannan, M.T. and J. Freeman (1984), 'Structural inertia and organizational change', *American Sociological Review*, **49**, 149–64.

Hazeu, C.A. (2007), *Institutionele Economie. Een Optiek op Organisatie-en Sturingsvraagstukken*, 2nd edn, Bussum: Coutinho.

Heckman, J.J. (1979), 'Sample selection bias as a specification error', *Econometrica*, **47** (1), 153–61.

Janod, V. and A. Saint-Martin (2004), 'Measuring the impact of work reorganization on firm performance: evidence from French manufacturing, 1995–1999', *Labour Economics*, **11**, 785–98.

Kato, T. and M. Morishima (2002), 'The productivity effects of participatory employment practices: evidence from new Japanese panel data', *Industrial Relations*, **41** (4), 487–520.

Lazear, E.P. (1998), *Personnel Economics for Managers*, New York: John Wiley & Sons.

Romme, A.G.L. and A. van Witteloostuijn (1999), 'Circular organizing and triple loop learning', *Journal of Organizational Change Management*, **12**, 439–53.

Sorge, A. and A. van Witteloostuijn (2004), 'The (non)sense of organizational change: an *essai* about universal management hypes, sick consultancy metaphors, and healthy organization theories', *Organization Studies*, **25** (7), 1205–31.

Van den Berg, A. (2004), 'The contribution of work representation to solving the governance structure problem', *Journal of Management and Governance*, **8** (2), 129–48.

Van den Berg, A., Y. Grift and A. van Witteloostuijn (2011a), 'Managerial perceptions of works councils' effectiveness in the Netherlands', *Industrial Relations*, **50** (3), 497–513.

Van den Berg, A., Y. Grift and A. van Witteloostuijn (2011b), 'Works councils and organizational performance. The role of top managers' and works councils' attitudes in bad *vis-à-vis* good times', *Journal of Labor Research*, **32** (2), 136–56.

Van der Veen, J., M. Engelen and M. van der Aalst (2002), *Naleving van de Wet op de Ondernemingsraden: Stand van zaken 2002, eindrapport*, Ministerie van Sociale Zaken en Werkgelegenheid.

Van het Kaar, R.H. (2008), *De Nederlandse medezeggenschap in een Europees perspectief. SER-Advies Evenwichtig Ondernemingsbestuur (Externe consultaties en (onderzoeks)rapportages)*, SER.

Wever, K.S. (1994), 'Learning from works councils: five unspectacular cases from Germany', *Industrial Relations: A Journal of Economy and Society*, **33** (4), 467–81.

Wigboldus, J.E., J.K. Looise and A. Nijhof (2008), 'Understanding the effects of works councils on organizational performance. A theoretical model and results from initial case studies from the Netherlands', *Management Review*, **19** (4), 307–23.

Williamson, O.E. (1967), 'Hierarchical control and optimum firm size', *Journal of Political Economy*, **75** (2), 123–38.

Zwick, T. (2002), 'Employee resistance against innovations', *International Journal of Manpower*, **23** (6), 542–52.

Zwick, T. (2004), 'Employee participation and productivity', *Labour Economics*, **11** (6), 715–40.

9. Corporate entrepreneurship in the non-profit sector: recombining resources to create social value

Maya Fiolet

1 INTRODUCTION

Non-profit organizations delivering public services are facing increasing upheaval, due to major changes in the social, political and institutional environment. These changes offer both opportunities and risks, thus fostering a rich environment for entrepreneurship. Entrepreneurs are poised to take advantage of the existing incongruities within the health care environment and are facing the challenge of how to transform their administrative focus by restructuring their companies into innovative organizations that can take advantage of opportunities. Corporate entrepreneurship is seen as a promising path to the future. It is well documented that entrepreneurship often fails because companies do not offer favourable organizational conditions for initiatives (Burgelman, 1983).

Research on strategic entrepreneurship, which is concerned with balancing the exploration of new opportunities and the exploitation of old certainties, is burgeoning in the profit sector (Birkinshaw, 1997; Hitt et al., 2001; Ireland et al., 2003; Luke and Verreynne, 2006; Covin and Miles, 2007). This research offers valuable insights into relevant organizational conditions; yet it has barely been explored in the non-profit sector. Entrepreneurial activities should be studied and understood in their context. Context provides resources and meaning to the entrepreneurial act. What is new or entrepreneurial is socially defined and constructed. Most studies in entrepreneurship have opted to measure only the extent of certain practices (for example, how many new products has the company introduced into the market over the past three years) rather then capturing the range of entrepreneurial variety. According to Zahra (2005), research is needed that relates the context to the variety of entrepreneurial activities being examined.

2 THEORETICAL BACKGROUND

Non-profit organizations are, by nature, situated between state, market and civil society (Alexander, 2000; Brandsen et al., 2006). New public management initiatives have changed the relations between government and non-profit organizations, and the entry of commercial providers leads not only to competition but also to cooperation between the public and the private sectors. To survive they must find ways to compete in markets that now often span all three sectors. Innovation enables non-profit organizations to anticipate and properly respond to these changes, and is essential for the improvement of public services (Klink, 2002; Toonen et al., 2003; Boekholdt, 2007). In all developed countries we see a restructuring of the health care sector (Saltman and Figueras, 1997; Van Der Grinten, 2004; Porter, 2006; De Gooijer, 2007). Discrepancies between consumer/client expectations and service delivery will produce opportunities.

Entrepreneurship is opportunity-seeking behaviour. The focus is on doing new things and departing from the customary. Key elements are: innovativeness, proactiveness and risk taking. Innovativeness refers to the seeking of creative, unusual or novel solutions to problems and needs. These solutions take the form of new processes as well as new products or services. Innovation is about new 'mean–ends' relationships (Shane and Venkataraman, 2000). It could be a completely new idea but also the introduction of (old) ideas that are new for the organization. Proactiveness is concerned with anticipating and then acting in the light of a recognized opportunity. It is acting on rather than reacting to. Risk taking involves the willingness to commit significant resources to opportunities having a reasonable chance of failure as well as success. Entrepreneurship can be defined as 'a process through which individuals, either on their own or inside established firms, pursue entrepreneurial opportunities to innovate without regard to the level and nature of currently available resources' (Ireland et al., 2006, p. 10).

The realization of entrepreneurship at various locations within the boundaries of the organization, rests on the premise that every individual in the organization has the potential to behave entrepreneurially. 'Initiative' is the key manifestation of entrepreneurship; it is a proactive undertaking that advances a new way for the organization to use or expand its resources (Kanter, 1982; Miller, 1983 in Birkinshaw, 1997). An initiative is essentially an entrepreneurial process that exists separately from the organization, mostly in the form of a project. This does not mean that they are not connected. Indeed, they are highly interdependent, sharing personnel, knowledge and capital. This is called a 'part–whole' relationship (Van De Ven, 1986) and is very relevant for us, as 'it indicates how the entrepreneurial activities of individuals combine to produce entrepreneurship at the level of the corporation, as well as how forces at the level of the corporation influence the entrepreneurial activities of these individuals' (Burgelman, 1983, p. 224).

The difficulties of entrepreneurial behaviour in existing organizations concern individuals who may explore and pursue opportunities in a corporate environment that is focused mainly on exploiting the existing resource combinations (Elfring, 2005). Initiatives face difficulties in being accepted into a hierarchical organization focused on exploitation. The administrative control system presents a hostile environment for uncertain and risky initiatives. Furthermore, the culture of large bureaucracies does not fit the needs of entrepreneurial individuals looking for creative ways to develop new ideas. They prefer the known static, bureaucratic model of service delivery.

Entrepreneurship often fails because companies do not offer favourable organizational conditions for initiatives (Burgelman, 1983). Organizations have to be able to achieve a balance between opportunity-seeking (exploration) and advantage-seeking (exploitation) behaviour (Hitt et al., 2001).

It is the task of management to shape the required organizational conditions, to create a work environment where all employees are encouraged and are willing to 'step up to the plate' to innovate in their jobs. Four critical elements are involved: structure, management support, resource availability and human resource management (Ireland et al., 2006):

- *Structure* Corporate entrepreneurship flourishes when an organization's structure has a restricted number of layers. This results in a broader span of control, which in turn creates opportunities for employees to act entrepreneurially. Authority and responsibility are decentralized and lateral interactions are encouraged.
- *Management support* The willingness of top-level managers to facilitate and promote entrepreneurial behaviour. Focus is on the future rather than the past, and the ability to develop and transfer knowledge is highly valued. Great importance is placed on being able to empower people in ways that allow them to act creatively, experiment and fulfil their potential.
- *Resource availability* Providing the resources (including time) people require to behave entrepreneurially. Controls promote and nurture entrepreneurial behaviour when they balance loose and tight properties. In this regard, controls are designed to strike a balance between encouraging individual action through flexible control and ensuring coordination, consistency, and accountability through tight control. Budgetary flexibility and slack resources are

Table 9.1   Organizational conditions

Element	Focus	Literature
Structure	Decentralization Broad span of control Open communication	Benner and Tushman, 2003; Gibson and Birkinshaw, 2004
Management support	Acceptance of uncertainty Promoting experimentation Tolerance of risk Focus on the future	Adler et al., 1999; Mom et al., 2007; Ireland et al., 2001
Resource availability	Formal/informal Rigid/flexible Tightness/slack	Ireland et al., 2006; Guth and Ginsberg, 1990
HRM	Appraisal and reward criteria Broad job description Process over task orientation Multiple career paths	Ireland and Webb, 2007

built into the firm's control system, providing room for experimentation. Strategic controls (which are concerned primarily with verifying that the firm is doing the right thing) are emphasized over financial controls (which are concerned primarily with verifying that the firm is doing things right).

- *Human resource management (HRM)*   The HRM system is a potent tool to encourage and reinforce entrepreneurial behaviour. Entrepreneurially friendly processes relate to recruiting, selecting, training and developing, and rewarding. Reward systems for corporate entrepreneurs should emphasize financial gains as well as formal recognition for their achievements.

Table 9.1 summarizes these organizational conditions.

3   METHODOLOGY

Process research is essential to gain insight into dynamic organization life and developing theories of entrepreneurship dynamics (Van De Ven and Engleman 2004). Process is seen here as 'a sequence of events or activities that describe how things change over time' (Van De Ven, 1992, p. 169). In the Netherlands, the long-term care for the elderly is traditionally provided by social organizations. These are private non-profit organizations that provide public services. The most striking feature of the non-profit organization is its mission to create social value for the public good rather than profit for shareholders (McDonald, 2007). Another important distinction lies in the different environmental dynamics, the environment being characterized by a different relation with (multiple) stakeholders and prominent political influence (Alexander, 2000; Morris et al., 2007). Research is needed on the influence of these factors on the process of entrepreneurship (Greenhalgh et al., 2004). The types of innovations produced warrant richer descriptions and categorizations (Morris et al., 2007).

We used theoretical sampling to select an organization involved in the long-term care for the elderly, because we wanted to be sure that the phenomenon under study, entrepreneurship, was indeed observable. We selected Vivium, an organization that was recommended by experts in the field as innovative and proactive. Similar to the studies of Burgelman (1983) and Birkinshaw (1997), the unit of analysis in this study is 'initiative'. A multiple-case study (Eisenhardt, 1989) was conducted because we are not so much interested in a single initiative as in the general pattern of a multitude of initiatives, allowing a comparative analysis.

Identification and selection of seven initiatives in the organization was based on the criteria innovation, risk taking and proactiveness, and done by studying relevant organization documents and interviewing all five top management personnel. The initiatives selected were at various stages of development: some had just started, while others were already completed. The combination of retrospective and real-time cases reduces researcher bias (Leonard-Barton, 1992). The research into the organization lasted approximately one year.

The first step after selecting the initiatives was to obtain baseline information for developing a retrospective case history of the context and events leading up to the present state of the initiative being investigated. We used project proposals, minutes of meetings, public relations material and so on. While the historical baseline was being developed, the real-time study began using a variety of data collection methods. A total of 25 interviews were held. Documentary and archive data (strategic plan, mission statement, HRM plan and so on) as well as observational material were also used in order to achieve triangulation. The topic of the semi-structured interviews was a specific initiative. Because in all instances various people were involved in any one initiative, there were always multiple key informants. For each initiative we spoke on average to three people.

One part of the interview concerned the content, goal, structure and results of the initiative and the people involved. The other part was about the supporting or constraining influences of the organizational factors on the specific initiative, and the environment and mission in general.

Initially the analysis focused on understanding each initiative separately. This within-case analysis familiarized us with the patterns of a single case, before we looked at patterns across cases. The second step was the cross-case analysis where the initiatives were compared with each other to detect general patterns and relate them to the various organizational conditions.

4   SELECTED ORGANIZATION

Vivium is a social organization that guarantees an acceptable quality of care. Its mission is to offer sustainable quality care and not to make a profit. Vivium is located in Gooi en Vechtstreek, a region in the western part of the Netherlands. The company runs a total of 11 nursing homes and homes for the elderly, and provides care at home, for a total of 1,322 residents and 2,441 employees (1,316 FTE, including care at home). Its organization comprises four working areas: Bussum, Huizen, Blaricum and Weesp. Our case study research takes place in Bussum, which has four nursing homes and homes for the elderly, providing residential care for 400 people. Bussum is considered to be Vivium's most entrepreneurial setup.

5   RESULTS

We start this section by describing Vivium's mission and the environment within which the organization operates, followed by a short description of the initiatives, summarized in Table 9.2. Subsequently we focus on the organizational conditions and the way they are influencing the initiatives.

Mission

Recently, the way in which service delivery takes place has been changing from supply to demand-driven care; the wishes of the client are the determining factor. This has led to a transformation in organization, way of working, competences and vision.

Vivium's ambition is to become an organization that fulfils the needs and wishes of elderly people by offering tailored arrangements that include living, care and well-being. An offer of services is made in close consultation with the client in order to suit personal wishes and circumstances. Such services have to remain within the range to which clients have a claim, and are determined by regulation and legislation. If the client is interested in services over and above those to which they have a claim, they have to pay for the extra service. Thus, Vivium offers both publicly and privately financed services. Furthermore, each employee is unique and has a personal motivation for working in the field of care for the elderly. Reconciling on the one hand the interests of client and employee, and on the other those of government and financier, is a constant challenge. The mission is therefore to be creative and caring.

The essence of the policy is demand-driven care, the starting point being the wishes of the client. With this as a basis, care and services are organized and offered. Furthermore, efficiency and productivity should be realized, which is only possible through product and process innovation. Therefore it is necessary that throughout the whole organization there should be a focus on awareness and creativity to stimulate entrepreneurial behaviour. The interests of the (vulnerable) client will always be paramount.

Environment

Vivium is located in a highly dynamic environment, where societal and political developments are occurring at a rapid pace. Increasingly, Vivium is facing uncertainty with respect to (future) regulation and legislation. The company's relationship with stakeholders (among whom are insurance companies, government and care partners) is subject to change. Moreover, the price/quality ratio is causing serious concern. Recent developments mean that Vivium has to prepare for:

- *Ageing of the population*   In the Bussum region the percentage of elderly people is increasing more than the average in the Netherlands. Planning estimates predict an increase of 25 per cent.
- *Individualization*   Clients take it for granted that the organization respects their individuality. In the near future standards for autonomy, privacy and quality will increase.
- *Change in financing*   In the new financing structure, organizations are no longer financed according to their capacity (number of beds) but by their performance, that is, services delivered to clients.
- *Labour market*   The average age of staff employed by Vivium is 46 years, and as such is relatively high. Attracting new personnel is very difficult because of the poor labour market.
- *Public/private financing*   Due to budget costs in health care, public-financed care is decreasing. This will lead to an increase of privately financed care.
- *Accountability and transparency*   The 'governance code' for health care is creating a demand for greater accountability and

transparency. This is also affecting the relationship with the various stakeholders.

Entrepreneurship is a context-dependent process. By describing the mission of the organization and the specific challenges in their environment, we have drawn a picture of the context in which the initiatives take place.

After providing a short description of each initiative in Table 9.2, we turn to (the influence of) the organizational conditions.

Structure

The organization's structure has only three layers – top management, middle management, and front-line employees – which results in a broader span of control. Top management includes a managing director who is responsible for all four locations, a facility manager also responsible for four locations, two care managers, each of whom is responsible for two locations and a quality manager responsible for the quality of all four locations. Each location has its own middle management and front-line employees.

Authority and responsibility are decentralized. The goal of the 'first-contact nurse' initiative is explicitly to delegate responsibility to those careworkers who have the closest contact with the clients. Demand-driven care begins with discovering and recording the wishes of the client. Assistant nurses have the most contact with the clients, so they should be responsible for this process.

Horizontal and lateral interactions and communication among employees are strongly encouraged. Top management has put much effort into stimulating cooperation – both between locations as well as within one location. Two years ago middle management meetings were instigated; three times a year all middle managers and top management come together to share knowledge and participate in discussions. These meetings improve the mutual cooperation between middle managers (of different locations) and reduce hierarchy: 'Because top management is always present and easily accessible, it is much easier to approach them throughout the year'.

The 'hostess' and 'place to eat/meet' initiatives are examples of initiatives that would not be possible without cooperation. In the former there is explicit cooperation between care and well-being, and in the latter between all three disciplines.

Table 9.2   Description of initiatives

Initiative	Description
Hostess	To successfully implement a new vision for psycho-geriatric clients, emotion-oriented care, a new function, that of 'hostess', has been created. The activities and competences of the hostess are different from those of the (assistant) nurse because the main focus of the hostess is on well-being and not on nursing care. Hostesses are experienced 'housekeepers' with empathy for older people; they don't have a nursing diploma. The main goal of the hostess initiative is to generate greater intimacy and warmth in common rooms and improve the well-being of clients. Creating such a job also had the explicit intention of diminishing the workload of the (assistant) nurses
Place to eat/ meet	This initiative plans to transform the dinning room from a place to eat into a place to meet. The goal is to increase the service level for the client. Currently, the dinning room is open only at noon and at 5 pm, and clients cannot have a cup of coffee or order a snack during the day. The shop, where clients can buy groceries, is open for only two mornings and one afternoon a week. The reception area is open only during office hours. By combining reception, shop and dining room in one place, all these functions will be available on a daily basis. An additional goal is to generate more income and increase the efficiency of the organization
Holiday	Vivium aims to fulfil the wishes of the client for extra (more or less luxury) services that have to be financed privately by the client. The company is offering an all-inclusive accompanied holiday to Spain. Clients are lodged in a private home for the elderly, a care hotel. Spanish staff provide nursing care and Vivium staff are responsible for coordination, extra activities and general well-being. This holiday initiative is the first attempt to offer a private service to clients
Front cooking	The goal of the 'front-cooking' initiative is to increase the service level by giving clients more freedom of choice. Allowing clients to choose when they eat and offering an 'à la carte menu', increases the service level. Clients can see how food is prepared and even smell the food to help them determine their choice. Personnel must now work in full view of clients and interact with them. Training for the new activities and competences – taking orders, serving and generally helping clients – is provided in-house
First-contact nurse	To prepare for the new way of financing and switch from supply- to demand-driven care, Vivium has created a new function of

Table 9.2   (continued)

Initiative	Description
	'first-contact nurse', which requires extra competences and training. An additional point is that in recent years the role of the assistant nurse has become much more complex and there has been little recognition of this. By introducing this new function, which commands a higher salary, these nurses finally gain the recognition they deserve
Clubs	Vivium Bussum recognizes that for increasing 'quality of life', the well-being of clients is at least as important as providing nursing care. One way of stimulating well-being is to offer various extra activities by introducing music, creative, sports, games and computer clubs. This initiative is also driven by the conviction that well-being leads to competitive advantage. Nursing care is the same everywhere, but the way well-being is realized is a means of distinguishing between different care providers
Life story	People living in a home for the elderly like to be in contact with young people. Secondary schools are obliged to promote a community internship for students. Combining these two has resulted in the 'life-story' initiative. During several meetings the client relates his/her personal life story to a student, who transforms it into a book. The client and his/her family are given a copy and another is added to the client's case file, so the (assistant) nurses, who are in close contact with the client, are aware of the client's history and can relate to the client in a more personal way

Management Support

Top management strongly encourage the generation of new ideas. Great value is placed on viewing change, and the uncertainty it often creates, as the foundation for opportunities to innovate and improve the organization's performance. All the initiatives listed are supported by management. All respondents, without exception, mentioned the support of the (top) management: 'They encourage experimentation and that's very motivating'.

There is room for experimentation, and top management supports many small and experimental projects, fully aware that some will undoubtedly fail:

> We wanted to increase our income in the dining room by inviting elderly people from the neighbourhood. We organized dinner and music for only €7.50. Unfortunately there were fewer neighbours than expected, so we had a financial loss. My manager's reaction was: it isn't a failure, you have succeeded in gaining positive (media) attention for the organization and we see this loss as learning money.

Employees who come up with innovative ideas receive management encouragement for their activities. The organization is very receptive to applying improved work methods that are developed by workers, and provide tools and guidance for workers to develop their ideas. People take up this challenge because they feel safe and protected and are allowed to make mistakes. It is important that they learn why things go wrong, communicate their mistakes and are able and willing to find out what has to be changed in order to succeed next time. The focus is on the future rather than the past, and the ability to develop and transfer knowledge is greatly valued. People who want to make a difference get the opportunity to test out their ideas. The 'place to eat/meet' is a good example of a bottom-up initiative that received full support: a new facility manager noticed that the dining room was spacious; he saw that the room was outdated but had lots of potential for creating new functions.

Resource Availability

Due to expenditure cuts in health care and changes in the way of financing there is no budget for innovation. This means that there are no extra resources (time and money) available for the initiatives. No extra resources means that you have to be creative with what is at hand – allocating the resources in another way, and making improved use of them.

Budgetary flexibility provides room for experimentation. The 'front-cooking initiative' had to be budget neutral, but include extended opening hours for the dining room. A 'solution' was found by looking carefully at the cost structure. As labour costs are much higher than food costs, costs can be reduced by buying more ready-to-serve food; fewer people were needed in the kitchen, leaving others to provide service directly to patients. In the 'life story' initiative, clients received much more individual attention, given by students. An additional advantage of this initiative is that some of the students 'stay' for working weekends and during their vacation, or continue as volunteers. Expenditure cuts in health care are leading to a decreasing quantity and quality of public services. Public services that are a right are restricted due to formal regulation by the government. For this reason, Vivium is also offering extra (more or less luxury) services that have to be financed privately by the client. This holiday initiative is a successful attempt to offer a private service to clients. Most people living in a home for the elderly no longer go on holiday, not because they cannot afford it, but because they think that they cannot travel and take care of themselves without (more or less) help.

The 'clubs' initiative is another example of a service that is not publicly financed but has to be paid for privately. Clients make a small contribution to participate. The 'place to eat/meet' initiative is a major project. Some investment money is available, but this is not enough. It is necessary to be creative with fund-raising or sponsoring. Typical of the initiatives is that the starting point is a vision or an idea; the needed resources are a concern for later:

> Many ideas in service delivering don't cost money, but take effort, a lot of communication and sometimes confrontation. If you are really interested in what is going on, giving an eye to the problems people are facing, you get their cooperation.

Human Resource Management

An entrepreneurially friendly organization does not have highly structured job roles – traditionally jobs/job descriptions in elderly care are very standardized and task oriented. The transformation from supply-to demand-driven care and the recognition that well-being is just as important as nursing care, has had a major impact. It implies another way of structuring, task differentiation, and creation of new functions. The 'first-contact nurse' and 'hostess' initiatives are examples of creating new functions. The new function of first-contact nurse requires other competences. Communication, for example is of importance. In consultation with the team manager, special training has been developed for this function prime. An additional point is that the duties of the assistant nurse in recent years have become much more complex and there has been little recognition of this. In the personnel structure there has been no opportunity for promotion. By introducing this new function, which commands a higher salary, these employees can now get the recognition that they deserve. The 'front-cooking' initiative changed the character of many jobs. Employees must now carry out their duties in full view of and interact with clients. Training for the new activities and competences is provided in-house.

A start has been made to institute a competence management system and new jobs/job descriptions are being created, with due observance of all regulations and protocols to meet the requirements of official authorities. Great importance is placed on being able to empower people in ways that allow them to act creatively and to fulfil their potential. The focus is now on process orientation and competences. The core competences of Vivium are creativity, integrity and client orientation. The Bussum region has added competence cooperation. The competences initiative, cuts and boldness are part of the new job descriptions to emphasize that top management truly attaches importance to these competences. Due to regulation and collective labour agreements, financial rewards are fixed and cannot be used to stimulate certain competences by offering extra bonuses. However, the motivation of most people working in elderly care is primarily to provide high-quality care, with financial rewards being of less importance. The most valued reward is to receive the freedom and support to behave creatively in order to directly increase the quality of life of elderly people.

6 CONCLUSION

Since entrepreneurship is a context-dependent process, we have researched how the unique context of this non-profit health care organization is influencing the way in which entrepreneurial activities are manifested (Bezemer et al., 2006; Luke and Verreynne, 2006).

This study gives a first impression of the context and variety of initiatives in the care for the elderly. It showed that within the organization there are a variety of innovation initiatives. Some aim at providing new services, others are process innovations. A few initiatives are location specific, others are implemented in all four locations. The initiatives originate top down (coming from top management) as well as bottom up (from the work floor): 'It does not matter who comes up with the idea, it's about the way it is communicated'.

Den Hertog (2000) has classified innovations in services into four dimensions: new service concepts, new client interfaces, new service delivery systems and new technological options. It is difficult to classify the initiatives under only one of these dimensions because all initiatives have multiple goals. For instance, the 'first-contact nurse': low responsibility in the organization, expressing appreciation, career development; 'place to eat/meet': increasing the service level and efficiency, 'hostess': greater intimacy and warmth for the client and a decreasing workload for (assistant) nurses, 'front-cooking': not only more freedom of choice for clients but also less loneliness. Eating in the dining room has an important social value; many people feel lonely in their own room, but when they come to the dining room they communicate with others and there is a change in routine. Another advantage is that personnel can assist with eating and drinking and ensure that everybody eats enough.

The fact that most initiatives combine two or more of Den Hertog's innovation dimensions shows the complexity of these initiatives. The reason why initiatives aim at multiple goals is due to the many stakeholders involved. Resources are scarce and to get commitment for initiatives, as many stakeholders as possible should benefit from the initiatives. Results show that non-profit organizations constantly have to balance the interests of their multiple stakeholders in pursuing initiatives. Because there are no extra resources available, creativity is the solution. A prominent finding in this research is that almost all innovations were implemented through the creative (re)combining of resources. The concept of 'bricolage' is very helpful in shedding light on the processes by which these organizations generate heterogeneous value from ostensibly identical resources (Baker and Nelson, 2005). Organizations were able to solve problems and exploit opportunities despite severe resource constraints. Often, initiatives even have unforeseen effects. For example, the 'hostess' initiative has reduced the need for tranquillizers. Because of the 'life story' initiative, some students have applied for weekend and/or vacation jobs or offered to work voluntarily. Some of the initiatives, which initially met with resistance, are now accepted as being very successful. Initiatives contribute to the recognition that change is an opportunity and demonstrate that innovation is necessary for creating public value, not an optional luxury (Albury, 2005): 'Nurses see for themselves how appealing it is to engage in activity with the clients and make real contact . . . Giving attention without providing nursing care'.

Preliminary results show that the organizational conditions are changing in a way that supports entrepreneurship. It is evident that top management and most of middle management feel the need for immediate action:

> You **have** to be dynamic; we have held back far too long. That really isn't possible any more. Society changes, the way of financing is changing. You have to perform, you can't afford to stand still, or else you won't have clients any more'.

The organization has become more decentralized and is becoming more process oriented. Top management has put much effort into stimulating interdisciplinary cooperation. Traditionally there was (nursing) care, well-being and facility management, which operated as three separate functions. Now there is the recognition by all middle managers that it is important to cooperate: 'We don't see each other as threatening but as supplementing'. These blurring of boundaries between disciplines has proved to contribute to more innovation.

Because Vivium is a large organization and there is a lot of cooperation in the Bussum, region top management is focusing on (the opportunities of) the changing environment. They are playing a very important role by carefully screening developments and information for their relevance to the organization – avoiding not seeing the wood for the trees, and reducing complexity by ignoring the things that do not yet make sense. They act as a shield to protect the organization from too much regulation and uncertainty, and by so doing they avoid a lot of internal unrest. This absorption of uncertainty by top management is definitely a supporting factor for entrepreneurship: 'It is important that they give their full attention to the client; it's our [top management] job to deal with the complexity and upheaval'.

Another important condition is that the manning level is sufficient. In the case of understaffing, people are too busy to get their work done satisfactorily, and there is no space for taking the initiative. Winning over everybody to this new way of thinking is a major challenge; emotional realization is very important for this transformation. If people are aware of *what* is happening, and *why* things have to change, it is easier to get their cooperation. Information sharing, transparency and demonstrating all help to reduce resistance: 'Now that (assistant) nurses actually see what the hostess does and the effect it has on the client, they find that there is another way of doing things – not to discredit nurses, but they need this concrete example'

The fact that there are no financial rewards for behaving entrepreneurially does not seem to constrain initiative. The findings support Gawell (2007), who finds that public sector entrepreneurs seem to be necessity driven; they are deeply engaged in their target groups and are committed to working for the patient's best interest, despite other offers. A perception of needs among people and/or in society, is essential, and connected to conviction.

7   CONTRIBUTION

This multiple case study in nursing homes and homes for the elderly has provided rich data on the way corporate entrepreneurship in non-profit organizations is manifested (Bezemer et al., 2006; Luke and Verreynne, 2006) by showing the variety in types of innovation and their relationship with organizational conditions. This study has shown that there are a variety of innovation types. Innovations often emerge in the wake of the actors' effort to cope more efficiently and adequately with the problems and challenges of everyday life. Because they have multiple goals they cannot simply be classified as just new service concepts, new client interfaces, new service delivery systems or technological options (Den Hertog, 2000). Innovations in this context are multidimensional due to the fact that they have to create value for as many stakeholders as possible. Furthermore, the study has contributed to the debate about the role of innovation in the public sector through our increased understanding of the role of innovation in creating social value (Albury, 2005). Innovation is necessary to develop 'personalized' public services, that is, services that are responsive to the needs and aspirations of individuals, 'One size fits all' services are not suited to an ever-more diverse and heterogeneous population. This study has identified that the internal (f)actors that stimulate and constrain strategic entrepreneurship in a non-profit organization are the same as these in a profit organization, with the exception of rewards (Ireland et al., 2009), which, due to legislation, are very difficult to disburse in non-profit settings, especially in financial terms. This distinction, according to our results, does not seem to constrain initiative and is in line with the research of Gawell (2007). The concept of necessities contributes to our understanding of entrepreneurship as not only acting on opportunities that are presented, but as being convinced of the necessity to institute changes. Necessity driven in this sense is often not mentioned either in mainstream or in public entrepreneurship research and supplements the discussion of opportunities.

Research into organizational conditions has also increased our understanding of how blurring boundaries inside the organization contribute to the creation of social value. Interdisciplinary cooperation between divisions provides new opportunities. Furthermore, we make a contribution to the theory of entrepreneurship in resource-constrained environments. A prominent finding in this research is the fact that almost all innovations were implemented through the creative (re)combining of resources. The concept of bricolage is very helpful in shedding light on the processes by which these organizations generate heterogeneous value from ostensibly identical resources (Baker and Nelson, 2005). The organizations showed that they were able to solve problems and exploit opportunities despite severe resource constraints.

REFERENCES

Adler, P., B. Goldoftas and D. Levine (1999), 'Flexibility versus efficiency? A case study of model changeovers in the Toyota Production System', *Organization Science*, **10** (1), 43–68.

Albury, D. (2005), 'Fostering innovation in public services', *Public Money and Management*, January, 51–6.

Alexander, J. (2000), 'Adaptive strategies of non-profit human service organizations in an era of devolution and new public management', *Nonprofit Management and Leadership*, **10**, 287–303.

Baker, T. and R.E. Nelson (2005), 'Creating something from nothing: resources construction through entrepreneurial bricolage', *Administrative Science Quarterly*, **50** (3), 329–66.

Benner, M.J. and M.L. Tushman (2003), 'Exploitation, exploration, and process management: the productivity dilemma revisited', *Academy of Management Review*, **28**, 238–56.

Bezemer, P., H.W. Volberda, A.J. Van den Bosch and J.P. Jansen (2006), 'Strategische vernieuwing in Nederlandse nonprofit-organisaties (Strategic renewal in Dutch non-profit organizations)', *Maandblad voor Accountancy en Bedrijfseconomie*, April, 190–97.

Birkinshaw, J. (1997), 'Entrepreneurship in multinational corporations: the characteristics of subsidiary initiatives', *Strategic Management Journal*, **18** (3), 207–29.

Boekholdt, M.G. (2007), *Maatschappelijk ondernemen in zorg: mythe en werkelijkheid* (Social entrepreneurship in health care: myth and reality) Inaugural address, Vereniging Het Zonnehuis/Vrije Universiteit Amsterdam.

Brandsen, T., W. Van De Donk and P. Kenis (2006), *Publiek Dienstverlening Door Hybride Organisaties* (Public services by hybrid organizations), Den Haag: Lemma.

Burgelman, R.A. (1983), 'A process model of internal corporate venturing in the diversified major firm', *Administrative Sciences Quarterly*, **28** (2), 223–44.

Covin, J.G. and M.P. Miles (2007), 'Strategic use of corporate venturing', *Entrepreneurship Theory and Practice*, March, 183–207.

De Gooijer, W.J. (2007), *Trends in EU Health Care Systems*, New York: Springer.

Den Hertog, P. (2000), 'Knowledge-intensive business services as co-producers of innovation', *International Journal of Innovation Management*, **4** (4), 491–528.

Elfring, T. (2005), *Corporate Entrepreneurship and Venturing*, New York: Springer.

Eisenhardt, K.M. (1989), 'Building theories from case study research', *Academy of Management Review*, **14** (4), 532–50.

Gawell, M. (2007), 'Activist entrepreneurship attacting norms and articulating disclosive stories', Dissertation, School of Business, Stockholm University, Stockholm.

Gibson, C.B. and J. Birkinshaw (2004), 'The antecedents, consequences, and mediating role of organizational ambidexterity', *Academy of Management Journal*, **47**, 209–26.

Greenhalgh, T., G. Robert, F. Macfarlane, P. Bate and O. Kyriakidou (2004), 'Diffusion of innovations in service organizations: systematic review and recommendations', *The Milbank Quarterly*, **82** (4), 581–629.

Guth, W.D. and A. Ginsberg (1990), *Corporate Entrepreneurship*, New York: Wiley.

Hitt, M.A., R.D. Ireland, M.S. Camp and D.L. Sexton (2001), Guest Editors Introduction to the Special Issue on Strategic: Entrepreneurial Strategies for Wealth Creation, *Strategic Management Journal*, **22**, 479–91.

Ireland, R.D., J.G. Covin and D.F. Kuratko (2009), 'Conceptualizing corporate entrepreneurship strategy', *Entrepreneurship Theory and Practice*, **33** (1), 19–46.

Ireland, R.D., M.A. Hitt, S.M. Camp and D.L. Sexton (2001), 'Integrating entrepreneurship, actions and strategic management actions to create firm wealth', *Academy of Management Executive*, **15**, 49–63.

Ireland, R.D., M.A. Hitt and D.G. Sirmon (2003), 'A model of strategic entrepreneurship: the construct and its dimensions', *Journal of Management*, **29** (6), 963–89.

Ireland, R.D., D.F. Kuratko and M.H. Morris (2006), 'A health audit for corporate entrepreneurship: innovation at all levels: Part 1', *Journal of Business Strategy*, **27**, 10–17.

Ireland, R.D. and J.W. Webb (2007), 'Strategic entrepreneurship: creating competitive advantage through streams of innovation', *Business Horizons*, **50**, 49–59.

Kanter, R.M. (1982), 'The middle manager as innovator', *Harvard Business Review*, **60** (4), 95–105.

Klink, A. (2002), 'Ondernemend met een missie' (Entrepreneurial with a mission), in P. Dekker (ed.), *Particulier initiatief en publiek belang: beschouwingen over de aard en de toekomst van de Nederlandse non-profitsector* (Private initiative and public interest: reflections on the nature and the future of the Dutch non-profit sector), SCP: Den Haag, pp. 139–52.

Leonard-Barton, D. (1992), 'Core capabilities and core rigidities: a paradox in managing new product development', *Strategic Management Journal*, **13**, 111–25.

Luke, B. and M. Verreynne (2006), 'Exploring strategic entrepreneurship in the public sector', *Qualitative Research in Accounting and Management*, **3** (1), 4–26.

McDonald, R.E. (2007), 'An investigation in nonprofit organizations: the role of organizational mission', *Nonprofit and Voluntary Sector Quarterly*, **36**, 256–81.

Miller, D. (1983), 'The correlates of entrepreneurship in three types of firms', *Management Science*, **29** (7), 770–91.

Mom, T.J.M., F.A.J. Van den Bosch and H.W. Volberda (2007), 'Investigating managers' exploration and exploitation activities: the influence of top-down, bottom-up, and horizontal knowledge inflows', *Journal of Management Studies*, **44** (6), 910–31.

Morris, M.H., S. Coombes, M. Schindehutte and J. Allen (2007), 'Antecedents and outcomes of entrepreneurial and market orientations in a non-profit context: theoretical and empirical insights', *Journal of Leadership and Organizational Studies*, **13** (4), 12–39.

Porter, M.E. (2006), *Redefining Health Care: Creating Value Based Competition on Results*, Boston, MA: Harvard Business School Press.

Saltman, R.B. and J. Figueras (1997), *European Health Care Reform: Analysis of Current Strategies*, Copenhagen: World Health Organisation.

Shane, S.A. and S. Venkataraman (2000), 'The promise of entrepreneurship as a field of research', *Academy of Management Review*, **25** (1), 217–26.

Toonen, T., G. Dijkstra and F. Van der Meer (2003), *Maatschappelijke onderneming. De waarde van de maatschappelijke onderneming geborgd* (Social enterprise: the value of social enterprise secured), working paper, Netwerk Toekomst Maatschappelijke Onderneming, Hilversum.

Van De Ven, A.H. (1986), 'Central problems in the management of innovation', *Management Science*, **32** (5), 590–607.

Van De Ven, A.H. (1992), 'Strategy process: managing corporate self-renewal', *Strategic Management Journal*, **13**, 169–91.

Van De Ven, A.H. and M. Engleman (2004), 'Event- and outcome-driven explanations of entrepreneurship', *Journal of Business Venturing*, **19**, 343–58.

Van Der Grinten, T.E.D. (2004), 'Sturingslogica's en maatschappelijk ondernemingschap in de gezondheidszorg' (Control logres and social entrepreneurship in health care), *Tijdschrift voor Gezondheidswetenschappen*, **2**, 123–7.

Zahra, S.A. (2005), 'Entrepreneurship and disciplinary scholarship: return to the fountainhead', in S.A. Aluarez, R. Agarwal and O. Sorenson (eds), *Handbook of Entrepreneurship Research: Disciplinary Perspectives*, New York: Springer, pp. 253–68.

10. Social and nonprofit marketing: issues and opportunities in marketing beyond business

**Charles B. Weinberg and
Hsin-Hsuan Meg Lee[1]**

1 INTRODUCTION

Since at least the 1960s, there has been increased recognition that marketing has a significant role to play in improving the performance of public and nonprofit organizations (for example, Kotler and Levy, 1969; Gallagher and Weinberg, 1991). Although there have been many successes in social marketing, there have been too many failures as well. The purpose of this chapter is to identify five key barriers to the successful implementation of marketing beyond business and discuss their implications for research and management.

To ensure that there is a common understanding, we begin by providing a definition of marketing that is not based on the business model. We further elaborate this by citing some key features of social marketing. As public and nonprofit organizations do not have a profit objective, we next discuss setting the objective or criteria for success in social and non-profit marketing. We argue that the key measure of success is changing behavior and we discuss briefly two programs, one concerned with sudden infant death syndrome (SIDS) and one concerned with drinking driving accidents in rural Wisconsin, for which the literature reports that they have successfully changed behavior. We next turn to a discussion of five important, but underappreciated barriers, to achieving marketing success in public and nonprofit organizations. These, as listed in Table 10.1, concern competition/collaboration, monetary prices, short-term focus, nature of benefits and costs, and usage of the word 'marketing', which has a pejorative connotation for some.

Table 10.1   Five underappreciated barriers to achieve marketing success in public and nonprofit organizations

Barrier	Description
Competitive effects and collaborative opportunities	Nonprofit organizations often underestimate the direct and indirect competition that they face as well as the opportunities for collaboration
Monetary price	Nonprofit organizations need to decide whether to charge a price, and if so, how to set that price
Short-term focus	Nonprofit marketing often has a short-term focus or focus on behavior change, not behavior maintenance
Nature of benefits and costs	The benefits for the 'consumers' are often to avoid something 'bad' happening to them or only occurring in the long term, while costs are often immediate
The M-word	Marketing is associated with organizational commitment and external publics, but the word itself often has a pejorative connotation

2   DEFINING MARKETING

Marketing is one of the key management functions and is primarily concerned with understanding people who will be the target market for the organization and who will adopt attitudes and behaviors that are mutually beneficial for the client and the organization. The following is an adaptation of the American Marketing Association's (2004) definition of marketing for organizations that are not in the business sector: 'Marketing is an organizational function and a set of processes for creating, communicating, and delivering *value to target markets* and for managing target market relationships in ways that benefit the organization and stakeholders.' We have modified the original definition from target customers to target markets to make it suitable to include non-business marketing. A key point in this definition is its emphasis on both providing value to target markets and the notion that benefits accrue to the target markets, the organization, and other concerned stakeholders. It is noteworthy that this definition does not simply state the functional aspects of marketing – for example, product development, pricing, distribution, advertising, and personal selling – but rather focuses on the development and delivery of value to clients in ways that are mutually beneficial.

To further clarify the meaning of marketing, consider the definition provided by Rothschild (1999, p. 30): 'voluntary exchange between two or more parties, in which each is trying to further its own perceived self-interest while recognizing the need to accommodate the perceived self-interest of the other to achieve its own ends'. The key point of this definition is that marketing involves voluntary exchanges. Rothschild argues that to be successful, it is necessary to recognize the self-interests of all the parties involved and to design programs which are mutually beneficial. Later in this chapter, we shall discuss the program to reduce drinking driving in Wisconsin of which Rothschild was a co-author, and we shall see those principles applied there.

The following is a list of key aspects of social marketing:

- behavior is the objective;
- awareness is only one step;
- social marketing is usually not financed by the user;
- target market selection;
- understand the nature of costs and benefits (to users) – product design;
- trust is key;
- role of branding;
- marketing programs (price, distribution, communication) to facilitate action;
- dual competitive–collaborative environment;
- public scrutiny and non-market pressures; and
- monitor, measure, and redirect.

In the case of social marketing, the providers of the service are usually government agencies, public sector groups, and nonprofit organizations, whose objective is not profit. A critical difference between business and non-business marketing is that the latter is focusing on human behavior and all the marketing activities are guided by behavioral objectives, as we shall discuss in the next section. In addition, there are other critical aspects that are common in social marketing. While some are similar to traditional notions of commercial marketing, such as the importance of establishing trust and designing consistent marketing programs, some are distinctive. For example, social marketing is usually not financed primarily by the user, but by private donors, foundations and governments. Social marketers often incur greater public scrutiny and more non-market pressures than do business executives. Among the similarities and differences listed above, this chapter will highlight six critical aspects of social marketing: awareness, target market selection, funding of nonprofit organizations, cost and benefits, the role of branding and the dual competitive–collaborative environment. The nature of benefits and costs and the competitive environment are discussed in the section on barriers (Section 4), so we briefly comment on the other areas here.

Awareness is Only One Step

Traditionally, social and nonprofit organizations aimed to raise awareness of specific issues with which they were involved. Organizations assumed that people would alter their behavior merely by becoming aware of these issues. For example, awareness of the damaging effects of smoking would result in fewer smokers; awareness of the global warming issue would result in more people consistently behaving in ecologically sound ways. Over a period of time it was realized that awareness itself is not enough. While awareness is usually a precursor of behavior, marketing campaigns that only target awareness or measure their performance by awareness are unlikely to lead to behavior change. In the next section of this chapter, we shall discuss changing behavior in social and nonprofit marketing more fully.

Funding of Nonprofits: Users Do Not Pay Their Full Costs

In successful businesses, over the long run, users pay the full costs of the products and services they consume and provide the business with a profit. Following Toyota's introduction of hybrid vehicles such as the Prius, one consequence of its widespread adoption would be the reduction of carbon emissions and other pollutants in the atmosphere. While achieving this goal would be considered by most to be a social benefit, Toyota is a profit-seeking business. In the long run, Toyota expects its revenues from consumers of its products to exceed its expenses.

Nonprofits typically operate under a different framework. The user is not expected to pay the full cost of the provided service. For example, if the Vancouver Symphony Orchestra were to sell all of the tickets available for its season of concerts, it still would cover only about half of its costs. As another example, Population Services International, a highly successful nonprofit which addresses health problems in the developing world, sold netting products to reduce the incidence of malaria in sufficient quantity to prevent approximately 34 million cases of malaria in 2005. Nevertheless, only about 10 percent of its revenues comes from earned income, with the vast majority coming from governments and foundations in the developed world. According to the Harvard Business School case study 'PSI: Social Marketing Clean Water', (Rangan et al., 2007) one reason for considering the option of not continuing their programs to reduce water-borne diseases is that PSI had not been able to convince donors to provide sufficient funding for this program.

In brief, the marketing challenge for nonprofits is complex. Not only must the nonprofit develop programs and services that meet the needs of target markets, as described in the definition above, but they need to market these programs to donors as well. While the topic of fund raising and resource attraction is beyond the scope of this chapter, successful nonprofits need to be concerned with both user markets and donor markets and to be sensitive to how these two markets may interact.

Target Market Selection

The third issue to take into consideration is that virtually all successful marketing programs involve the notion of targeting a market segment. The selection of the target market is often a difficult practice in the social and nonprofit sector where the notion of serving the whole public is deeply rooted in the culture of these organizations. Industry descriptions such as 'mass transit' and 'public service' reflect such thinking. Such notions, however, under careful inspection, are typically incorrect. The reality is that not everyone is served by the public health system or by mass transport. Most organizations will find it more useful to fulfill the needs of a series of target markets, rather than developing one strategy for the entire market.

Market segmentation is a common marketing practice in business sectors that represents a compromise between developing a specific market program for each person, which is naturally too costly, and treating everyone alike, which misses the point that people are different. So it is typically best to group relatively similar people together. At the basic level, this can happen by targeting young people, people who live in a certain area or people who are vulnerable to a specific disease. Given the objective of nonprofit marketing to achieve behavioral changes, more developed programs target people who can be grouped by more behaviorally oriented characteristics. For example, the EX program from the American Legacy Foundation, specifically targets people who have decided that they want to quit smoking, but need an effective way to do so. The EX program does not, for instance, attempt to convince smokers that they should quit or make them aware of the dangers of smoking, as those people who have not yet decided they want to quit smoking are different from those who need to be convinced to do so (for more details about this program, see www.becomeanex.org).

Role of Branding

Branding has evolved from its humble beginnings as an extension of product packaging to its current status as a key component of organizational strategy. It has long been recognized that brands provide some measure of strategic benefit to the organizations that use them, but the full magnitude of this contribution in nonprofit marketing has only recently been acknowledged.

Although brands have traditionally been seen as instruments of commercial firms, as discussed in Ritchie et al. (1999), brands are increasingly finding a home in the nonprofit sector. The rise of well-known brands, such as the Red Cross, the World Wildlife Fund, Oxfam and Greenpeace are prominent examples of successful nonprofit branding. While the social merits of branding remain a matter of some debate, two major benefits for users have been broadly acknowledged. First, brands provide a simple and effective vehicle to convey the benefits offered by organizations and the goods and services they offer. This reduces consumer search costs by distinguishing one good or service from another, making it possible to arrive at image decisions more quickly and with less effort. Second, brands offer an assurance of quality and consistency, both of which may be difficult for users to evaluate prior to consumption. By offering such assurances, brands facilitate the development of mutual trust between supplier and user – especially important when there are high costs associated with a poor or incorrect choice.

In addition to the benefits they provide to users, brands also play an important strategic role for the providers of goods and services. Specifically, they make it possible for organizations to differentiate their offerings in the mind of the consumer. This differentiation forms the basis of enduring relationships with customers, establishing competitive advantages that endure over time.

It should be noted that for a brand to provide the benefits described, it must offer more than a recognizable name and image. There must be a corresponding organizational commitment to deliver products (whether goods, services or programs) that are consistent with the brand's positioning.

Moreover, when comparing commercial and nonprofit brands, it is important to note that nonprofits often naturally involve a very high emotional component. For example, the commitment to the environment as expressed by Greenpeace and the commitment to the society as exemplified by Save the Children resonate with the public. On the other hand, brands such as Apple and Nike invest substantial sums of money to achieve high emotional involvement with their brands.

3 BEHAVIOR IS THE BOTTOM LINE

Businesses have one advantage as compared to nonprofits. They have a clearly defined bottom line – profits! While there are arguments in the economics literature and the financial press about long- and short-term profits, stock market values and business performance, and various accounting approaches, there is little doubt that businesses focus on achieving profits.

What then is the metric for non-business organizations? As these organizations serve social ends, for a long time, the focus was often on the efforts made by such organizations and their personnel. Nevertheless, there has been increasing realization that the focus has to be not on inputs, however well-intentioned, but rather on outputs. Placed in a marketing framework, initial efforts on output measures focused on intermediate measures of success. One measure was awareness. As noted earlier, under the mistaken notion that mere awareness was enough to result in desired behavior, organizations concentrated on informing people about the organizations, their services, or the desired behavior change. However, as awareness or attitude change was not sufficient, management has increasingly focused on behavior as the goal. As Andreasen (1995) and others have argued, 'behavior is the bottom line'.

Social and nonprofit organizations that focus on behavior have often been successful. In the following paragraphs, we briefly summarize two such successful programs.

In 1992, the American Academy of Pediatrics (AAP) recommended that healthy infants be positioned to sleep on their back (supine position) or side (lateral position) when being placed down for sleep to reduce the risk of SIDS. Epidemiological studies had reported an association between infants who were positioned to sleep on their front (prone position) and SIDS. Traditionally, parents put their children to sleep on their front, so if the babies coughed up at night they would not be in danger of choking. This was a very logical and intuitive behavior. However, in the late 1980s a series of scientific discoveries showed that the probability of a child dying from SIDS was lower if the baby were put to sleep on its back. The US 'Back to Sleep' program was highly successful as the 'market share' of children put to sleep on their backs went from 30 percent in 1992 to 83 percent in 1998 (see Hornik, 2001). In Europe, a similar campaign in the Netherlands also showed extraordinary success in changing behaviors.

What accounts for this remarkable success? In the first instance, the focus was on behavior change. The behavior that needed to be changed was clearly identified and (relatively) easy to do. Moreover, it was the parents who made the decision. Parents, particularly first-time parents, are typically in an information-seeking mode and quite receptive to logical arguments. Although their own parents may have used a different approach and common sense would suggest that sleeping on the stomach is more logical, there was little controversy about the scientific studies.

Furthermore, the needed behavior was consistently reinforced by health workers, friends, and even on disposable diapers, where the 'Back to Sleep' logo, showing a baby sleeping on the back, was printed on a leading brand providing reinforcement at the point of use (see http://www.sids. org/index.htm).

Another program, the 'Road Crew' campaign, deals with reducing drink in rural Wisconsin in the United States. The goal of the program was a behavior change to reduce the level of drunk driving. The goal of the program, however, was not to reduce drinking, so that marketing approaches that would allow equal levels of drinking, while reducing drunk driving, would be considered as successful.

Market research revealed that in these communities, many young men who were aware of their excessive drinking claimed they did not have a reasonable way to avoid drunk driving. While in some areas it might be appealing to have a designated driver program, this did not seem applicable here. A taxi ride home was expensive and it still left them with the problem of how to retrieve their cars. As described in Rothschild et al. (2006), the Road Crew program was designed to provide older, luxury vehicles that looked 'cool' to pick up the young men from home, drive them to the bars, and then return them home at the end of the evening. The cost for the service is set low and is paid in advance. The underlying benefit was that people would have more fun drinking without worrying about the ride home. This benefit is explicitly illustrated in one of their advertising posters, which shows a half-stripped man partying in a bar, having a tagline of 'guess who's not worried about driving tonight'. The program resulted in a decrease in the number of men charged with drunk driving, fewer women driving with drunk drivers, and no change in the level of drinking overall (Rothschild et al., 2006). (For more details about this program, see www.roadcrewonline.org.)

A number of factors account for the success of this program: first, following the definitions of marketing provided earlier, the program offered a clear benefit to the target market; second, the program itself had a clear focus on behavior; and third, other stakeholders saw it in their best interest to support the program. Thus local bar owners endorsed the program and at least one Wisconsin beer company provided support for it.

4   BARRIERS TO SUCCESS

While many social marketing programs are highly successful, many others do not succeed. In this section, we discuss the following five barriers: (i) underestimating competitive effects and collaborative opportunities, (ii) the role of monetary price, (iii) businesses' short-term focus, (iv) the nature of benefits and costs, and (v) the pejorative connotation of the 'marketing' word.

Underestimating Competitive Effects and Collaborative Opportunities

Initially, nonprofit and social organizations arose because there was no alternative way to solve a problem. Over time, different groups found distinctive ways to help people or to provide different but related services which have been lacking in the society. For example, a food bank would be started to provide food for people with little or no income when there is a lack of other better options, such as government benefits or food cooperatives. Yet, many different food banks may arise for this same purpose but use different approaches. A recent study exploring the providers of food and meals for low-income people in Toronto, Canada, found that there were more than 300 providers of such meals (Tarasuk and Dachner, 2009). These organizations differ on when they provide services, the type of food offered, the level of preparation required, and related services involved. More broadly, in the US, there are more than 1 million nonprofits, and in the EU, more than 11 million people (nearly 7 percent of the labor force) work in the so-called 'social sector'. The number typically indicates a crowded market which, in the commercial sector, usually results in intense competition. The following list indicates a number of possible reasons why these many organizations find themselves at times competing with each other:

- entrepreneurial drive – individuals passionately committed to their cause;
- different organizations emerge to meet the distinct needs of different groups or to champion new causes;
- organizations differ in their definition of 'social good';
- limited consumer time and attention makes many pro-social behaviors substitutes to some degree;
- providing complete service to clients means that organizations expand into areas of others or seek alliances;
- performance-driven management leads to focusing on achieving specific goals; and
- competition for funds which leads to competition in service.

However, at other times, despite their differences, the nonprofit organizations find that they can better accomplish their goals through cooperation. In some cases, competition is inadvertent. To return to the Road Crew example, in order to reduce drinking driving accidents, the campaign stressed that the young men in the target market could drink as much as they wanted. For people concerned about alcohol abuse and the dangers of binge drinking, this campaign is a powerful competitor. While the data did not indicate an increase in drinking among those participating in the program, these were individuals who were already heavy consumers of alcohol (at least as represented by the young man in the poster).

At other times, competition arises just because there are so many social cause organizations arguing that people should change their behavior. In the style of a famous US Army recruiting poster, 'The US Army Wants You', the *New York Times* published an editorial cartoon that listed the following activities that social organizations wanted people to do: stop smoking, wear your seatbelt, eat your vegetables, stay out of the sun, lose weight, buckle your kids in the back seat, talk about race, use a condom, volunteer, and eat less red meat! As can be readily seen, engaging in all these behaviors would tax the mental resources, time availability, and energy of most people. In essence, all these social causes are competing with one another, not only for the attention, but for the actual capacity and allowance of individuals to change these behaviors.

At the extreme, social and nonprofit competition can be deliberate and very intense. For example, in the US, there are fierce advocates of gun control and on the opposite side, those who assert their second amendment right to bear arms. These organizations compete directly with one another and one's success is the other's failure. Another illustration concerns organizations that advocate the right of a woman to have an abortion and those who oppose that right. Often, the opposing organizations are driven by moral imperatives, and the competition can be more intense than that in the business sector.

While managers in nonprofit organizations often recognize the competition for funds, they frequently do not consider the nature and intensity of the competition that they face in service provision or behavior change. Ritchie and Weinberg (2000) identify five types of competition (see Table 10.2). In combative competition, each organization's success often depends upon the failure of its competitor. By contrast, in collegial competition, such as disaster relief, the organizations realize that success depends upon their working together. In alternative competition, different organizations provide alternative ways of solving the same underlying problem. For example, deaf people can choose among such alternatives as sign language and cochlear implants. Each approach and many others have strengths and weaknesses and may appeal to different market segments, but all are competitors (and possible collaborators) as well. In directional competition, some organizations may be more inclined to find joint solutions. For

Table 10.2 Types of nonprofit competition

Type	Key characteristics	Examples
Combative	Aggressive and adversarial; focus on winning at expense of rivals	Gun control
	Organizations have different fundamental goals or define problem differently and / or	
	Market conditions endanger survival of organizations in product market	Cases where social services are contracted to a single supplier
Collegial	Widespread sharing of knowledge personnel and resources	
	General agreement on both problem and solution; need is often massive, urgent and life-threatening and / or	Disaster relief efforts
	Cooperation necessary to marshal resources or win client trust	Improving childhood nutrition
Alternative		
Preference based	Occurs when individual differences in preference are great, or when variety of alternatives is needed for full impact	Summer camp for children
	Organizations act as independent agents, using multiple methods to achieve a common goal	Drinking driving campaigns
Technology based	Occurs when a single need can be met using multiple types of skill sets	Communication for the deaf
	May be well entrenched, or emerge suddenly with the development of new capabilities	Internet libraries
Directional	Stems from disagreement on appropriate balance between ideology and practicality	Protecting the environment
	Pragmatists willing to lose clients to ideologically stricter alternatives, but reverse does not hold	Elimination of sexually transmitted infections

Source: Ritchie and Weinberg (2000).

example, organizations concerned about safer sex would see themselves as successful if people choose abstinence, but organizations concerned about no pre-marital sex, would not view as successful the consistent use of condoms or other birth control or disease prevention procedures.

Nonprofits also need to be much more open to the opportunity to collaborate with other nonprofits and with businesses. In the first instance, what would be considered as unwarranted collusive behavior might be encouraged in the nonprofit sector. If the opera, ballet, and symphony orchestra in a city were to agree to coordinate their schedules so that only one event were performed each night, many would laud this as benefiting music goers and avoiding unnecessary conflict. Conversely, if two major soft-drink companies were to coordinate their promotion campaigns, that would be considered collusive. Although it is beyond the scope of this chapter, the growth of corporate social responsibility provides new opportunities for nonprofits to collaborate with businesses. For example, since 2002, TNT, a leading logistics company has partnered with the World Food Programme (WFP), a major humanitarian aid agency. WFP has benefited from the technical and monetary support from TNT, while TNT has enjoyed the increasing employee engagement and its known better social performance as a result. These kinds of social alliances or social partnerships have moved the collaborations or interactions between business and nonprofit sectors beyond philanthropy. (For further reading, see Austin, 2000 and Ireland and Pillay, 2009.)

Lack of Understanding of the Importance of Monetary Price

Many social marketers are reluctant to discuss the issue of pricing, as they regard money as an 'ugly necessity' to maintain their operations. Often the issue of pricing comes at the end of planning a marketing program. However, when a price is charged, its impact both on clients and on the organization needs to be carefully considered. Even when a price is not charged, the user may still incur a cost in adopting the advocated behavior. For example, professional roofers, who chose to use safety gear to lower the risk of falling from roofs, would need to buy equipment costing $250 to do so. In a focus group done for an organization advocating for safer sex practices, one woman commented: 'I have a limited budget and if I have to choose between a six pack of beer and a package of condoms, I'll choose beer'. (See Dahl et al., 1998 for a discussion of barriers to condom acquisition.) In this subsection, however, we shall concentrate on the issue of pricing by the nonprofit itself. We shall follow the approach of Oster et al. (2004) who suggest that there are two main pricing issues to consider: when should a price be charged and if a price is charged, how should that price be determined?

There are three main reasons for not charging a price: ideological, practical (too difficult to charge a price), and high price sensitivity (key market segments will not use the product if a price is charged). To illustrate the first, consider Doctors Without Borders, which offers medical care to victims of disaster regardless of race, politics and religion. Although they could charge a fee for the services they provide, doing so would not reflect the organizational norms and its core values. At times, societal values are the dominant reason for avoiding monetary payments. In the case of blood and organ donation, in some countries, Holland for example, selling of the human body is prohibited by law but also contradicts the people's culture and ethics. In other cases, pragmatic considerations make it difficult to charge a fee. One needs to be careful that the cost of collecting the fee is not higher than the fee itself. In some cases, such as convincing people not to smoke or to be environmentally sensitive, there is just no service for which a charge can be made. Ironically, some organizations need to avoid charging a price because their key market segments are so price sensitive that charging a price would drive demand to near zero. Meal services for seniors might consider charging a price for meals with high nutritional value to reflect the higher cost of ingredients for such meals, but the likely effect would be to cause low-income seniors to choose the less nutritious meals, a perverse outcome to be avoided.

On the other hand, there are several benefits to the organization arising from charging a price. One is that price provides a revenue stream to the social organization that gives the organization some independence from funders, and provides it with the flexibility to make product-market choices and set quality levels that funders might not agree with. Charging a price may also encourage commitment from buyers to use the product. For example, those paying for a counseling service may be more likely to follow the advice given if they paid for the service than if they got it for free. In a small-scale study, Yoken and Berman (1984) found that clients who paid for counseling services were more likely to follow the advice given, and also that psychological counselors provided higher-quality service to clients who were being charged for the service as compared to those receiving the counseling at no charge. Another advantage of pricing is that it provides a way of regulating demand. Public services that charge no fee at times regulate demand by waiting lines, that is, people wait a long time to be served. By charging a differential price based on demand patterns, organizations are able to shift demand to times when the facility is less crowded or even limit some demand. As noted above, care has to be taken not to set prices in a way that overly discourages demand from critical segments. Finally, in some cases, consumers may use price as an indicator of quality. Kotler and Roberto (1989), provide an example of a clinic which found that its demand increased when it started charging a price for its services. However, given that many of the target markets for nonprofits are low-income people, care must be taken not to overgeneralize from this example.

Once an organization decides to charge a price, it must determine what price to charge. The critical distinction between business and nonprofits is that the business pricing strategy is driven by the goal of profit, whereas the nonprofit's decision is driven by its mission and objectives, which are decidedly not profit driven. However, as described in Oster et al. (2004) and in Liu and Weinberg (2009), there are many similarities in developing an appropriate pricing program. One nonprofit manager quoted in Oster et al. commented that his pricing strategy is driven by current price, demand sensitivity, competition and its pricing, costs that need to be covered, providing sufficient funds to ensure ongoing product quality, and the perceived need for incrementalism.

Short-term Focus

Another barrier to the successful use of marketing in nonprofit organizations is that too often the focus of the organization is on solving immediate problems and not on committing resources for the long term. In part, this is due to the nature of the funding of such organizations. They often do not have sufficient funds to engage in long-term activities, as they need to avoid a deficit each year. Another issue, as we shall discuss in the next subsection, is that they underestimate the difficulty of changing behavior. Convincing people to change their behavior and then to adopt a 'safer' or 'healthier' lifestyle often takes a number of years. In addition, as many behaviors are age specific, there is always a new cohort to target. For example, in attempting to reduce/eliminate teenage smoking, tobacco control groups need to recognize that there are continually new groups of teens who are at the age when smoking is most enticing.

In the following paragraphs, we shall demonstrate this barrier with two examples. The first concerns Rescue 911 in New York City, which had a very successful program in terms of reducing inappropriate calls to 911, but then stopped investing in the program and saw the number of inappropriate calls rise again. (Our description is based on Lovelock and Kahn, 1975, in Lovelock and Weinberg, 1990.)

While we shall use the New York City program as an example, many cities around the world have the same problem – less than half the calls to 911 are true emergencies. In the Netherlands, for example, the main emergency number is 112, which is the common EU emergency number. In 2007, there were 5.3 million calls to the 112 line, of which 3.4 million were misuses of the 112 system. By the end of 2008, the Ministerie van Binnenlandse Zaken en Koninkrijksrelaties (BZK) ran a campaign called '112 Als Elke Seconde Telt' ('when every second counts'). As a continual effort of ongoing media campaign focusing particularly on 10–13-year-old children, the effect of such a campaign is as yet unknown. As many countries in the EU are facing the same problem, the EU has formed the European Emergency Number Association which organizes an annual workshop to discuss information and education actions preventing inappropriate 112 calls (see http://www.eena.org/).

When 911 was introduced in New York, the number of calls to 911 rose from 12,000 calls per day to 18,000. Not only were less than half of the calls true emergencies, but the system did not have the capacity to answer this number of calls. This resulted in many true emergency calls being left unanswered. To improve this situation, the city of New York tried to understand the behavior of the people who call 911 unnecessarily. Four main reasons were found for the misuse of the 911 service:

1. Abusers and pranksters misuse the service on purpose.
2. There is ignorance of when exactly to call 911, as the product is not well defined.
3. Calling 911 is easier than other numbers.
4. The cost of using 911 inappropriately is not realized by the public.

In order to solve these problems, New York City officials developed a campaign titled 'Save 911 for the real thing'. First, they defined the product precisely by making 911 exclusive for dangerous emergencies. To make clear what these emergencies are, they launched an intensive campaign showing examples of what is a dangerous emergency and what is not. For example, the campaign indicated that calling 911 because of a noisy party nearby, a fire hydrant being broken, or a car being stolen were not dangerous emergencies. Furthermore, inside the phonebook, they provided a list of phone numbers to call for these non-dangerous emergencies. The focus of the campaign was on reasons 2, 3, and 4 in the list above, as they were most amenable to change. The result of these actions was that in the first year the total number of 911 calls dropped by 20 percent but the number of true emergency calls stayed the same. However, city officials, facing budgetary pressures, apparently decided that the problem was solved and did not invest funds in continuing the program. As a result, the number of non-dangerous emergency calls to 911 increased to their previous levels. Few behavior change programs can be successful without constant reinforcement and adaptation to changing conditions. We next turn to a case study where these factors have been recognized.

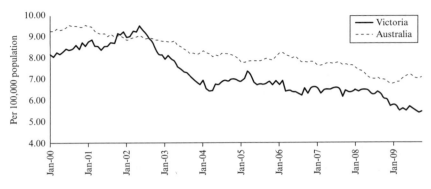

Source: Australia Transport Accident Commission (TAC), www.tac.vic.gov.au.

Figure 10.1   12-month moving fatality rate – Victoria versus Australia

The second case study concerns the Transport Accident Commission (TAC) campaign in Australia. Starting in 1989, the TAC developed a program to promote safe driving in the state of Victoria. As compared to the 911 program, the TAC program has been continuously and regularly funded at relatively high levels. While advertising is only one of the marketing strategies used, TAC has been one of the leading advertisers in Victoria since the program began. Based on extensive market research, the organization created highly emotional and graphic TV ads which have been shown with high frequency for more than 20 years. TAC also set a clear sustained focus on key market targets, including drunk driving, speeding, fatigue and young drivers. While there has been much discussion about the graphic nature of the ads employed, the key point is that the program has been running for more than 20 years and management has continually invested in the marketing program and adapted it to changing needs and priorities. Consequently, as shown in Figure 10.1, Victoria has a lower rate of fatal accidents than the rest of the country. Moreover, the program does not rely merely on advertising, but also includes coordination with law enforcement and the use of web-based activities.

Many factors account for TAC's willingness to spend continuously on this program. One is that the benefits appeared relatively quickly, so that TAC could see the value of the program. Moreover, as TAC also acts as the auto insurance provider in Victoria, the financial benefits of the campaign accrued directly to the organization. While many nonprofit organizations do not have a direct link between safe and healthy behavior and financial returns, they are still well advised to focus on the long term and the need for continuous programs to achieve behavior change.

Table 10.3   Nature of benefits and costs

Category	Characteristics
Benefits	Long term in nature Relate to avoiding bad things happening to me Impact society in general
Behaviors	Deeply ingrained or *apparently successful*, e.g., Drinking driving – I have avoided accidents and police; Safer sex – I can choose disease-free partners
Costs	Immediate – money, time, effortful, psychological

Nature of Benefits and Costs

In the business sector, benefits and costs are typically closely connected. For example, if a person is thinking of buying a new bike so that their ride will be easier, faster, or more comfortable (for example), then this person can spend a certain amount of money to buy that bike and have an easier, faster, more comfortable ride. Not everyone will value those benefits equally and not everyone will have the same amount of money to spend on a bike, but most people can see a direct relationship between the benefits of a new bike and the cost. Such a direct exchange relationship is often not the case in fostering social change as shown in Table 10.3.

Typically, the benefits from social programs are long term in nature and often impact on society in general rather than on a person individually. For example, the benefits of green energy are not immediately realized by the person; often people have to pay a premium for this alternative option, so there is not even an economic gain. Moreover, the benefits from a social change program are often designed to avoid something bad happening, as compared to an immediate gain. If, for example, a person drives more slowly than usual and does not break the speed limit, he/she will get to his/her destination later, but the benefit is that this person is less likely to have an accident. This makes convincing people to change their behavior even more difficult, especially since behaviors are deeply ingrained and related to successful past practices. For instance, people can (inappropriately) claim that drinking and driving is not dangerous for them as they always choose quiet and easy routes and drive slowly. Therefore, it is hard for the general public to realize the dangers of a certain behavior, when the harmful results are apparent only in the long term.

Achieving significant behavioral change in such cases is extremely difficult, so that marketing programs need to be long term in nature and

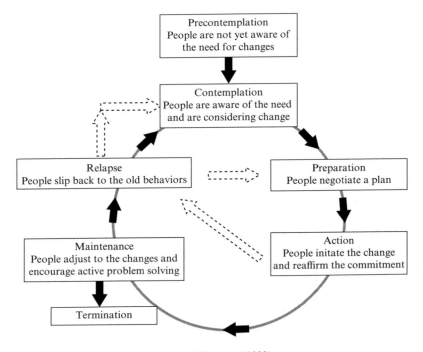

Source: Adapted from Prochaska and DiClemente (1983).

Figure 10.2   Transtheoretical model: stage of change

guided by a comprehensive model of behavior change. While there are a number of available models, as suggested by Andreasen (1995), one of the most successful for social marketing is the transtheoretical model developed by Prochaska and DiClemente (1983). This model takes the view that people do not suddenly change from one behavior to another, but that they go through a series of stages before adopting a new behavior on a permanent basis. These steps or stages are referred to as the 'Processes of Change'. The model is summarized in Figure 10.2.

Prochaska and DiClemente argue that there are six steps to consider in the change process. During the contemplation stage, the person evaluates the recommended behavior and considers what needs to be done. In the preparation and action stages, actual behavior occurs. After the action has happened, the person may then move on to the confirmation stage where he/she is committed to the new behavior and to maintaining it. After this stage, the person enters the termination stage where the new habits have formed and the stages of change have been completed. However, a linear progression through these stages is rare, as people often slide backwards. This often occurs after the stage of action, where the person returns to the old habit instead of maintaining the new behavior, that is, relapses. Many people, for example, have attempted to change their eating patterns, but then slip back to their previous behavior. Even the person who goes though the full cycle of the stages may re-enter this cycle in the future. Nonprofit marketers who have adopted the model need to pay particular attention to choosing their target markets relative to the person's current stage, and then develop appropriate programs.

EX, a program that we discussed earlier in this chapter and that is designed for people who have decided to quit smoking, serves to illustrate a number of the characteristics of the stages of change model. The campaign simplified the quitting process to eight steps: (i) choose a date on which to quit, (ii) make a list of your five biggest reasons to quit smoking and look at them often, (iii) for five days, make a list of each cigarette you smoke, and the triggers to smoking, (iv) in the days before you quit, separate smoking from the triggers, (v) think about what you will do instead of smoking, (vi) strategize about stress, (vii) research smoking cessation aids, and (viii) call 800-QUIT-NOW for one-on-one counseling. The success of this program lies in the fact that the program does not rely on explaining the dangers of smoking but focuses on people who have already decided to quit. Instead of focusing on the benefits of quitting smoking or the bad effects of this habit, the program approaches the issue from a behavioral change perspective and recognizes that change is a difficult process, but then provides a systematic approach to change.

The M-Word

The final barrier to be discussed here is that 'marketing' as a word has a pejorative connotation to some. Many social and nonprofit organizations avoid using the term 'marketing' for their department and instead opt for other titles. For example, in universities, 'Marketing Department' is replaced by 'Admissions Office' or in the case of blood banks by 'Donor Recruitment Department'. A consultant quoted in Lovelock and Weinberg (1989, p. 382) mentions that 'the negative conception of marketing prevails among many in local government. It is important for me to define marketing and dispel misconceptions of marketing as immoral, propagandistic selling'. While that quote is more than two decades old, the underlying misconception is still held by some. Especially for marketing in the social sector, many issues are raised because of this problem.

To avoid the misperception of marketing from limiting their effectiveness, some managers position themselves and their strategies as being involved in social changes, not social marketing. Another approach is to simply adopt existing organization terminology and not use the term 'marketing'. For example, blood banks have long been concerned about donor recruitment without recognizing that this is actually marketing. As the definitions at the start of the chapter made clear, marketing concerns facilitating voluntary exchanges in which both parties are better off. And, of course, this is what donor recruitment is.

By using the term 'marketing', an organization can gain a number of advantages. First, it facilitates the transfer of knowledge that underlies successful marketing research and practice. There is also much greater opportunity for cross-organizational learning. Use of the term also clarifies for the organization and its funders the difference between marketing and other methods of behavioral change. Marketing comes with a distinctive set of approaches that are important to recognize. Not using the term can limit the scope of activities that can be managed and implemented.

5   CONCLUSION

As mentioned earlier, behavioral change is the bottom line of the social sector. Marketing is one among different approaches to achieve this change, along with education, technology, and regulations and law. Marketing needs to be seen as an organization-wide orientation, involving strategies and tactics, increasing the organization's ability to work and collaborate across the private, nonprofit and government sectors. Marketing has much to offer to social and nonprofit organizations and it is a powerful tool to bring change.

The potential of marketing beyond business will grow over time. As illustrated with a number of successful marketing programs, marketing can and should be utilized in the social and nonprofit sectors. While barriers and pitfalls in using marketing successfully in achieving change need to be recognized, awareness of these barriers and developing methodologies to overcome them can lead to improved performance.

NOTE

1. The financial support of the Social Sciences and Humanities Research Council of Canada is gratefully acknowledged.

REFERENCES

American Academy of Pediatrics Task Force on Infant Positioning and SIDS (1992), 'Positioning and SIDS', *Pediatrics*, **89**, 1120–26.

American Marketing Association (AMA) (2004), available at: http://www.marketingpower.com/_layouts/Dictionary.aspx?dLetter=M (accessed 10 March 2011).

Andreasen, A.R. (1995), *Marketing Social Change*, San Francisco, CA: Jossey-Bass.

Austin, J.E. (2000), 'Strategic collaboration between nonprofits and business', *Nonprofit and Voluntary Sector Quarterly*, **29** (1), 69–97.

Dahl, D.W., G.J. Gorn and C.B. Weinberg (1998), 'The impact of embarrassment on condom purchase behavior', *Canadian Journal of Public Health*, **89** (6), 368–70.

Gallagher, K. and C.B. Weinberg (1991), 'Coping with success: new challenges for nonprofit marketing', *Sloan Management Review*, **33** (1), 27–42.

Hornik, R. (ed.) (2001), *Public Health Communication: Evidence for Behavior Change*, Mahwah, NJ: Lawrence Erlbaum Associates.

Ireland, P. and R. Pillay (2009), 'Corporate social responsibility and the new constitutionalism', unpublished working paper, Kent Law School, University of Kent at Canterbury.

Kotler, P. and S.J. Levy (1969), 'Broadening the concept of marketing', *Journal of Marketing*, **33** (1), 10–15.

Kotler, P. and E. Roberto (1989), *Social Marketing: Strategies for Changing Public Behavior*, New York: Free Press.

Liu, Y. and C.B. Weinberg (2009), 'Pricing for nonprofits', in V.R. Rao (ed.), *Handbook of Pricing Research in Marketing*, Cheltenham, UK and Northampton, MA, USA: Edward Elgar, pp. 512–34.

Lovelock, C.H. and J.S. Kahn (1975), *911 Emergency Number in New York* (Case study), Boston, MA: Harvard Business Publishing.

Lovelock, C.H. and C.B. Weinberg (1989), *Public and Nonprofit Marketing*, 2nd edn, Danvers, MA: Boyd & Fraser.

Lovelock, C.H. and C.B. Weinberg (1990), 'Public and non-profit marketing: themes and issues for the 1990s', in Lovelock and Weinberg (eds), *Public and Non-profit Marketing: Readings and Cases*, San Francisco, CA: Scientific Press, pp. 3–16.

Oster, S.M., C.M. Gray and C.B. Weinberg (2004), 'Pricing in the nonprofit sector', in Denis R. Young (ed.), *Effective Economic Decision-Making by Nonprofit Organizations*, New York: The Foundation Center, pp. 512–34.

Prochaska, J.O. and C.C. DiClemente (1983), 'Stages and processes of self-change of smoking: toward an integrative model of change', *Journal of Consulting and Clinical Psychology*, **5**, 390–95.

Rangan, V.K., N. Ashraf and N. Bell (2007), *PSI: Social Marketing Clean Water* (Case study), Boston, MA: Harvard Business Publishing.

Ritchie, R., S. Swami and C.B. Weinberg (1999), 'A brand new world of nonprofits', *International Journal of Nonprofit and Voluntary Sector Marketing*, **4** (1), 26–42.

Ritchie, R. and C.B. Weinberg (2000), 'A typology of nonprofit competition: insights for social marketers', *Social Marketing Quarterly*, **6** (3), 64–71.

Rothschild, M.L. (1999), 'Carrots, sticks, and promises: a conceptual framework for the management of public health and social issue behaviors', *Journal of Marketing*, **63** (4), 24–37.

Rothschild, M.L., B. Mastin and T.W. Miller (2006), 'Reducing alcohol-impaired driving crashes through the use of social marketing', *Accident Analysis & Prevention*, **38**, 1218–30.
Tarasuk, V. and N. Dachner (2009), 'The proliferation of charitable meal programs in Toronto', *Canadian Public Policy*, **35** (4), 433–50.
Yoken, C. and J.S. Berman (1984), 'Does paying a fee for psychotherapy alter the effectiveness of treatment?', *Journal of Consulting and Clinical Psychology*, **52** (2), 254–60.

Index